'A beautiful book with engaging stor[ies] on the edge of faith and those for whom [faith is a] rious friend.'
Rev Kate Bottley, Radio 2 presenter

'This book *is* a beacon – it gives us hope, it shines a light, it is a warning and it is a comfort. All are wrapped seamlessly into every glorious page through the generous and insightful writing. We may not have realized it yet, but we all need this book.'
Professor Dame Sue Black, Baroness Black of Strome

'This wonderful book will inspire many to play their part in the transformation of society. Wherever we are, we have the opportunity to be carriers of hope. Practical, inspiring, vulnerable and joy-filled, this book will help us all to play our part more effectively in reaching the nation for Jesus.'
Gavin Calver, CEO, Evangelical Alliance

'This book has warmed my heart, informed my mind, inspired my spirit, and strengthened my will. It's done that by liberating my imagination to exercise its God-given role in giving space for the longings of my heart to reach beyond conformity to the immediate cravings of our culture. It's raised my eyes to pray and work for the better future God has planned for broken people, churches, communities and nations. It's full of humble and self-disclosing personal stories from Bishop Jill's own life as a scientist, wife, mother and church leader among the most broken. It's grounded in deeply thoughtful reflection on Scripture and packed with learning from the examples of Christians from other generations and cultures. It's punchy in style and impact. It offers new hope and rekindles faith. It's life-changing. Buy at least two copies – one to change your own life and one to give to someone else to change theirs!'
John Coles, Chair of New Wine

'All of us have hopes and aspirations. We dream of what could be, should be, what might have been. So often we live in the land of "If only". And the longings live. They change with our years, growing, diminishing, changing. But what if these dreams could be realized? What if they really were meant to be?

If you have a dream of a better life, this book is for you. Within these pages you'll meet people whose stories will inspire and encourage you that the life your deepest self wants really is possible. It's not too late. It's never too late.

Inside each of us is a kindling fire that God longs to fan into flame. His heart is ablaze with love for you, your desires, your purpose, your future.

The Lord of the universe is the father of miracles. He has a history of supernatural transformation. And your situation is ripe for change. Just imagine what this might mean.

There's a light in the window of the heart of God guiding you home. And as you journey, along the way you'll light a trail of fiery torches in the lives of others.

Be brave. Read this magnificent book and then simply pray this prayer: "Not my will but yours be done." And watch your miracle happen.'
Peter Kerridge, Chief Executive, Premier Christian Media Trust

'*Lighting the Beacons* is a high-energy fix of joy, ideally suited to an age when so many are speaking gloom over our church. Bishop Jill's accessible style and heady mix of illustration, autobiography and Scripture will both lift the heart of the weary Christian and challenge the enquirer with the power of the gospel. This whole book, laced with an honest and perceptive wisdom, is itself a beacon that can lead the reader home to that place Jesus has prepared for them.

I really love the book.'
Philip North, Bishop of Burnley

'There is no doubt that we find ourselves living in confusing and challenging times. In this winsome and accessible book, Jill Duff introduces us to the possibility of hope, the pin pricks of light that point to the real and tangible love of God who has not given up on us. *Lighting the Beacons* is a must-read for any who are curious, or on the brink of losing heart, for there is indeed hope.'
Dr Amy Orr-Ewing, author, speaker, theologian and Honorary Lecturer in Divinity at the University of Aberdeen

'*Lighting the Beacons* is a cracking book, full of insight, wisdom and grace for our journey toward the heart of the Father.

God has placed a beacon in each one of us . . . a "homing beacon" if you will, that as we learn to listen, will open our hearts to his perfect plan for our lives

If you are new to the Christian faith, a committed believer, or someone who's just exploring, then let Jill walk alongside you in this deeply personal book, as the Father lights a fire in each one of us that will become beacons of faith and hope to a lost and hurting world.'
Fergus Scarfe, Regional Director, GOD TV

'Simple language. Clear purpose, to inspire faith. Touching stories and examples from real lives. Humbling and courageous autobiographical details. Bishop Jill Duff has given us an engaging account of how Christian faith is relevant in these times, and how it can deepen within us.

Never shying away from the thornier aspects, she patiently builds a picture of how faith works to change individual lives and the lives of those we live amongst. It is a book that challenges anyone who has been living their faith more as a hobby than a full life-commitment.

She draws on rich and proven traditions of spirituality, making this book suitable for individual reading and group-sharing. It will easily find its place within ecumenical settings.

One book can never tell it all. She leads us to a conclusion that does indeed inspire faith. This becomes a possible departure point for what could be her next volume, namely, how faith must be infused with love for it to bear fruit that will last.

I commend *Lighting the Beacons* to all who sense a need to refresh their faith in Christ and grow in confidence.'
Paul Swarbrick, Roman Catholic Bishop of Lancaster

'Jill Duff is an inspiring leader who spreads hope wherever she goes. This book is deeply grounded in a gritty sense of place, yet is alert to the signs of God's presence in our culture and breathes the kind of hope and longing that will lift your eyes and your heart.'
Graham Tomlin, theologian, author and McDonald Agape Director of the Lambeth Palace Library

Jill Duff is the Anglican Bishop of Lancaster in the Diocese of Blackburn in her home county of Lancashire, as well as an Assistant Bishop in the Diocese of St Asaph in Wales.

She is a sought-after speaker, passionate about communicating the good news of Jesus in everyday language, and committed to finding ways for people to 'come home' spiritually.

A chemist by background, Jill worked in research and management in a multi-national oil company before being ordained into the Church of England. Until becoming a bishop, she served all her ministry in deprived areas of Liverpool Diocese. She was the founding director of St Mellitus North West – the first full-time ordination training college in the region for over forty years – where she taught mission, evangelism and New Testament.

Jill is mum to two teenage boys and wife to Jeremy. She enjoys long walks, long lunches and writing fun lyrics to well-known songs, as the occasion demands. She has wanted to write a book for as long as she can remember. This is her first.

LIGHTING THE BEACONS

Kindling the flame of faith in our hearts

Jill Duff

First published in Great Britain in 2023

Society for Promoting Christian Knowledge
36 Causton Street
London SW1P 4ST
www.spck.org.uk

British Library Cataloguing-in-Publication Data
A catalogue record for this book is available from the British Library

ISBN 978-0-281-08777-8
eBook ISBN 978-0-281-08778-5

1 3 5 7 9 10 8 6 4 2

Typeset by Fakenham Prepress Solutions, Fakenham, Norfolk NR21 8NL
First printed in Great Britain by Clays Ltd

eBook by Fakenham Prepress Solutions, Fakenham, Norfolk NR21 8NL

Produced on paper from sustainable sources

This book is dedicated with love and thanks to

Jenny Hellyer, my spiritual director, my beloved spiritual Mum.
All I have the joy to baptize and confirm.

Contents

Foreword

This is a book written with a vision at its heart, a burning fire calling us home. It is about light in darkness, about beacons burning brightly.

Over the years, these images have spoken to Jill; indeed, they continue to speak to her. Hers is a fiery faith, lit by the fire of the Holy Spirit. She writes about home, her home and the home to which we are all called. She weaves a message of hope in the midst of the struggle that is life. And this calling to come home is the strand throughout the book that holds it together. The fire in God's heart which she speaks about lights beacons that send out the message: 'We miss you, please come home.'

With God, there is a place for each one of us to call home, our home with God. Jill calls us to be attentive to God's call, both in our own lives and the lives of those we meet. She wants us to live out our faith in the living God boldly, unashamed of being Christian, declaring God's love in every word and action.

There is discipline in this: prayer, reading your Bible, going to church and participating in the sacraments of Holy Communion and baptism. None of this just happens. We need to practise. We need to develop holy habits. We need to keep our gaze fixed on heaven, because then we will learn how to call heaven down to earth. And because we are surrounded by the great cloud of witnesses, we are on this journey with our friends and our faith communities.

Jill's faith is unashamedly bold. She speaks of the Holy Spirit, of visions and dreams, as a normal part of her life. Miracles are expected, people come to faith; this is, quite simply, what God does.

Years ago, there was an arson attack on the church where I served. The fire brigade were called in time. The damage was contained, the fire put out. Next morning, as the clearing up began, one member of the congregation said this to me: I hope the fire in this church never goes out.

May this also be true for those who read this book and the churches they serve. Take time to ponder the questions at the end of each chapter. Accept Jill's invitation to allow God to work in your life. Then grab the challenge with both hands; go out and light beacons yourself. Join with God in inviting people home.

Stephen Cottrell
Archbishop of York

Acknowledgements

In a pride of lions, many are needed to bring a lion cub to maturity. My heart swells when I think of the pride who have nurtured this book.

First of all, I would like to thank my colleagues in the Diocese of Blackburn for generously making space so that this book could see the light of day. Bishop Julian Henderson for his gift of study leave in January and February 2022. I hadn't realized how much I would love space in my hermitage to write – one of the many ways in which he has encouraged me to be myself. Bishop Philip North, whose conversations have coaxed many of my ideas out of their shells and has helped me find my voice as a bishop ('Are you ready to roar?'). Thanks go especially to Archdeacon David Picken who stepped into all my bishop's work while I wrote; Archdeacon Mark Ireland, who has most persistently encouraged me to write; and my PA Judith Henderson who kept the emails, phone calls and diary at bay. Many others in Lancashire have prayed me on to this runway. I am particularly grateful for Joy Rushton, whose prayerfulness and careful observation have been a constant encouragement to me; and for Ronnie Semley, who told me as a very new bishop to 'speak from the heart' and made me write a weekly column for the *Lancaster Guardian*.

Which brings me to my next panoply of saints, who read chapters in the clunky early days: Mike Hill from the *Lancaster Guardian*, Prof. Edwige Camp-Pietrain, Jo Warren, Sharon Collins and the Revd Rachel Bedford.

Four readers have distinguished themselves by being prepared to read the full version on short turnaround times. I am grateful for their insightful comments and encouragements: the Revd Dr Nicholas Heale, the Revd Dr Jordan Hillebert, Dr Iman Riad and Dr Helen Moon.

Acknowledgements

Helen's exuberant enthusiasm couldn't help weaving its way into the pages which follow; you would enjoy meeting her for lunch as much as I have. Iman's deep wells of Egyptian wisdom overflow across many chapters. Jordan's beautiful insights into Christology and Augustine have added depth. Finally, over the last two years, Nicholas has quietly introduced me to his friends, most notably the English mystics, who you will meet for yourselves in many chapters. His letters to patiently answer my questions (which have sufficient content for several books) have been the fertile soil for our 'Held in God's gaze' quiet days offered at Whalley Abbey.

Many people have prayed for this book. Two in particular have been its spiritual midwives: Jo Wylie and Jan Abiru. Your gems of wisdom have been invaluable. I am deeply grateful that many people pray regularly for me across Lancashire and beyond. One in particular stands tall as my spiritual mother: Jenny Hellyer. So much of what I have written is the fruit of her spiritual direction over nearly half my lifetime.

One of the best things about study leave was more time spent with my two favourite sons. Harry has been a superb pacesetter, monitoring progress, gifting me a light-up globe 'For the Indoor Adventures', which has lit up my desk while I wrote. When we first looked round our current house, Robbie pointed out the boxroom where 'Mum, you'll write your books.' He also told me with great faith this book needs to be read by the rugby dads. I raise a glass of frothing beer to toast the dads of the Chester RFC U17 Junior Colts for all their cheering from the touchline as I wrote.

I am grateful to Alison Barr, Publisher at SPCK, who has wonderfully believed in this from the start. It was only after signing the contract that I learnt about Thomas Bray's vision for the founding of SPCK – to help the poor and disadvantaged to have a better life. This is fundamental to my vision for the land of light and glory (see Chapters 5 and 12).

And finally, my most heartfelt roar of thanks goes to my husband, Canon Professor Jeremy Duff. Basically, he made me do this. Ever since I became a bishop, at key public moments, someone from the crowd has come up to me and asked, 'Are you married to Jeremy Duff?' His bestselling New Testament Greek textbook is used across the world, in multiple languages. He is a teacher par excellence. He has read and commented in detail on three full drafts. This is just a tiny glimpse of his unstinting support which gives my life such colour and courage. Maybe one day, it will be his turn to be asked, 'Are you married to Jill Duff? I read her book about the beacons . . .'

Beacons are lit in the darkest places. So it is fitting that I finish writing on Good Friday. That darkest day of history. When the Lion of Judah was led like a lamb to the slaughter. He bore our pain, our suffering, our punishment. He went with courage to the darkest gates of hell. And roared them off their hinges. He is the Great Beacon Lighter. His light shines in the darkness and the darkness will never have the last word.

1

Lighting the beacons

A vision

This book has emerged from a vision. Not a 3D bolt-upright-in-the-night vision, complete with surround sound. But a series of corner-of-the-eye, yet-another-coincidence promptings over the last decade. A deep longing in my heart coming into focus all around me. A reality which is just a trailer of the full-blown blockbuster film to come.

It is best introduced with a clip from the film version of Tolkien's *The Lord of the Rings*.

In the film of the third book, *The Return of the King*, when the darkness seems greatest, a little hobbit manages to scramble up to light the beacon. Then there's this amazing cinematography of a chain of beacons being lit all across the hills. And Gandalf breathes a sigh of relief that hope has been kindled.[1]

Our films are often astonishing windows into the purposes of heaven (and, of course, the purposes of hell). God has placed longings for the eternal into our human hearts. 'You have made us for yourself, and our hearts are restless until they rest in you', to quote the famous fourth-century African theologian, Augustine.[2] Our savvy film industry makes billions at the box office each year, because they know how to resonate with our deepest hopes. Their films have glimpses, previews, of our home in heaven.

When I first noticed this film clip, it was in a student presentation I was marking at St Mellitus College in 2014. Our final-year students had to give a talk about where they were going to serve as newly ordained ministers. Ashley was going to Liverpool, to St George's Church on the hill in Everton, overlooking the city. The local primary school was the Beacon school. My role as tutor was to assess her presentation for theological content and clarity of speech. But as she played the film clip, I found myself quietly overcome by tears. The sort of tears that come from a very deep place inside. This was my hope for Liverpool, my husband's home city, which had become my beloved home and the birthplace of my boys. This was my hope for the North West of England, my family's home for generations. This was a picture of my hope for the nation. Beacons of hope lit in the darkest places across our land.

Then I remembered a stray comment from the previous year. I was being interviewed for the post of Director, to set up St Mellitus College North West in Liverpool Cathedral, in partnership with bishops in the North West of England. When it came to 'Any questions for us?', I asked the panel: 'What would success look like in ten years' time?' Bishop Graham Tomlin (then Dean of St Mellitus) answered self-effacingly: 'When I pray for the college, I see this picture of little lights coming on round the country wherever our students are sent.'

And, like scrolling through the showreel on a phone or a timehop on Facebook, this picture of the beacons has come back to me again and again and again.

Scroll forward through time six months. In one of our Half Nights of Prayer for the North West, student Rachel said: 'As I am praying, I imagine beacons being lit across the North, fanned into flame by prayer.' Really?

Scroll forward another six months. At the end of a long phone call with the Bishop of Carlisle, James Newcome, as a throwaway comment, he said, 'When I came here, I found people who had been praying for years for Cumbria; they had seen fires on the hills all around.'

Scroll forward another year, I am in Truro Cathedral to talk about the potential of a partnership to form St Mellitus South West. On the wall I spot a picture of dawn breaking over Cornwall, painted in the 1980s, marking ancient Christian churches. Each was marked with a beacon.

The image was so persistent, it came to a point when I concluded that I must be going mad. Over-interpreting coincidences. Fantasy land. That very morning, my spiritual director, Jenny, emailed me out of the blue. 'Jill, when I was praying for you, I had a distinct image of you being called to light beacons.'

The beacons have continued unabated since I became the Anglican Bishop of Lancaster in 2018. In fact, Lancashire is a county of beacon sites. I grew up in Bolton in Lancashire. My parents' ashes are scattered on Winter Hill, north of the town, near a prominent beacon site, Rivington Pike. At the end of the day of my consecration as bishop in York Minster – a hot summer day in June – a friend came up to me: 'Did you spot those two fires on the skyline of Winter Hill?' Then on Remembrance Sunday, 100 years since the end of the First World War, I found myself at a civic ceremony on the hill in Lancaster by the castle and ancient priory where one of the 1,000 beacons were being lit around the country. My dear colleague, the Roman Catholic Bishop of Lancaster, Paul Swarbrick, was standing next to me. He knew my beacon story. He whispered from his deep wells of faith: 'This is a sign of your prayers being answered.'

I am also an honorary assistant bishop in the Diocese of St Asaph in the Church in Wales. Leading the ordination retreat the following year, I mentioned the beacons in passing. I immediately received an email: 'Bishop Jill, I have been praying for beacons all along the Clwyd valley.'

I had to smile. While writing this very chapter, I happened to be leading a day at Whalley Abbey for our new ministers on healing and deliverance. As I prayed with the team before the day started, Alison Fleetwood, GP and the Diocese of Carlisle's Healing Advisor, said: 'Gosh, I have this beautiful picture of little lights coming on across Lancashire and joining together into a bigger light.' Yes!

Trailers of 3D reality

We often need reassurances that our instincts, our dreams, are socially acceptable. We can be tempted to commit anything that is not fully rational to the lonely lunatic asylum of the 'supernatural', safe to be ignored. It seems only in the dimmed light of the cinema that we are allow ourselves to relish these fantasies.

But what if our dreams were no fantasy? What if our dreams are trailers of 3D reality to come?

For me, the beacons are men, women and children who have caught fire, who bring light, hope and love in their families, communities and networks. I see pinpricks of light and trailers of this vision in lives everywhere. Some like tall lighthouses, giants of faith on the cliffs in the storm; some like tiny flickering candles, their very fragility giving hope; some like fires crackling in the hearth, gently inviting others home to the warmth of God's love.

How have they caught fire? What is the fire that lights the beacons? Or should I say, who is the fire?

God's own Spirit. He's the gift that Jesus promised when he left so that men, women, children in all times and all places could experience that he is with them and, incredibly, living inside them. He's described as the deposit guaranteeing what is to come (2 Corinthians 5.5); I like to think of the Spirit of Jesus giving us a trailer of that welcoming heavenly fire, burning in the heart of the Father.

Trail of torches

What if our dreams had already found their way on to paper, even before we dreamed them? What if the clues to the adventure trail had been around for thousands of years? What if our deepest unformed instincts had found already their way into the bestselling book of all time?

Here's a trail of fiery torches through the Bible:

John the Baptist, the forerunner to Jesus, tells his followers: 'I baptise you with water for repentance. But after me comes one who is more powerful than I, whose sandals I am not worthy to carry. He will baptise you with the Holy Spirit and fire' (Matthew 3.11).

'Baptize' was just a normal everyday word in John's time. You would use it about dyeing cloth. You would baptize it in the dye, so that every fibre of the cloth was soaked in the new colour.

John was offering a baptism of water – a soaking of every fibre to wash away the dirt.

Jesus would bring a baptism of God's Spirit and fire – a soaking of every fibre with his Spirit; a soaking of every fibre with his fire.

Being soaked in fire sounds rather scary. I confess that when I first came across this verse as a teenager and heard about the Holy Spirit and fire, this evoked a paralysing sense of fear in my heart. Fear that I couldn't shake . . . Until I came across this in Romans 8.15: 'The Spirit you received does not make you slaves, so that you live in fear again; rather, the Spirit you received brought about your adoption to sonship. And by him we cry, "*Abba*, Father."' (*Abba* was the word for Dad in the Aramaic language Jesus spoke.)

As Jesus soaks us in his Spirit, he wants to set us free from fear, fear that is often nesting inside, free to know deep in our hearts that we are sons and daughters of the King. When Jesus was baptized, we are told that heaven was opened.

As soon as Jesus was baptised, he went up out of the water. At that moment heaven was opened, and he saw the Spirit of God descending like a dove and alighting on him. And a voice from heaven said, 'This is my Son, whom I love; with him I am well pleased.'
(Matthew 3.16–17)

What does it mean, an open heaven?

Lancashire is famous for many wonderful things. Stunning landscape, friendly people, homely cuisine. And yes, our Lancashire rain.

The lovely green hills encourage mist, clouds and rain as warm air rises from the sea and cools. Good for our famous cotton industry. Not so good for outdoor parties.

Last summer, I was driving to an outdoor baptism on one of our council estates in Blackburn, a church that was meeting on an allotment. As I drove, it poured with rain. The mist was low, I couldn't see the hills, my heart was braced for a miserable morning. The rain stopped as I pulled up – it was just grey and overcast. That'll do, I thought. Paisley (aged 9) bounded up to me. She said: 'I want to be baptized because I want to open the door to Jesus.' My heart unbraced itself a little. Then wonderfully, as I baptised Paisley, the clouds parted and the sun broke through. By coincidence we had just read the story of Jesus' baptism about heaven opening. It literally was an open heaven over the estate. So easy to speak of how sometimes the clouds come in and we can't see or hear properly, but my prayer for that day was that there would be an open heaven. So that friends and family could hear for themselves, 'You are God's own dear sons and daughters and he is really pleased with you.' I could spot tears glistening in people's eyes. Even the lads who gathered round the edge of the allotment – the first ones to light up in the fag break. One older widow, who had also lost her son, said to me afterwards: 'It really was like heaven was opened, I could see my husband and son watching me in peace.'

Sometimes the veil between heaven and earth becomes just a bit thinner. Often, we haven't got words for it, let alone a language for how this happens. All a bit of a mystery. We can be embarrassed to speak of it; we fear people saying, 'She's a bit doo-lally', as we do in Lancashire.

My story of coming to faith is exactly this.

I grew up in a family who didn't have faith or go to church, but I went to the local Church of England primary school. When I started in Reception, aged 4, I saw pictures of Jesus on the walls and started to dream about him. When I was in the Juniors, aged 7, I was given a Bible and started to read it. I was fascinated by the stories of Jesus and started going to church. When I was 11, I went for a week away on a Christian activity camp in the summer holidays. I distinctly remember my dorm leader asking me: 'Have you ever heard of the Holy Spirit?' I'd heard of God the Father and Jesus, but I didn't really know about the Holy Spirit. She advised: 'Don't just read the Bible like it's a normal book, ask the Holy Spirit to open your eyes.' I did this, and it was as if Jesus walked off the pages of the Bible and into my life – like a real and living person.

After the camp, my first week away from home in my life, I remember meeting my mum at Manchester Piccadilly station. I bounded up to her and said: 'Mum, I have given my life to Jesus!'

She was horrified. She thought I'd been brainwashed by the Church of England.

This view continued for many years, especially when I left my career in the oil industry to train to be a vicar. But to finish her story ... Back in 2012, I went to see her. She was in a hospice in Manchester because she was suffering from cancer. When I arrived, she said: 'You've got to come along the corridor with me to the chapel.' So I went. That wasn't the sort of sentence my mum would normally say. When we got to the chapel, she said: 'I was here last night, asking God to make my back better' (she'd had a bad back with the cancer). Then she continued with words that I'll never forget: 'It was like Jesus was here and he was telling me it was going to be OK.' She said: 'That's what you've been trying to tell me all these years, isn't it?' I don't know what happened to my mum that night. But I do know we were from a family of worriers. If we could worry about something, we would worry about it. And to our amazement, she approached her death, four months later, on Easter Day, with an incredible sense of peace. Although she had lived her life under a dark cloud of worry (which is a whole other story; see Chapter 12), that night she had glimpsed that, with Jesus, one day it was going to be OK.

It's fair to say our view is often clouded. And not just in Lancashire. This happened even right at the very beginning of the Christian faith. The day Jesus came back from the dead, he appeared to two friends walking on the road to Emmaus just outside Jerusalem. It wasn't until they sat down for food together and Jesus broke the bread that 'their eyes were opened and they recognised him, and he disappeared from their sight. They asked each other, "Were not our hearts burning within us while he talked with us on the road and opened the Scriptures to us?"' (Luke 24.31–32). There was something about the presence of Jesus that made their hearts burn with fire.

As I said earlier, the first time this fire appears in the New Testament is with Jesus' cousin John the Baptist. Intriguingly, the Bible is explicit that John moves in the spirit and power of Elijah (Luke 1.17) – that fiery Old Testament prophet who called down fire from heaven. What is the point of his fire? So 'these people will know that you, LORD, are God, and that you are *turning* their hearts back again' (1 Kings 18.37, italics added).

And if we look further back in history, where is this image of fire first sparked? It's the beautiful promise that God makes in the night with Abraham, after showing him all the stars in the sky – an image promising countless descendants to come. How could this possibly be? But as we fast forward through time, we see the breath-taking fulfilment of that promise, Jesus. He is 'the first among many brothers and sisters' – not just blood descendants of Abraham, but descendants by faith.

But all this is far beyond Abraham's sight. God confirms his mind-blowing promise, with something tangible, his signature, if you like, to seal the deal: 'When the sun had set and darkness had fallen, a smoking brazier with a blazing torch appeared . . .' (Genesis 15.17f.).

We are inheritors of God's promise to Abraham. We are inheritors of that blazing torch. We take up the baton in our day.

This helps explain why Jesus is so insistent that he is baptized by John, not the other way around.[3] John is passing on the fiery baton. Jesus longs for this fire to spread: 'I have come to bring fire on the earth, and how I wish it were already kindled!' (Luke 12.49). Then Jesus, risen and ascended, sends his Spirit on his Church on the Day of Pentecost. What's the significance of Pentecost? It's the very festival commemorating when God came with fire on Mount Sinai to give the Ten Commandments to Moses. The New Testament scene is equally electrifying: 'They saw what seemed to be tongues of fire that separated and came to rest on each of them. All of them were filled with the Holy Spirit . . .' (Acts 2.3–4).

Jean Darnall spent her life as a missionary, after a miraculous healing as a teenager awakened her to the realities of faith. In 1967, she had a vision of the British Isles:

Suddenly, a vision appeared within my mind – for the third time. I saw the British Isles glistening like a clump of jade in the grey seas surrounding. Trees upon the hills and clustered clouds hid the people. Suddenly, small, flickering lights appeared, scattered all over the isles.

The light was firelight, burning from the top of Scotland to Land's End on the tip of Cornwall. Lightning streaked downward from the sky above me, touching down with flashing swiftness, exploding each of the fires into streams of light. Like lava, they burned their fiery path downward from the top of Scotland to Land's End. The waters did not stop them, but the fire spread across the seas to Ireland and to Europe! . . .

'What is to come, Lord?' I asked, wondering why He should show this to me. 'I will penetrate the darkness with a visitation of My power. With lightning swiftness, I will release the power of My Spirit through a renewed people who have learned to be led of the Spirit. They will explode with a witness that will reach every part of the society of Britain. I am strategically placing them to touch the farms, villages, towns and cities. No one will be without a witness whether they be children in the schools, farmers in the fields, workers in the factories and docks, students in the universities and colleges, the media, the press, the arts or government. All will be profoundly moved and those who are changed by My power will alter the destiny of the nation.'

'And the streams of fiery light into Europe, Lord?'

My mind seemed to see an army of all types of people moving into the Continent with a compassionate ministry. This ministry was not mass meetings, led by powerful personalities preaching to spectators, but participating, caring communities involved with each other at grass roots level, sharing the love of God everywhere. I saw the empty cradles of Europe – her churches – holding a new generation of Christian leaders.[4]

I find it intriguing that one of the most popular Christian songs today in schools is Graham Kendrick's 'Shine, Jesus, Shine'. Unexpectedly, teenagers at the school where I was chaplain loved to belt it out on coach trips: 'Blaze, Spirit, blaze, set our hearts on fire.'[5] Our popular #HomeGrown conference in Blackburn Diocese took as its theme, 'Hearts on fire with love for you', a line from the Church of England's daily Morning Prayer. #Homegrown meant all our contributors were home-grown from Lancashire. My instincts told me that there were already many poems and songs, hidden away; I was astonished to find so many already written were on the theme of fire. Many hearts were warmed.[6]

Beacons of hope today

In 1975 two men each committed to spend time in prayer for a month. They were seeking an answer to a big question: 'How do we see transformation in a nation? Which spheres of influence are significant for this?' They met for lunch a month later to compare notes. They came back with exactly the same seven spheres of influence: family, religion/church, education, government and law, media, celebration (arts, entertainment and sport), and economics (business, science and technology).[7]

Across different spheres of society often spurred into action in desperate situations, when the darkness seems greatest, unlikely 'ordinary' people, with fire in their hearts, are lighting beacons of hope and releasing chain reactions which bring tasters of the heavenly atmosphere into all spheres of our society.

Most will never make the headlines. But, when you look down on land at night from an aeroplane, the more pinpricks of light there are, the brighter the map. And the closer you come to those pinpricks, the more you realize how significant the light is for individuals. For example, the football teams we're running on our estates in Lancashire might be a drop in the ocean for British teenagers. But for those 50 kids with purposeful, fun, hope-filled engagement from adults each week – well, that could make a difference. We saw this with the story of the 2019 winning South African rugby team captain, Siya Kolisi. His story brought hope across the world – a teenager from a township captaining such a prestigious team to victory. A cross tattooed on his wrist, narrating his story: 'I decided to lose my life and find it in Christ.'

The first sphere of influence, family life, barely gets a mention today, even though it is the biggest determining factor in the well-being of children and society. The charity Home for Good has been mobilizing hundreds of church families to foster or adopt vulnerable children, widening their support base with the family of the

Church.[8] My friend Kate, who has written extensively about single-ness (chosen and not so chosen),[9] tells such heart-warming stories about the difference that her volunteering with Safe Families for Children makes – on her, as well as the children – another charity helping vulnerable families by offering respite care and resources.[10]

In business, small gestures can make a big difference. Timpson has become one of the largest employers of ex-offenders in Britain after CEO James Timpson visited a prison and saw the potential in a young man called Matt who is now one of its most successful branch managers. Peter Vardy motor corporation donates 10 per cent of profits to local community charities that help children reach their potential and employs a group chaplain to take personal well-being seriously.

In sport, it is becoming hard to watch significant sporting events without seeing beacons of faith on the international screen. Liverpool Football Club's Jurgen Klopp speaking naturally about his faith; one couldn't escape seeing a number of the LFC team being baptized in the 2020 winning season, with film clips shared all over social media. The 'three lions' of the feted England football team who reached the Euro 2020 final, Rashford, Saka and Sancho, spoke publicly of their Christian faith.

There are endless examples. These are just the tip of the iceberg that make the news.

If we expand our gaze internationally, there are some heart-stopping stories of how Christians, praying in unity for the transformation of their cities, have astonishing stories to tell. For example, in the mid-1990s, the Christians in Cali, Colombia, decided they didn't want to put up with their city being the drug capital of the world. They started to pray. With ambition. Asking for insight into the spiritual landscape and history of the city (see more in Chapter 8). Six months later, the police unexpectedly stumbled across a lead which led them to round up the leaders of the drug cartels. Twelve months on, significant numbers of Christian teachers moved into the schools. Two years on, churches were seeing significant growth such that all night prayer rallies took place in the main football stadium. Cali is a city that has seen astonishing transformation in all its spheres of society. Through prayer. These stories happen slowly, never at a pace that makes the news. Little lights come on, and gradually, imperceptibly, cities and regions are transformed with light.[11] But just as films can be astonishing windows into the hopes of heaven, sometimes even the news becomes a trailer of the hopes in our hearts.

As this book was being edited, I attended the Lambeth Conference – a once-every-ten-years event, with 600 bishops from 165 countries around the Anglican Communion. I met giants of faith from across the globe, carrying the fire of God's love in war-torn situations of persecution, corruption and opposition. I have read a diocesan annual report which made me weep. Extraordinary faith that is seeing 'Christ-centred, Holy Spirit-filled and holistically transformed lives and communities' in the poorest parts of the world. Many fire-filled bishops from across the Anglican Communion spoke from the heart about the Church of England – that their own grandparents had come to faith because of Anglican missionaries from England. They were like fiery beacons of faith, burning brightly in the most unlikely places across our globe. I found myself praying for this chain of fire to return to our shores, to rekindle the faith which lit beacons from here only two generations ago.

Fire can be quenched. This is written large across the twentieth century in Britain. But fires can be rekindled from grey embers. On the eve of the United Kingdom's entry into the First World War, British Foreign Secretary, Sir Edward Grey, was looking out of his window in the Foreign Office, which overlooked The Mall in London. The gas lamps were being lit. He famously remarked: 'The lamps are going out all over Europe. We shall not see them lit again in our lifetime.' He was not far wrong: 1914 marked an extraordinary tide of darkness.

Russia invaded Ukraine as I was finishing this book. One of my school-mum friends, Helen, who was reading it for me, emailed me very movingly:

I conjured up visions in my head of the whole world lighting up fiery beacons to support those courageous Ukrainians and breathing waves of peace towards Russia to try to stem the tide of violence and war!

If ever we needed the Holy Spirit to intervene it's now! So inspired by all the stories of miracles, I shall be praying for miracles tonight!

More than 3,000 Jubilee beacons were lit across the British Isles and the Commonwealth as a cornerstone of the late Queen's Platinum Jubilee celebrations in June 2022. 'Like a beacon, the Queen's leadership has provided warmth and light.'[12] It was a spine-tingling moment of unity and thankfulness, reaching across time and space. For me, it was a real-time glimpse of my heartfelt prayer. For the Father to send his Spirit to light beacons to call many home, through the night, to his fiery heart of love. The next morning, in a last-minute change to schedule, the Archbishop of York preached at St Paul's Cathedral to an estimated audience of more than 1 billion. His sermon, comprising horse-racing wit, made the front page of the broadsheets. He finished with this winsome invitation:

What I see in Her Majesty the Queen is someone who has been able to serve our nation faithfully because of her faith in Jesus Christ. Perhaps there is no better way of celebrating her Platinum Jubilee than by doing the same ourselves.[13]

Figure 1 **The Platinum Jubilee beacon at Lancaster Castle, 2 June 2022**
(Photo by the author)

This book is trying to strike a tiny match as part of that beacon-lighting that resonates with the hopes of so many. My hope and prayer is to see beacons lit across Lancashire, across our nation and beyond.

Going further

For group discussion

1 What parts of the chapter have most resonated with you? Where would you disagree or have questions?
2 Where do you see the gospel appearing through film and culture? (If you're meeting as a group, you might like to play a song or film clip that means a lot to you.)
3 If you looked forward ten years in your community, church, workplace or sphere of influence, what would a 'golden age' look like? What would a 'dark age' look like?
4 Thinking of the different spheres of influence, where do you particularly spot beacons of light?
5 In the Church of England's Daily Prayer each morning is the line, 'Set our hearts on fire with love for you.' Many of us pray this, but what does it mean?

For personal devotion

Read: Isaiah 60.1–5

With each of our devotions, read the Bible passage through slowly twice, inviting Jesus by his Spirit to open your eyes, ears and heart. See what strikes you and sit with this in prayer. As you become more settled in prayer, allow the Spirit to pray in you.

Prayer to conclude: Jesus, may I carry your torch of fire – the good news of your love in my life and work today. Amen.

2

We miss you, please come home

The heart of the book

Beacons are lit to carry a message. But I warn you, every time I speak on this message, I find a deep emotional response.

Messages vary. Beacons can signal danger: for example, the beacon at Rivington Pike near my childhood home was used to warn that the Spanish Armanda were in the English Channel. Beacons call for help: in *The Lord of the Rings*, the beacons of Gondor rally the troops of the Rohirrim. Beacons announce a celebration: the Platinum Jubilee beacons celebrated the 70-year reign of Queen Elizabeth II, which was the longest in history.

This chapter is the heart of the book.

If, like me, you skim read books to get to the main point, it is this.

The fire in God's heart which lights the beacons is all about sending this message: 'We miss you, please come home.'

Emotion! No emotion please. How interesting that I felt to preface this chapter with a health warning. A near apology. Fire – handle with care! Watch out – you might get emotional. We like to keep things in our head. I certainly do. It's neater and tidier. I have assured my colleagues I will never cry in front of them. That would be unprofessional. Out of control. A shaming sign of weakness. So far, so good. Thirty years in.

There is only one occasion in my working life when tears have surfaced in a business meeting. Maybe because it was all about this message: we miss you, please come home.

The background to the meeting is best plotted with three data points.

Data point one. The North West of England is the most populated area of the country outside the South East. Major cities, industry, innovation, as well as some of the most stunning land-scape in the country.

Data point two. The most significant factor in church growth and community transformation is leadership. This isn't to make a churchy or religious point; this is true in all spheres of society. My colleague Joy once asked a senior researcher at Church of England HQ what was the number one factor in church growth. He smiled and replied simply: 'The vicar's nice, it makes them think God is nice, and so they want to come back.'

Data point three. Back when this story starts in 2011, the last college in the North West of England to train young leaders full-time for the C of E had closed its doors in 1969 (St Aidan's College, Birkenhead; more about this story in Chapter 5). This meant that we had a shortage of good young leaders in the North West for our churches and Christian leaders for civil society. There were part-time training courses (tricky to juggle alongside a busy career or young family) so they attracted much older candidates, with the average age of starting on the course over 50. The other full-time training options were outside the region. A barrier to families. And when younger leaders left the North West to train, often they never came back.

To cut a long story short, my husband, then I, had tried to find ways to remedy this over the previous five years. And hit the political buffers. Ironically the main argument was this: surely if there were full-time training for leaders in the North West that would be bad for the other colleges elsewhere in the country?

My favourite comedienne, Victoria Wood, did a brilliant set about how when she was growing up in Bury in Lancashire, her mum would always say, 'You've just got to put up with it. That's what we do in the North West, isn't it?' She then lists all the industry that has closed over the years . . . the pits, the mills, the textile industry… 'Ah well, you've just got to put up with it. At least in the North East, they marched down to London and complained!'[1]

But back to our attempts to start full-time training in the North West. When the last big buffer was hit, when it looked like it had all died a death, it drove me to serious prayer for our region. And in the secret place I became more and more convinced Jesus meant what he said, that people are hungry and lost, longing for home. And this is still true today, despite all the noise about a secular age (which we'll come to in Chapter 9).

In my heart, in prayer, I was drawn back again and again to these words:

> When [Jesus] saw the crowds, he had compassion on them, because they were harassed and helpless, like sheep without a shepherd. Then he said to his disciples, 'The harvest is plentiful but the workers are few. Ask the Lord of the harvest, therefore, to send out workers into his harvest field.'
> (Matthew 9.36–38)

So, I tried again. With a modified idea. The first bishop I met with listened carefully. Then said something along the lines of: 'Great idea. But it'll never work – the other North West bishops will never agree.' At which point, against all my principles, I burst into tears. 'But the harvest fields are plentiful and the workers are few,' I sobbed, thinking of all the people across the North West who wouldn't be able to hear how loved and missed their were by their heavenly Father, how they might never realize he was longing for them to come home. I was deeply embarrassed by my tears at the time; it is embarrassing to tell such a story now.

A week later, I plucked up the courage to write to apologize. And he sent the most unexpected reply. 'Please don't apologize for your tears. The Desert Fathers and Mothers saw tears as a sign of the Holy Spirit. Bon courage as you go to speak with other bishops.' (The Desert Fathers and Mothers were hermits who lived in the Egyptian desert from the third century; out of their silent prayer has come an astonishing wisdom which endures through time.)

This opened a door for the start of St Mellitus North West, which over the next years would train hundreds of leaders, picking up the fiery baton from St Aidan's College, and now passing this to the new Emmanuel Theological College as I write.

I find this response of Jesus electric: 'When he saw the crowds, he had compassion on them, because they were harassed and helpless, like sheep without a shepherd.'

In English, the word 'compassion' can sound ever so pastoral, even sickly sweet: 'There, there, have a cup of tea.'

In the original Greek, it is much more visceral, more painful, more agonizing. You might say something more like 'his guts were twisted'.

It's the same word Jesus uses in his famous parable of the Prodigal Son. Here, we have the Father, whose heart has been broken by his younger son leaving home with his share of the inheritance. The old man waits in agony every day, straining for a sign of him on the horizon. Then the day comes when he spots this tramp on the road home. The son has spent all his father's money on prostitutes and wild living. He comes back armed with self-centred excuses. He's taken his father for a ride, big time. But his father misses him so much, he just wants him to come back home, no questions asked.

> But while he was still a long way off, his father saw him and was filled with compassion for him; he ran to his son, threw his arms round him and kissed him.
> (Luke 15.20)

And it's this agonizing longing in the heart of the Father for his lost sons and daughters that impressed itself on me in the secret place of prayer. We can think in our heads: 'Surely God knows everything?' He knows exactly where his sons and daughters are. We assume he's like some kind of headmaster, waiting, fists clenched, to tell us off. Standing in judgement on our society. But it's not like that – we couldn't be more wrong. Our Father is missing us and longing for us to come back home. And that's why we need the Scriptures. God is not as we think he is.

Notice how it is 'while he was still a long way off' that the father saw him. This was such a signature of Jesus' ministry. It was all the people who were a 'long way off' – the sex-workers and tax collectors – who were getting into the kingdom ahead of the religious teachers and bishops. Note this!

In short, the incredible revelation – as shocking today as it was then – Jesus is saying that the agony in the heart of God for us is the same as that of a father who has lost his son.

When a child goes missing, the 24-7 news picks it up with heart-stopping detail. When the Manchester Arena bomb went off at 10.30 p.m. on 22 May 2017, following the news was unbearable. I had been leading one of our Half Nights of Prayer till midnight, so we prayed as the news came in on social media, and then unusually I tuned in to the radio at 1 a.m., then 2 a.m. as I drove home. Then the next morning I immediately tuned in. Parents of lost children were interviewed on their doorsteps, harassed and helpless. 'Perhaps Naomi is with her friends' in the first update. Then, 'Perhaps Naomi has lost her phone.' Then, 'Perhaps, perhaps . . .' And as the hours tick by there's the dreadful realization that Naomi is not coming home. Ever.

Most of us have some limited, temporary experience of something or someone going missing. As I write this, we have lost our pet snake. He was in his tank outside my study. Looking a bit bored, nose up against the glass. He doesn't move fast. Usually. So I opened the glass door. He likes to slide out and tuck himself behind his tank against the wall near the radiator, nice and warm. I am only feet away, but ten minutes later he was nowhere to be seen. A week later he still hasn't turned up. Every time I pass a sofa, I feel the need to look under it just in case. But a pet snake is nothing compared to the human tragedy of a loved one going missing.

I was at a meeting of Christians in Lancaster a few years ago. I told this story about the fire of love in the heart of God for his missing sons and daughters. One older couple came up to speak with me in the coffee break, tears glinting in their eyes. 'You weren't to know this, but today is the twentieth anniversary of our son's death. It all started when he went missing.' We were all in tears by the end of it. They were happy for me to share this with the gathered company. It seemed a wonderful serendipity of the Spirit to honour them, their bereavement and their beloved lost son.

This is the heart of the book. The heart of God's blockbuster film. From the fire in the heart of God, the Spirit is calling out: 'We miss you, please come home.'

Forcing into our culture

And this agony is so intense that it is forcing its way into our culture. Sometimes loud and clear, like hilltop beacons blazing against the clear night sky. At other times, just the faintest whisper, like tiny flickering candles guiding the way home through the fog. Here are some examples from the worlds of film and advertising. You can probably think of many more – once you tune in, they're everywhere:

Home in our films

There's a heart-wrenching scene which caught my breath in *Star Wars VII*. Han Solo finally tracks down his estranged son, Kylo Ren. He pleads simply, with tears in his eyes, his voice cracking in desolation: 'We miss you, please come home.' Moments later something terrible happens and they are lost to each other for ever.[2]

Then there's Bridget Jones, struggling to articulate why Mr Darcy has her heart, despite their comically numerous failed attempts to get together: she loves him because he feels like 'home'.[3]

My favourite is *Paddington 2*. His hapless, heartfelt longing to find a home tugs at heartstrings throughout the film. I have yet to watch the end without crying. We think the film has nearly ended: the baddie is thwarted; Paddington is rescued from near drowning by his jailbreak mates turned good. But something's incomplete. We need to come home. We next see him waking up, back at the Browns' home after several days' sleep. With a desperate jolt, he realizes it's Aunt Lucy's birthday and he never sent her a present. 'Come downstairs,' urges Mrs Brown. The Browns have gathered all Paddington's friends, each one thanking him for help he never realized he gave them. Then the doorbell rings. 'Paddington, you answer it . . .' It's Aunt Lucy! He couldn't get home to Darkest Peru, so she came home to him in London. I have lost several important family members, 'before their time' so to speak. This scene feels like how I imagine it is to arrive home in heaven. Discovering people we didn't realize we'd helped; being reunited with loved ones we never expected to see again.[4]

Home in our advertising

So much of our advertising revolves round that magical concept of home. Ikea will sell you 'a happier life at home'. Rightmove will help you find your 'for-ever home'. How many of our Christmas Day disappointments stem from the longing for that one perfect day 'at home' with all the family? I think that at the root of many of our Christmas Day stresses lurks those unwelcome reminders that we haven't yet arrived at the perfect day of the rose-tinted adverts. Presents can be disappointing, turkeys aren't defrosted on time, relationships are frayed, loved ones are bone-achingly absent. But should we blame the advertising agents, when the flat-pack wardrobe fails to deliver the happier life at home, the for-ever home turns out not to be for ever, and there's a massive family fall-out over the Christmas dinner?

No. We have these instincts, these hopes, these longings deep in our hearts, that someday, somewhere over the rainbow . . . it will all be OK . . . because, quite simply, those hopes are put there by God. Because there really is a for-ever home he's making ready for us.

Longing for home

Jesus told his friends again and again not to be afraid of the future. Trust in him. He underlined this with beautiful imagery just before he left them:

'Do not let your hearts be troubled. Trust in God; trust also in me. In my Father's house are many rooms; if it were not so, I would have told you. I am going there to prepare a place for you.'
(John 14.1–2, NIV 1984)

21

I love the idea that Jesus is preparing a place specially for me. Home at last. Safely to the hearth where his fire burns for his loved ones whom he longs to come home.

In retirement, my mum managed wonders in the garden. She'd grown several giant blue lupins, impressively glorious. After her death, I was cleaning out her house, my childhood home in Bolton. I noticed with fresh eyes a cheap china plate mounted on the kitchen wall. A little thatched cottage, tucked away, smoke curling from the chimney, giant blue lupins in the front garden. It made me smile – I like to think of it as a preview of her home in heaven.

God gives us trailers of the heavenly 3D blockbuster film to come (see Chapter 1). Tasters of home. Not just in our advertising and films, but shafts of heavenly dawn breaking in for real. Into the here and now. I love how Bill Cahusac observes in his inspirational book, *That Gentle Whisper*,[5] that so many people speaking to him say, 'I feel like I've come home.'

As a teenager and an adult, I am thankful that my experience of church has been as a wonderful place of home. Especially when you're new to a city. Family of all ages where you genuinely are a sister or a brother. Sons and daughters of the King.

I recall the early bedraggled days when my husband Jeremy was vicar of St Paul's Church in the centre of Widnes. We came super-low on the deprivation indices. We just about managed to pull off Christmas dinner in our church hall on Christmas Day for those who find the day difficult. Only 30 of us. I'm no chef and cooking with our assorted band of volunteers was a minor miracle in itself. Single mum Amanda ('my little sis' as she has come to be to me) brought her two young daughters along. They were nearly as energetic as my young sons. Which is saying something. It was a delight to have them with us. As they left, the younger 3-year-old daughter simply said: 'Mum, this is a family.' Lesslie Newbigin in his beautiful book *The Household of God* writes: 'Is there a family of God on earth to which I can belong, a place where all people can be truly at home?'[6]

In Welsh, there is a beautiful word that doesn't exist for this in English: 'hiraeth'. The nearest translation is homecoming. But any

Welsh native speaker will say the word has a deep heartfelt longing for not just home but for the people, landscape, community, language. A profound longing for home, blended with nostalgia, tinged with loss. (Not for nothing is Welsh known as the language of heaven!)

No home is perfect. The church as we see it on earth is far from a perfect home. Like all families there are arguments; and on rare occasions, terrible things happen behind closed doors, made all the worse by reasonable expectations of our duty of care. Dutch priest and writer Henri Nouwen said in his down-to-earth-way: 'Often it seems harder to believe in the Church than to believe in God.'[7] Bishop Charles Gore wrote: 'The visible Church has to be borne with, because it is the Spirit's purpose to provide a home for the training and improvement of the imperfect.'[8] Even pearls are improved by the grit of imperfect family relationships – both at home and at church.

But all that said, I am continually astonished and grateful for the real-life loving reach of what is one of the nation's largest volunteer-based charities, reaching all ages and with the ambition to be a Christian presence in every community. A living, breathing manifestation of that Christmas 'peace on earth and goodwill to all' in every city, town, village, estate, suburb in the country. And then there are our wonderful chaplains; serving on the frontline of our hospitals, prisons, universities and in the armed services. No wonder we can be easy targets for lampooning. Like a home in heaven, with a heavenly Father whose heart burns for you, that must be too good to be true. Fairy tale.

Waking up

But here's the thing. It's actually the other way round. It's as if we are waking up, as a nation, from a deep sleep in a fairy tale where the world is secular, scientific, rational, and no one cares about the big questions in life, like what happens after you die. It's just the end. We're just a set of chemicals recycled into the melting pot of the anonymous universe. Those narratives are unravelling. People are waking up to the real world.

The BBC commissioned a recent survey and to their surprise found that three out of five people believe in miracles; and the younger you are, the more likely you are to believe.[9] I was interviewed about this on local radio around the country one Sunday morning. When it came to the slot for BBC Radio Cornwall, I could tell the question had been set elsewhere in the country. It was something like, 'In our secular age, does it surprise you that people believe in miracles?' I couldn't help laughing out loud. 'Of course it doesn't surprise me. We're in Cornwall, the land of the saints.' People come to Cornwall because it's a place of miracles, a 'thin place' where heaven seems close to earth.

Our media may mistakenly presume that the 'secular' viewpoint is somehow a neutral, majority view in our country. I'm afraid that's rather out of date if you follow the academic research. This is not the language of our films, our advertising, or even our hard-bitten sports commentators. As a Boltonian, I can't forget the incredible story of Fabrice Muamba, Bolton Wanderers footballer, peak of his fitness, who collapsed on the pitch. BBC commentator, Adrian Childs, said, 'You can feel the whole stadium praying.' Seventy-eight minutes later, Muamba's heart restarted.

The late Queen Elizabeth II spoke to the hearts of many in our nation with her broadcasts, full of Christian faith. At the height of the pandemic, she reached for the line from Dame Vera Lynn's wartime song, 'We'll meet again.' We are a nation intrigued by faith. We are hungry for hope, for our home in heaven.

Just across the water in France, in theory one of our most secular European countries, there were astonishing scenes on the streets following the tragedy of the fire at the twelfth-century Cathedral of Notre Dame. Candlelit vigils with people crying out to God. Last year, I was thrilled to receive a call from an old friend of mine, Edwige, now Professor at the Universite Polytechnique des Hauts-de-France. She asked if she might interview me about my faith for an academic article on geopolitics. She kindly read some of this book for me. She was keen to point out that even France is losing its secular edge – 'Your article is published in a geopolitical journal edition all about Christianity!'[10]

Burning brighter

Meanwhile, if there's a way to sum up the effect of the Covid pandemic, for me it's been 'burning brighter'. Here are three quick examples.

Burning brighter in relationships – with councils, government, NHS, faiths – all working together for the common good. From providing meals for kids in the holidays to food-bank support; in welcoming asylum seekers and advocating on the ground for our poorest communities.

Burning brighter online. Did you know that an astonishing proportion of under-30s have participated in Christian worship services online? One of our vicars in Lancashire, the Revd Anne Beverley, even appeared on BBC's *The One Show* after gaining 2 million followers on TikTok @ChristChurchWesham. Anne said to me: 'I dared to switch the comments on and I couldn't believe it; people were asking such big questions, like "What happens after I die?" and "Can you pray for healing for me?"'

This brings me to my final burning brighter – an acceleration in people asking those big questions in life. This might be in a pub discussion; on an Alpha course (run by many local churches to introduce people to the Christian faith);[11] through weddings and funerals. The big questions are also asked in schools' work. I joined a Year 4 class in Preston recently. They'd been reading one of my favourite books, *The Lion, the Witch and the Wardrobe*, and the children had prepared questions for me, such as, 'Can Aslan help us in the dark times?'

C. S. Lewis answers this movingly in *Prince Caspian*:[12]

'You have listened to fears, child,' said Aslan. 'Come, let me breathe on you. Forget them. Are you brave again?'

Lucy buried her head in his mane to hide from his face. But there must have been some magic in his mane. She could feel lion-strength going into her. Quite suddenly she sat up. 'I'm sorry, Aslan,' she said. 'I'm ready now.' 'Now you are a lioness,' said Aslan. 'And now all Narnia will be renewed.'

We are waking up. Jesus is spot on. People are harassed and helpless like sheep without a shepherd. The harvest is plentiful, and the workers are few.

Harassed and helpless far from home

Sadly, the most harassed and helpless, and often voiceless and invisible, are our children and young people. It's not hard to see the damage done when people don't have a home or are dislocated from their home. In Lancashire we have the highest number of children in the country in the care system. Growing up without a stable home makes it significantly more likely that you will spend time in prison.

The charity Home for Good advocates for the plight of 4,000 children needing homes each year. Every 15 minutes a child comes into care.[13]

- 23% of adult prison population grew up in care;
- 40% of under-21 prison population grew up in care;
- 25% of women leaving care are already pregnant.

Is it telling that a popular series on CBBC, *The Dumping Ground*, is a dramatization based on Jacqueline Wilson's bestselling 'Tracy Beaker' books about a children's care home? Children are gripped with plots about dealing with rejection; in fact, serial rejection from home.

The Mothers' Union might appear to be out of fashion, but its founding documents are potent. Mary Sumner wrote in 1887: 'The prosperity of a nation springs from the family life of the homes.' 'A true home should be a light-house, shedding its quiet beams far and wide.'[14] How little we talk about what makes for good relationships and family life. If people are struggling to find ways to communicate and live well together at home, where do they go for back-up? It's as if this is off limits and all we're left with is a trail of edited highlights of happy, smiling families on Facebook and Instagram.

In her books *Call the Midwife*, Jennifer Worth tells the compelling story of a 10-year-old girl she knew, who had grown up in the workhouse. She stood out from all the other girls with her glossy hair and confident, optimistic character. Even harsh treatment could not break her spirit. When a new Master of the workhouse arrived, he found her ebullience irritating, a challenge to his authority. She didn't blend into the grey, docile, submissive mass of the other women and girls. He found out more about her story. From a young age, she believed that she was the daughter of a rich and powerful man, who had to leave the country on business. He had promised that one day he would come back to claim her and take her home. The new Master hatched a plan. He invited one of his wealthy business associates to come to the workhouse. He posed as this girl's long-lost rich father. He was convincing. She was thrilled to see him. And then in front of all the other women and girls he disowned and shamed her. She was no daughter of his, how dare she believe this ridiculous story. The girl's spirit was broken. She wasted away, her hair lost its shine, within a year she had died. She had lost all hope.[15]

I love Christian comedian Milton Jones's definition of hope.[16]

> Perhaps hope is like ordering something on Amazon. Every so often you get little messages saying 'It's on its way'. Then one day the doorbell will ring! But if you don't answer, your hope might disappear to the depot for ever and ever.

It's like the semaphore telegraph chain along the North Wales coast, starting on Anglesey. They were built in 1826 on 11 prominent sites, starting at Holyhead, to carry the message to port in Liverpool, that the ship was nearly home.

Of course, this theme of 'coming home' is richly woven throughout the Bible. Adam and Eve lost their home in the Garden of Eden; their descendants wandered in the wilderness looking for home in the promised land; this longing for home is echoed by the Old Testament prophets, particularly the book written by the prophet Hosea.

Hosea is told by God to marry a prostitute, so he can speak with integrity about the unremitting agony in the heart of God. Hosea's beautiful bride deserts him, she commits adultery, she sells her body and soul as a prostitute to passing strangers, before his very eyes, breaking his heart into pieces. But he will not give up on her. Hosea evocatively writes of how God longs for his adulterous, but much-loved, bride to come to her senses and come back home:

> 'How can I give you up, Ephraim?
>   How can I hand you over, Israel . . .
> My heart is changed within me;
>   all my compassion is aroused . . .
> [The LORD] will roar like a lion.
> When he roars,
>   his children will come trembling from the west . . .
> I will settle them in *their homes*.'
> (Hosea 11.8, 10–11)

If you're new to the story of Hosea, it's been wonderfully dramatized in *Redeeming Love*, a novel by Francine Rivers, now a Universal Pictures film.[17]

Jesus speaks of home especially in John's Gospel: 'Anyone who loves me will obey my teaching: My father will love them, and we will come to them and make our home with them' (John 14.23). Jesus' closest disciple Peter speaks of being exiles, longing for the heavenly inheritance 'that can never perish, spoil or fade' (1 Peter 1.4). And then the culmination of the Bible at the end of time with the heavenly city coming down to earth where, note again, the *home* of God is with people. And he will wipe every tear from our eye. The city of light, full of bright heaven's bright sun.[18]

Home is foundational to our well-being. But home isn't usually like the picture-perfect glossy images of *Hello* magazine. Our homes are flawed and broken, but at the best of times they carry shafts of light from heaven where all is well.

Beacons of hope guide us home. Sometimes they are just pinpricks in the darkness. Faintest whispers of the warmth of the heavenly hearth, retuning us for the wonder of the heavenly love song from the fiery heart of our Father in our home in heaven. He is longing, with deep fiery love in his heart, for his lost sons and daughters to come home, safe at last.

Going further

For group discussion

1 Home. When you hear the word 'home', what does that conjure up for you? (Go for your gut reaction, trying not to think too hard.) Do you have a favourite film, song, poem about home?
2 Can you share a story about losing something or someone?
3 'Tears are a sign of the Holy Spirit.' What do you think?
4 What does God think of you? When my friend read this chapter, she said: 'I realize now that God loves us like I love my boys.' What would you say is God's opinion of you?
5 'We are waking up. Jesus is spot on. People are harassed and helpless like sheep without a shepherd. The harvest is plentiful.' How do you react to this?

For personal devotion

Read: Luke 15.11–32

Prayer of St Cuthbert: Almighty God, who called your servant Cuthbert from keeping sheep to follow your Son and to be a shepherd of your people, graciously grant that we, following his example and caring for those who are lost, may bring them home to your fold, through your Son Jesus Christ our Lord. Amen.

3
Wonders of God in their own languages

How do we hear about home? Our real home? And the big family we actually belong to? How do we catch a glimpse of how things really are? How do our hearts sense the fiery love in the heart of God for his lost sons and daughters? How can they come back home, if they haven't heard where it is?[1] How do our minds begin to grasp this incredible news? How do our beacons convey this message?

The first glimpse of all this that I remember was when I was four years old. I spotted pictures of Jesus on the walls of my classroom, and I started to dream about him. In the dreams he was my friend. He asked me to help him with a rescue. When you're four, you're rarely asked to help with anything significant, so this made quite the impression on me.

Dreams are powerful. Who hasn't woken up from a dream and had to pinch yourself to check that what you were dreaming isn't reality? Dreams have real currency in our culture. Listen to 'A Million Dreams', the hit song from the 2017 film *The Greatest Showman*.

Films, songs, pictures, dreams – these can all give us clues to the way back home. We reach out to find the way, over the rainbow. In the last chapter, we saw how the longing in the heart of the Father for his missing daughters and sons is so intense and so agonizing that it forces its way into our culture through films, advertising, songs. Listen to the beautiful coming-home lyrics of 'The Prayer', written for the 1998 Disney Film *Quest for Camelot*.

Live on air

There's a moment in live broadcasting when the producer announces: 'We're live on air.' I can't say I'm a regular on the airwaves, but I have experienced that moment – and it is a particular moment – when the red light comes on and we switch from being 'off air' to 'on air'.

When it comes to hearing about our real home, there really was a moment in history when everything changed. When the heavenly comms switched to 'live on air'. Red light on, eureka moment, curtain rising on the blockbuster film. This moment is so important, yet it's often overlooked or lost in translation, so I'm making it the focus of this chapter.

So when was this moment?

If we go back in time to the Old Testament part of the Bible, we find there are previews of the 3D film that are 'ticket only' – only certain people are invited to preview the trailer; only certain people received the transmission, so to speak. Giants of faith like Abraham, leaders like Moses, prophets like Elijah. There was always the hope that, one day, more people would get an invitation. This hope stretched over a thousand years.

Then came Jesus, God's Word in the flesh, the long-awaited Saviour. Was this the moment? Surely if you'd been with Jesus for real, it would have been like getting a front-row seat for the blockbuster? Red light, on air. But strangely, despite his following at the time, those who heard Jesus speak in person didn't seem to get what he was talking about, not even his closest friends. His death was a disappointment. His resurrection was confusing. His friends ran away frightened. He appeared to them in person, but when asked directly – 'Is this the time when the kingdom will be restored?' – Jesus was evasive (Acts 1.6–7). And then, all of a sudden – he left. So no, that wasn't the moment then.

Just wait, Jesus said mysteriously, 'until you have been clothed with power from on high' (Luke 24.49).

Wait again? Really? Anti-climax. Such a disappointment.

But they waited. Ten days his followers waited and prayed. In hiding. In an upper room. Behind locked doors.

Then came the moment. Finally. Then came the game changer. Red light – on air. The doors were literally flung off their hinges. By wind and fire. On the Day of Pentecost. Here's what happened, carefully recorded from eye-witness accounts:

> When the day of Pentecost came, they were all together in one place. Suddenly a sound like the blowing of a violent wind came from heaven and filled the whole house where they were sitting. They saw what seemed to be tongues of fire that separated and came to rest on each of them. All of them were filled with the Holy Spirit and began to speak in other tongues as the Spirit enabled them.
> (Acts 2.1–4)

They were filled with the Holy Spirit, the Spirit of God, the same 'power from on high' that brought Jesus back from the dead.

And the result?

> Now there were staying in Jerusalem God-fearing Jews from every nation under heaven. When they heard this sound, a crowd came together in bewilderment, because each one heard their own language being spoken. Utterly amazed, they asked: 'Aren't all these who are speaking Galileans? Then how is it that each of us hears them in our native language? Parthians, Medes and Elamites; residents of Mesopotamia, Judea and Cappadocia, Pontus and Asia, Phrygia and Pamphylia, Egypt and the parts of Libya near Cyrene; visitors from Rome (both Jews and converts to Judaism); Cretans and Arabs – we hear them declaring the wonders of God in our own languages!' Amazed and perplexed, they asked one another, 'What does this mean?'
> (Acts 2.5–12, NIV UK 2011 adapted)

What was the result of this wind and fire of God's Spirit? Incredibly, it was that people, from all over the known world, heard them declaring *the wonders of God in their own languages* (Acts 2.11).

People from all sorts of backgrounds could suddenly hear and understand. Live on air. The lightbulb eureka moment.

Lost in translation

We all can relate to what it feels like to lose something in translation.

During the Covid-19 lockdown, I found myself running a secondary school at home and a school canteen in my spare time. My older son asked me if I could help him with his GCSE RE lesson. 'Yes, of course. What's the topic?' 'Mission, evangelism and church growth.' Brilliant! I leapt up like a Labrador to help . . . that's exactly my brief as Bishop of Lancaster. 'Right, Mum, what do you think of this question about evangelism?' He played a YouTube clip he'd been given by his teacher. My heart sank. Men on streets of New York with big cross and placard. 'Repent, the end is nigh.' I laughed – that's not evangelism. Can you imagine that working? It's really embarrassing and off-putting. (And I'm not sure even Jesus himself could have made that work, but that's another story for later.)

Our heart-wrenching, life-changing message of home can so easily be lost in translation. Morse code without the code book. We need to hear it in our own language. The language we understand.

The challenge is that we all hear differently and speak differently. Even within one country there are thousands of subcultures. Age, gender, geography, ethnicity, social setting . . . the list stretches on. Our advertisers are well tuned in. For example, the marketers at YouTube seem very savvy about targeting adverts appropriate to my age and gender. It jars when their algorithm gets it wrong. I'm not sure what led them to suggest enticingly with cute smiley baby that it was time for me to buy a pregnancy test: 'One more smile.' It stands out in my memory, because it jarred so much. That said, I then received a news feed about supermodel Naomi Campbell having a miracle baby at 51 ('Even more ancient than you, Mum!', assured my son), so perhaps it was a subtle encouragement to follow the celebrity trend.

Humour is one of the most obvious examples of getting lost in translation. Here the airwaves can easily get tangled. I spent ten formative years growing up in an all-female environment at an all-girls school in Bolton. I was fortunate that, for me, school was a very happy place. My instincts for relationships have been forged in that context. Number one rule – never say anything negative about another girl's appearance. Compliment or keep quiet. In fact, complimenting can be a great way to authentically build relationships. My friend, Kate, has just posted me a luscious set of stick-on nails to try, simply because when we met for dinner it was the first thing I complimented. It turns out she's an evangelist for them, so it really was a win–win: I genuinely meant I liked her nails; she took pleasure in sending me a free pack. Compliments are king in an all-female setting. Turns out that's not the rule in an all-male context. In fact, pretty much the opposite. I find myself unnecessarily leaping to the defence of male colleagues being teased about their new jacket. But I've checked and double-checked: my colleagues genuinely find that teasing builds relationships. That simply isn't a first line of communication that would have occurred to me to build mutual appreciation. My son happily says, 'But when you get teased about what you look like, Mum, it's a sign people like you.' Really? Eessh – I'd never try to negotiate that minefield with other women. Unexploded bombs everywhere.

It's a damp squib when humour gets lost in translation. Jokes often tread a fine line – it's the daring that makes them funny and builds the team. But more important messages can get lost in translation too.

Here's the incredible thing about 'that moment', about the coming of God's Spirit on the Day of Pentecost. The gift of God's Spirit, his breath (the word 'spirit' and 'breath' are interchangeable in the original languages) – to everyone – flicked a switch to 'live on air'. Now people could hear the wonders of God in their own languages. No more need for lost in translation. The Spirit of God is wonderfully creative. The creator of language, the original translator, can loosen tongues to speak and unblock ears to hear. He can connect our speaking with their hearing, and vice versa.

Let's unpack the two ways God's Spirit is described in this hinge moment of heavenly comms in Acts 2: wind and fire. These are two metaphors that are close to my heart. They both signal the way back home.

1 Wind

When Jesus first speaks of the Spirit, he says he's like the wind:

> The wind blows wherever it pleases. You hear its sound, but you cannot tell where it comes from or where it is going. So it is with everyone born of the Spirit.
> (John 3.8)

Then at this hinge moment in history, in Acts 2, when the wind blew, quite unexpectedly, people could hear the wonders of God in their own languages.

My experience in the UK is that God's Spirit has a wonderful way of unbinding tongues so that they can speak the wonders of God in new languages. Let me give you an example.

In the seventh century, there was an incredible flowering of the Christian faith across the North, as people heard the message of Jesus for the first time. You may have heard of St Hilda – schools and colleges are named after her, even today. She was founder and abbess of a mixed-gender monastery in Whitby that sent out bishops and evangelists all across Britain. You may not have heard of Caedmon. He was a cattle herder, who looked after the animals in the monastery. He was shy and tongue-tied: he found it very difficult to make himself understood. But one night he had this dream that he could sing a heavenly song about the creation of the world. When he woke up he could remember the song – in fact he could still sing it. He told his boss and his boss told Hilda, who invited Caedmon to sing at the feast. This was the start of an incredible ministry – Caedmon would sing the gospel in the local Anglo-Saxon language in words that the ordinary people could understand.

Here's the thing: I keep spotting Caedmons everywhere. Often in hiding, tongue-tied, unable to get their words out, but it seems the Spirit of God releases them to speak the wonders of God in their own language. It is beautiful to behold.

In Preston, Lancashire, Smith Wigglesworth used to preach in the 1930s. He was 'a straight-talking Yorkshire lad with little education, no training and no credentials, but he shook the earth with his miracle-producing faith. For four decades spectacular healings and deliverances followed his preaching of the Gospel in many nations of the world.[2] Early on in his story, he was so fearful to speak he used to leave the preaching to his wife because he couldn't get his words out.

Across our nation today there are people hiding away, tongue-tied, but I believe the Spirit of God wants to come to call you out of hiding, to release your tongues so that people can hear the wonders of God in their own language. A Pentecost, today and every day.

What if we had people on fire with the Spirit of Jesus alight in every sphere of influence in our society: in our families, in our churches, in our schools and universities, in the media, in business, in law, in government, in entertainment and sport – so people could hear the wonders of God in their own language? What might this look like?

What would it look like for Jesus to breathe his Spirit on our nation today?

C. S. Lewis describes this with beautiful imagination in his children's book *The Lion, the Witch and the Wardrobe*.

The lion Aslan, back from the dead, ransacks the White Witch's fortress where she has taken hundreds of creatures captive by turning them into stone. Aslan bounds up to a stone lion and breathes on him.

At that moment Lucy said, 'Oh, Susan! Look! Look at the lion.' I expect you've seen someone put a lighted match to a bit of newspaper which is propped up in a grate against an unlit fire. And for a second nothing seems to have happened; and then you notice a tiny streak of flame creeping along the edge of the newspaper. It was like that now. For a second after Aslan had breathed upon him the stone lion looked just the same. Then a tiny streak of gold began to run along his white marble back then it spread – then the colour seemed to lick all over him as the flame licks all over a bit of paper – then . . . he opened a great red mouth, warm and living, and gave a prodigious yawn . . . Then, having caught sight of Aslan, he went bounding after him and frisking round him whimpering with delight and jumping up to lick his face . . . Everywhere the statues were coming to life. The courtyard looked no longer like a museum; it looked more like a zoo . . . And instead of the deadly silence the whole place rang with the sound of happy roarings, brayings, yelpings, barkings, squealings, cooings, neighings, stampings, shouts, hurrahs, songs and laughter.[3]

For many years, I have found that when I pray for our nation, I feel I am tuning in to hear a choir singing in amazing harmony with so many parts that I cannot count them. A choir made up of the Church present and the Church past, plus many of the heavenly hosts. And as this choir find their voice, sing from their hearts in gorgeous harmonies, the land literally is sung back to life. Like a heavenly Eisteddfod! I am praying for tongues to be unbound, so that people can hear the wonders of God in their own languages.

Here's a lovely example from living memory. In the twentieth century the Church of England declined for most decades. Apart from one. After the national trauma of the Second World War, the Church grew in the 1940s and early 1950s. Why? Not because of great bishops. But research suggests that there were a number of writers and artists who were able to communicate the gospel in everyday language: for example, C. S. Lewis, Dorothy Sayers, Simone Weil, T. S. Eliot. I am praying for writers, artists, musicians, after this national trauma of the Covid-19 pandemic, to find their gifts with fresh courage and verve. And more than this, for those with gifts who have never used them to come out of hiding (see more on this in Chapter 4). All in ways never been imagined before: all the colours in the palette; all the instruments in the orchestra; the beats in the band; textures from heaven, on frequencies that people from all our marvellously varied subcultures can tune into and find their hearts warmed by the fire of his love.

Who would have thought that a wordless picture book would have made it on to the bestseller list and into hospital wards across the country? Don't miss Charlie Mackesy's homely drawings of *The Boy, the Mole, the Fox and the Horse*.[4]

Common frequency?

Of course, God's Spirit doesn't just transmit on one frequency. He made the universe, in all its glorious and extravagant beauty. The painter of stripes on the okapi or the voice coach of the song thrush – he's not 'one size fits all'. He knows full well that people speak and hear well on many, many different frequencies. He's a master translator.

In this book, I talk of beacons, fire, 'Come home', the Father's breaking heart. That's just a tiny take on the message. Scripture is packed with countless more images – debts paid, acquittal in the law courts, the heavenly banquet, the homecoming, and some more alien to our culture – lambs slaughtered in the Jewish sacrificial system, slaves ransomed. It can be like trying to imagine a glass of vintage wine by reading the tasting notes, or a holiday from write-ups on Tripadvisor. Whatever words you pick, they never do justice to the real thing. Understandably, we often get attached to the way we first heard the message, the frequency on which we first tuned in. We want others to love that holiday hideaway on Tripadvisor as much as we did. But we are all different. Wonderfully different. My taste in music is different from my teenage son's. God's Spirit enables people to speak and hear the message in their own individual way. The chef of the heavenly banquet creates many different courses; the conductor of the heavenly orchestra has countless melodies and harmonies under his baton.

On first blush, like Aslan's releasing of the stone animals in the White Witch's fortress, this might sound rather chaotic. Just as this sudden deluge of the Spirit on the Day of Pentecost caused quite the commotion. Defied expectations. Some dismissed Jesus' followers as drunk. We all have an instinct for order and control. This Pentecost hinge moment can be dismissed as a crazy one-off. But it was necessary to literally blow the doors off their hinges. God's good news isn't just for one particular people, in one place at one time. He can't possibly just broadcast on a common frequency in a common language, common prayers, common worship. Everyone is welcome in God's family. Opening the floodgates can seem chaotic.

But this was the divine plan all along. Peter grabs the microphone, so to speak, and he takes his Jewish audience back to the words of the prophet Joel, centuries earlier:

In the last days, God says,
I will pour out my Spirit on all people.
Your sons and daughters will prophesy,
   your young men will see visions,
   your old men will dream dreams.
Even on my servants, both men and women,
   I will pour out my Spirit in those days
   and they will prophesy.
(Acts 2.17–18)

Across our nation, I am convinced the Spirit of God is and has been giving prophecies, visions and dreams. But people think they're mad, they're too ambitious and it'll never happen.

- You are not mad if you are seeing visions from God. We desperately need you in the Church in our society. In part, we have rationalized away the wonderful things of God, even though many scientists, like me, find science speaks volumes about God. We apologize for 'god-incidences'. But these are the calling cards of his Spirit. The book of Acts was full of visions. Vision of a man from Macedonia – precisely guiding a whole shift in missionary work – key in bringing the message of Jesus to Europe from the Middle East (Acts 16.8–9). I'm really pleased that Ananias listened to his vision in Acts 9, telling him to go to Straight Street and ask for a man from Tarsus called Saul. If you are seeing visions please do not apologize. You are being given them for a reason. Act on them. Don't keep them to yourself. You are like the spiritual GCHQ, like troops who have those special night-vision goggles to spy out the terrain ahead.

- You are not ambitious if you have dreams from God. I think there are people reading this chapter who have had dreams from God that seem so big that you have consigned them to fantasy land. They can't possibly happen. No . . . he is the One who is able to do immeasurably more than all we can ask or imagine (Ephesians 3.20). Dreams from God are always far beyond us. I am praying that he will wake up our dreams today. Remind us of his beautiful whispers in the night.

A twentieth-century heroine of mine is Henrietta Mears. Born in North Dakota in 1890, she is virtually unknown, but she was convinced of the spiritual significance of good leadership. From a place of hiddenness, she had an astonishing influence on a generation of significant male leaders in US Christianity. You may not have heard of her, but you may well have heard of Billy Graham, and Campus Crusades, whose missions have had astonishing influence across the world. When she was interviewed as an old woman, she was asked if she had any regrets. She answered: 'I wish I had asked Jesus for bigger mountains; I wish I had dreamed bigger dreams.'[5]

I would love to see Jesus unleash his bigger dreams today.

- You're not mad if you prophesy – 'eagerly desire spiritual gifts, especially the gift of prophecy' (1 Corinthians 14.1, NIV 1984). I remember this verse jumping off the page in my twenties and thinking, what's that about? What is prophecy today? I simply had a sense that Jesus wanted to coach me. To tune into Scripture for those verses which seem to resonate into that situation you're in, to expect his words, his promptings, his pictures. When I was Director of St Mellitus NW, training vicars for the Church of England, I remember my first year of writing student reports for the bishops. Overwhelmed by the size of the task, I came to God in my weakness. I felt his whispered, 'Ask for a word for each one.' For my group of eight, I asked for a word – a Bible verse and/or image – ten seconds each. I was so desperate I just went with what I heard. Each time I met a student to talk about their report, I'd waffle on for half an hour then have the courage to say the verse or picture. Does this mean anything to you? Every single time, it unlocked a new deeper level in our conversation. Now I don't wait for half an hour. I ask for words and pictures and prophecies the moment I start speaking to people. If you want to grow in this area, I recommend Bill Cahusac's book, *That Gentle Whisper*.[6] There you'll find beautiful stories of how his tuning in, gently and without fuss, unlocked hearts and undammed tears. Prophecy is much more than a word or picture. It also includes the courage to challenge the injustices of the present with a vision of the kingdom; the insight to apply Scripture to the context you find yourself in. Maybe Jesus is wanting to give you the gift of prophecy today. It's a gift that can shape organizations, churches, workplaces, governments.

In a late-night conversation with a key religious teacher of his day, Nicodemus, Jesus used this analogy for the Spirit: 'The wind blows wherever it pleases. You hear its sound, but you cannot tell where it comes from or where it is going. So it is with everyone born of the Spirit' (John 3.8). This is a beautiful invitation. I love the sense that living the life of the Spirit invites me into his gentle wildness. To speak on the wind of his Spirit. To tune into his breath which created everything I see out of nothing. I like to tune in and see what questions I should ask people when I'm out and about. I was in a taxi – only a ten-minute ride from the railway station. We got chatting. As you do. I felt prompted to ask the taxi driver about his dad. Every fibre of Britishness in me fought back. I can't possibly ask a stranger that sort of question. But the prompting intensified. I couldn't hold it in. 'When did you last see your dad?' The dam burst and out poured this incredible story of pain, misunderstanding and longing for reconciliation. I paid the fare. 'Maybe you could tell your dad what you told me. I bet he'd like to know. I will pray you'll find a common frequency.' There were tears in his eyes as he left. The atmosphere felt like that release after a lightning storm.

2 Fire

They saw what seemed to be tongues of fire that separated and came to rest on each of them.
(Acts 2.3)

We highlighted the trail of fire in Scripture in Chapter 1.

Just like the wind, the breath of God, the purpose is the same. Fire to turn hearts towards home, like a lighthouse bringing hope to ships lost in dark seas. Fire so that people could hear the wonders of God in their own languages. We've heard about fire in this way already. For example, when Elijah calls down fire from heaven on Mount Carmel, the purpose is so that 'these people will know that you, LORD, are God, and that you are *turning their hearts* back again' (1 Kings 18.37). Similarly, another baton carrier of the fiery torch, John the Baptist, is to 'go before the Lord, in the spirit and power of Elijah, to *turn the hearts* of the fathers to their children and the disobedient to the wisdom of the righteous' (Luke 1.17).

I have found it so encouraging to trace this fiery baton handed down by those who have gone before us in the race of faith. Here are a just few resting points on the journey to warm your heart. The testimonies of the great cloud of witnesses, the stadium of the saints, those unseen heroes of the faith who surround us with their encouragement, cheering us on.[7]

Fire to set us all aflame. From around the third century in Egypt, several generations of monks and nuns lived simple lives of prayer as hermits in the desert of Egypt. The *Sayings of the Desert Fathers* (or Abbas) shows how they tuned in on astonishing spiritual frequencies and people sought out their wisdom from far and wide. One saying tells how Abba Lot went to see Abba Joseph and said to him: 'Abba, as far as I can, I say my [prayers], I fast a little, I pray and meditate, I live in peace and as far as I can, I purify my thoughts. What else can I do?' Then the old man stood up and stretched his

42

hands towards heaven. His fingers became like ten lamps of fire and he said to him, 'If you will, you can become all flame.'[8]

Fire that lights cities. John Chrysostom, Archbishop of Constantinople in the fourth century, said: 'If but ten among us lead a holy life, we shall kindle a fire which shall light up an entire city.'

Fire to defy the darkness. Part of St Patrick's story in ancient Ireland is captured by contemporary band Rend Collective's 'Revival Anthem'. The song is introduced with the story of a defining moment for Patrick. In AD 433, a fire was lit in honour of the sun god Bel by the High King and druids of Ireland, who commanded that there should be no other flames lit in the land during the time of their festival. But in direct defiance, Patrick courageously lit a fire to celebrate Christ, the High King of Heaven and light of the world. The rest is history.

Fire that is catching. Two centuries after Patrick, the fire leapt across the sea to Columba's mission base on the remote Scottish island of Iona, still a popular pilgrimage destination today. Aidan, an Irish monk from Iona, was invited to bring the gospel to the Northumbrians by his friend, King Oswald, who had lived in exile on Iona as a boy. Aidan led the way for an incredible flourishing of mission across the north of England in the seventh century. He called out such a significant number of leaders that he was named as 'the apostle of England' by Bishop Lightfoot (a nineteenth-century bishop of Durham). Aidan was famed for his gentleness. Wherever he went, he would simply ask people if they knew Jesus. If they did, he would encourage their faith. If they didn't, by then they were already intrigued and he would simply introduce them to Jesus. Aidan is always depicted with a torch of fire in his hand.

Fire that is enduring. Cuthbert, a shepherd boy in Northumbria, watching sheep by night on the Lammermuir Hills, saw a vision of a fiery chariot in the sky. He concluded that some saint must be on their way to heaven. In the morning he discovered that Aidan (who by then had become Bishop of Lindisfarne) had died in the night. This vision was enough for him to leave his sheep and train to be a monk. Cuthbert became known for his healing miracles, his wrestling with demons in prayer to reclaim the Farne Islands as his place of hermitage, and his gentle persistence in the face of opposition – 'He wore them down with his patience.'[9]

Fire that warms up our love. Richard Rolle was a hermit from Yorkshire. His book *The Fire of Love*, written in 1343, has inspired generations. He begins with beguiling openness:

> I cannot tell you how surprised I was the first time I felt my heart begin to warm. It was real warmth too, not imaginary, and it felt as if it were actually on fire. I was astonished at the way the heat surged up, and how this new sensation brought great and unexpected comfort. I had to keep feeling my breast to make sure there was no physical reason for it! But once I realised that it came entirely from within, that this fire of love had no cause, material or sinful, but was the gift of my Maker, I was absolutely delighted, and wanted my love to be even greater.[10]

Fire that comforts. Margery Kempe, from Norwich in the following generation (1373–c. 1438):

> Our Lord gave her another token, which endured about sixteen years, and it increased ever more and more, and that was a flame of fire, wonderfully hot and delectable and right comfortable, not wasting but ever increasing of flame, for though the weather was never so cold, she felt the heat burning in her breast and at her heart, and verily as a man should feel the material fire if he put his hand or finger there in.[11]

Fire that inspires. Catherine of Siena, across in Italy, also in the fourteenth century (1347–80) had much to say about fire in her pithy soundbites: 'The devil fears hearts on fire with the love of God.' 'Be who God called you to be and you will set the world on fire.' Catherine has been a special accompanier during the writing of this book. I used this last quotation on the first ordination cards I sent to our new priests in Lancashire. Several years on, Emma, one of our priests with a gift for crocheting, sent me my very own crocheted Catherine, through the post, complete with a globe on fire. She is sitting on my desk as I type.

Fire to be handled with care. Teresa of Ávila, a Spanish nun, 200 years later in the sixteenth century, warns us to handle this fire carefully:

> This love must flow into interior reflection, not boil over like a cooking pot that has been put on too fierce a fire, and so spills its contents. The source of the fire must be controlled. An endeavour must be made to quench its flames with gentle tears.[12]

Fire that cauterizes our wounds. Her companion, John of the Cross, another Spanish mystic, highlights the related property of fire to cauterize our wounds in his poem *The Living Flame of Love*: 'O sweet cautery, O delightful wound! O gentle hand! O delicate touch . . .'[13] We will explore this beautiful work of cauterization more in Chapter 11.

Fire that gathers crowds. John Wesley, a depressed Anglican priest, found himself at a meeting of the Moravians[14] in London on 27 May 1738. On hearing Paul's letter to the Romans read from the Bible, he famously describes how his heart became 'strangely warmed'. This experience transformed him. He became a fiery preacher whose preaching translated outside the usual Church of England congregations. He was once asked how he managed to gather such crowds outdoors to hear him preach. His answer? 'I set myself on fire and people come to watch me burn.'

Fire that warms us with radiance. Seraphim of Sarov (1750s–1833) spent most of his life as a hermit in a log cabin outside Sarov. He's one of the most revered Russian saints. A meeting with him in

1831 is recorded by Motovilov in *The Aim of the Christian Life*. As the young man encountered the presence of God with the elderly saint, there had been peace, inexpressible sweetness and unspeakable joy. It is followed by this intriguing conversation. Seraphim asked:

> 'What else do you feel?' 'An unusual warmth,' replied Motovilov. 'How warm?' 'As in a sauna, when they pour hot water on the hot stone.' Seraphim continued: 'But how is it warm? It is now the end of November; it is winter and there is snow under our feet and there is a sprinkling of snow on our heads, and it is snowing and the wind is blowing; how can it be as warm as in the sauna?' Then he added, 'It is warm, Lover of God, not in the air, but in ourselves. This is the same warmth about which we speak to God in our prayer: 'Warm us with the radiance of Thy Holy Spirit.'[15]

In all these examples, fire communicates the presence of God. A presence which is catching. One of my home-grown heroes, Samuel Chadwick, a cotton-worker from Burnley in Lancashire, who became in turn President of the Methodist Conference (1919–20), wrote this:

> Spirit-filled souls are ablaze for God. They love with a love that glows, they shine with a faith that kindles, they serve with a devotion that consumes, they hate sin with a fierceness that burns. They rejoice with a joy that radiates. Love is perfected by the fire of God.[16]

Beacons and Caedmon

Just like beacons, the fire of the Holy Spirit starts a chain reaction. And like beacons, you only get to see part of the chain. When a beacon is lit on a hilltop, others see it from a distance and light their beacon. But the point of this communication is that the original beacon is out of sight.

Hilda at Whitby didn't have the language to pass on the gospel message to local Anglo-Saxon farmers. She needed Caedmon to do this. There will be many of you with friends, family, colleagues who wouldn't understand what I'm trying to say in this book. But if you understand me, you could translate the message for them. I would love this book to light many beacons. Not just to inspire faith in our readers, but like a chain of beacons, my prayer is that faith inspired in you will catch fire and reach people of different ages, stages, languages, backgrounds, so many more can hear 'the wonders of God in their own language', so many lost daughters and sons might hear their Father's calling from his fiery heart of love: 'We miss you, please come home.'

Going further

For group discussion

1 Lightbulb moments: can you give an example where you've experienced one of these – either fun or serious?
2 Dreams and visions: have you had a memorable or persistent dream or vision that you would be able to share with the group?
3 Lost in translation: when have you got lost in translation? What gets lost in translation in the message of Jesus today?
4 Caedmon was once tongue-tied. Something happened in his dream so that when he woke up he could sing the wonders of God in a language that the local people could understand.
   (a) Might you be a Caedmon?
   (b) What does it look like to find fresh ways of singing the wonders of God in a language that people can understand today?
   (c) Do you have favourite examples of writers, artists, film-makers, who manage to convey the gospel in everyday language like some of our writers in the 1940s and 1950s did?
5 Torches of fire: were there quotations which particularly warmed your heart, and why?
6 Breath of God: what would it look like for Jesus to breathe his Spirit on our nation today?

For personal devotion

Read: Acts 2.1–24

Prayer to conclude: Jesus, would you fill me with your breath, so I may speak on the winds of your Spirit. Always for your glory. Amen.

4

Breathing the oxygen of peace

At Pentecost, this hinge moment in time, the Spirit of God came like fire and wind. The breath of God on all his people. Fire and wind are popular manifestations of God's Spirit in Scripture. But there is a third.

Completing the picture, the Bible gives another description of this hinge moment when the Holy Spirit came as a gift for everyone. Like most of the world's incredible events, the Bible contains accounts from different vantage points. This one is John's account. We have every good reason to think John was one of Jesus' closest disciples.

Here's what John witnessed on the first Easter Day in the evening:

> On the evening of that first day of the week, when the disciples were together, with the doors locked for fear of the Jewish leaders, Jesus came and stood among them and said, 'Peace be with you!' After he said this, he showed them his hands and side. The disciples were overjoyed when they saw the Lord.
>
> Again Jesus said, 'Peace be with you! As the Father has sent me, I am sending you.' And with that he breathed on them and said, 'Receive the Holy Spirit. If you forgive anyone's sins, their sins are forgiven; if you do not forgive them, they are not forgiven.'
> (John 20.19–23)

The third manifestation of the breath of God is – peace.

After the commotion of fire and wind in the previous chapter, this manifestation is gentle and tender; you might even say, intimate. 'He breathes out, we breathe in' – I love this description from

'The Vision' poem, which came from the first ever 24-7 Prayer Room.[1] Bernard of Clairvaux (1090–1153) described this with even more intimacy – 'the kiss' of Jesus. His loving presence is so close.

As a scientist, I couldn't resist this chapter title – 'Breathing the oxygen of peace'. Oxygen is what makes fire burn. Perhaps you tried that experiment in chemistry at school. Put a lit candle under a glass jar. It burns for as long as there's still oxygen in the air trapped under the jar.

The third manifestation of the Holy Spirit is peace. He calls us home with a taster of the atmosphere of heaven. The oxygen of heaven. Peace.

Through history, again and again, the presence of God brings peace. Moses found this. Elijah found this. Isaiah found this.

And in each of our four accounts of Jesus' life, when the Holy Spirit first comes on Jesus, he appears – unusually – in exactly the same way – as a dove, the symbol of peace.[2]

I only noticed this prominence of peace when I started teaching about evangelism. I based my teaching on the 'go to' passage for Jesus' teaching about mission – Luke 10 – when he sends his disciples out into the towns and villages ahead of him. His top tip is to look for a 'person of peace'. If your peace rests, then stay with that person; if not, just move on.

This advice was a big relief to me. Growing up as the only Christian in my family, then working in a secular workplace for my early adult life, I had noticed there were some people who were more open to engaging with the big questions in life; and some people who just weren't. This could change at different times. My mum had been unwelcoming to such conversations about faith since the moment she'd thought I'd been brainwashed . . . until the very end, 30 years later, in a very beautiful story (see back to Chapter 1).

I kept finding that peace would often precede an encounter with God. So I decided to be even more proactive about it. Walking into new situations, new places, new meetings, I always try to remember to invite his peace. I have got used to ending a conversation with: 'Can I pray for you?' People rarely refuse. And I always invite Jesus to send his peace from heaven. Even grown men have wiped away tears. I remember our under-14 rugby tour. Fascinating conversation with one of the dads at breakfast. He'll still say to me sometimes: 'I feel quite teary remembering that time.' The peace from heaven is so very near.

Here are my three favourite stories about this peace drawing near. All in very different areas of life.

The girls

From 2010 when our boys were small, we used to live in a vicarage in the middle of Widnes, an ex-chemical industry town on the River Mersey. The glory days of industrial might had transformed a sleepy village into an industrial 'hell on earth' (as the town plaque winsomely commemorated in 1905). These days were long since passed. The stunning town hall across the square from St Paul's Church, where my husband was vicar, was now a nightclub. There were seven others within spitting distance. Many with licences to play very loud music till 5 a.m. The downside was it was very noisy to be there on a Friday or Saturday night (usually time to escape to our caravan in North Wales). The plus side was that there were plenty of takeaways on tap.

One Friday night in February, when it was too cold to stay at our caravan, I was walking the 100 yards from the vicarage to pick up our Friday night curry. It was dark, 7 o'clock. I bumped into three teenage girls. I felt sorry that they were out on such a cold night. 'What are you doing out on a night like this?' They couldn't go home ''cos Mum's out at bingo and Chloe's been kicked out of school'. I didn't have much to offer them, so in desperation I offered to pray (it had become my habit to pray for peace with teenagers when I was a chaplain at a school in Liverpool). I prayed simply that Chloe would get back into school, and that they would know the peace of Jesus. When I looked up, their heads were up, alert like meerkats. Like me, they had noticed a change in the atmosphere. Something of a heavenly peace. They were intrigued. 'So where are you from?' I explained that I lived over there in the vicarage and invited them to come to church on Sunday afternoon to *St Paul's@4* – our weekly all-age service at 4 p.m.

Sunday afternoon came, and I was leading the children's work at church. That sentence sounds more impressive than it was. I had about five kids between the ages of 5 and 11 on random chairs around a table in an old room at the back of church. Suddenly, in walked the three teenage girls. My heart sank. I was struggling as it was. We were looking at a story in the Bible where Jesus asks a blind man, Bartimaeus: 'What do you want me to do for you?' (Mark 10.51). I had got the kids drawing pictures in response. This was so age inappropriate for teenagers. There was nothing for it. 'Ahem – would you like to draw what you would like Jesus to do for you?' The first girl tossed her hair, resentfully grabbed a felt tip pen, and wrote: 'I would like Jesus to give me £1.20.' The second girl copied her mutiny and wrote exactly the same. And so did the third. 'This is SO boring,' they rolled their eyes at each other ('I know it is,' I inwardly groaned), got up and left. I assumed that would be the last I'd see of them.

That evening, the girls were walking down the street near church. A tramp crossed the road; he shoved some money in their hand. It was £3.60. Chloe was allowed back into school. The following week, she came back to church with her friends and this time brought her boyfriend too. 'This is SO boring,' he moaned, right in front of me. But Chloe was quick off the mark: 'Yeah, but she prays and things happen!'

The dentist

Then there was the conversation with my dentist. It was the end of the first lockdown. I could feel the stress from the dentist's chair. And it wasn't fear about my teeth. What I learnt was that dentists had been classified with beauty therapists so there hadn't been the financial support given to other medical businesses. And now there was so much cleaning and sanitizing and spacing out of appointments. So I said simply, I believe that Jesus can bind up fear and in its place release the opposite – his peace from heaven. Can I pray for you? So I prayed a very simple prayer. When I looked up, I could feel the atmosphere had shifted. The dentist and her nurse were wiping tears from their eyes. When I went back, six months later, for my next check-up, she said: 'Your prayers had such a profound effect on me and Julia. Even thinking about them now makes me cry.'

The school

As a chaplain at Liverpool College, I used to pray daily that when our pupils (aged 4–18) came to chapel they would encounter a sense of God's peace. Not that they would 'learn about' or 'know about' Jesus, though of course I longed for this too. But quite simply that they would encounter the peace of Jesus for real. Because I wanted them to meet him.

One moment stands out. It was senior school chapel, when the head of house and I walked out at the end of the service down the aisle (senior chapels were fairly formal). I felt a deep wave of peace. 'Did you notice that?' she gasped. Once she'd experienced this, she wanted more. I soon found she was sneaking into chapel, ahead of a busy teaching schedule, 'to get my head in the right place'.

As a bishop, it's a beautiful honour to call down God's blessing at the end of services. I often use the words from Philippians 4, which have meant so much to me personally: 'May the peace of God which passes all understanding keep your hearts and minds in the knowledge of God and of his son, Jesus Christ, and the blessing of God Almighty, Father, Son and Holy Spirit, be upon you and remain with you. Amen.' Jesus never disappoints.

Very movingly I was recently invited back to be the guest speaker at the Liverpool College 185th Founders' Day in 2021, held in the dramatic setting of Liverpool Cathedral, the largest Anglican cathedral in Europe. I knew the cathedral well – we used to worship there as a family when we lived in Liverpool city centre. For me it had memories, not of grandeur but of scrabbling on the floor chasing my two wriggly toddlers as a young mum. This time was a different vantage point. I preached about peace – the peace of heaven. Then at the end, I stood in the pulpit to call down God's blessing on more than 1,000 children, teenagers and staff. I give all the glory to God for this, but I lost count of the number of people who came up to me at the end. They were struggling to find words but trying to say something along the lines of – when you asked for God's blessing, what happened made me cry. Like the girls in Widnes, heads were up and the peace was tangible. ,

Seraphim, our Russian orthodox hermit (Chapter 3), puts it wisely: 'That I am a monk and you are a layman is of no importance – rather that we are both in the light of the Holy Spirit. *Acquire Peace*. And thousands around you will be saved.'³

Because here's the thing. The peace of heaven isn't just about a future reality. Peace is the atmosphere of heaven, and it breaks in now. Jesus breathes the peace of his Spirit now.

This is one of the things I love about the stories of Jesus in the Bible. With Jesus, the time is always now.

And this still applies today. Our nation is interested in the gospel, the good news about home. The harvest fields are plentiful. We have spiritual amnesia; we can be short-sighted in our reading of church history. We think that the Golden Age for faith and the gospel is in the past. That's a lie. Faith, in our nation, has always fallen and risen over time. For example, in the late eighteenth century, some studies suggest every fifth woman in London sold her body as a prostitute, the banking system corrupt. Forty years later, there'd been Christian reformers in Parliament, a swell of faith in churches of all traditions, and what's different? Slavery is abolished, working conditions for children and women significantly changed, London becomes the international centre for banking it is today because a gentleman's word was his promise. Truth had broken in.

And Jesus still says: 'The time is now.'

In Mark's fast-paced Gospel, there are no angels, shepherds, wise men, growing up. Jesus bursts on to the scene in a simple sentence:

> Jesus went into Galilee, proclaiming the good news of God. 'The time
> has come,' he said. 'The kingdom of God has come near. Repent and
> believe the good news!'
> (Mark 1.14–15)

We see this longing for that peace from heaven all over our media –
a longing for the kingdom of God to come near. Death was the
number one topic on my newsfeed yesterday. People are facing
death and reaching out for hope, peace and healing. Reaching out
for a bigger story. They are wanting to know it's going to be OK. It's
as if our nation has been covered with a scab of years of turning
the other way from God, but underneath there's the fresh skin of a
nation of giants of faith (see Chapter 8).

There was a beautiful interview on the TV breakfast show, *Good
Morning Britain,* in the middle of the January 2021 lockdown by
Holly Willoughby and Philip Schofield. They interviewed the Poor
Clare nuns from their enclosed convent in Arundel. These are
women who spend all their lives in lockdown. They have produced
an album which went viral: *Hope for the World.* It is absolutely
worth a listen. But the interview ended with Holly Willoughby in
tears . . . 'When you speak to people like that, they make you think
it's going to be OK.' Those nuns are singing the gospel.

Across our nation today, children, teenagers, men and women,
old and young want to know 'it's going to be OK'. This is the good
news from the heart of God. If you come home to Jesus, it's – going –
to be – OK. And Jesus says that the time for this news is now:

> Jesus went into Galilee, proclaiming the good news of God. 'The time
> has come,' he said. 'The kingdom of God has come near. Repent and
> believe the good news!'
> (Mark 1.14–15)

But hang on a minute, it could seem a bit weird nowadays to stand
on a street corner and say, 'The time is now. Repent and believe.'
It doesn't make sense, does it? In the last chapter, I described the

example of my son's RE classwork – a shouty man on a street corner in New York – 'Repent, the time is nigh.'

But, you might say, isn't that what Jesus did when he appeared on the scene? No! We've missed out the vital connecting ingredient: the kingdom of heaven is near.

Telling people that the time is now only makes sense if they *experience* it for themselves.

We might think that people are argued into the Christian faith. There is a place for intellectual wrangling, but all the data shows that people need to *experience* for themselves that the kingdom of God is near. And it is near now.

What do I mean by 'the kingdom of God is near'?

Another way of putting it is: heaven is drawing near. The place where God is King, where everything comes under his rule.

Humans are wired with an instinctive sense of what the world would look like when 'it's all OK'.

It bursts through in our films, our stories, our music, our art – that longing that one day, over the rainbow, it will all be OK, there will be the happily ever after. As you might have noticed, my favourite narratives (now wonderfully brought to life by film) are *The Lord of the Rings* trilogy and *The Chronicles of Narnia*. Evil is defeated. The humble hero ushers in the final scene where all is put right, people can live safely and securely. For me, the Bible describes this ultimate horizon with the most potent imagery I've ever heard. Here's a taster:

> Then I saw 'a new heaven and a new earth,' for the first heaven and the first earth had passed away, and there was no longer any sea. I saw the Holy City, the new Jerusalem, coming down out of heaven from God, prepared as a bride beautifully dressed for her husband. And I heard a loud voice from the throne saying, 'Look! God's dwelling-place is now among the people, and he will dwell with them. They will be his people, and God himself will be with them and be their God. "He will wipe every tear from their eyes. There will be no more death" or mourning or crying or pain, for the old order of things has passed away.'
> (Revelation 21.1–4)

Heavenly grandeur encompassing earth. Not in pomp and ceremony, but with the vulnerable homely love of a husband for his bride. The tenderest love imaginable, which reaches out to wipe every tear away. From every eye. No more death. No more mourning. No more crying. No more pain.

When I pray, I have a glimpse, an image in the corner of my eye, of the heavenly Lancaster, the heavenly Blackpool, the heavenly Blackburn. Coming down to earth. Yes of course it's quite hazy. But it's a place where children are fed, have fun and laugh; men and women flourish in harmony with joy; where different backgrounds, races and languages bring dynamism in place of division; where families and communities are fully alive, in all their colours, gifts and songs; creation is fresh, green and healthy; justice is done; where there is no more death or mourning or crying or pain.

All that can seem a bit hazy.

But it is possible for people to experience part of this now.

How? Not in the pomp and ceremony of the visitation of a heavenly choir. Ta-dah! But as we go deeper in the ways of Jesus, as we let him guide us (see Chapters 6 and 7) through prayer and Bible study, it's as if our senses subtly start to change. We start to see things through the eyes of Jesus; we start to feel with the heart of the Father; we start to hear promptings of the Spirit. It's hard to put into words. Like trying to describe a glass of the finest vintage wine – words fail. At the end of the day, you just have to try it.

Peace and *shalom*

And here's the more wonderful thing.

The Hebrew word for peace, *shalom*, is much bigger than peace in your heart, tears in your eyes. It's about the goodness, the wholeness of God soaking through all of society . . . in our businesses, schools and universities, our homes, the arts, media and sports, our health service, our government, our legal system . . . *Shalom* is not just inviting God's peace into individual lives, but rivers of peace overflowing from hearts wherever people find themselves. Not neat and tidy canals, but rivers in flood, bursting their banks to drench the very fabric of society. Healing and deliverance, reconciliation and restoration in whole communities and spheres of influence.

Deliverance is one of those words that is often lost in translation. For many it conjures up freaky elements of horror movies. Most famously, the 1974 film *The Exorcist*. This box-office hit featured the demonic possession of a young girl and her mother's attempt to deliver her of a powerful demon who was actually living inside her. She invites some priests to conduct an exorcism.[4] The big impression: this is a threatening world.

More widespread, on airport bookshelves – especially for teens – are books crammed with angels and demons. The big impression: this is a fantasy world.

Deliverance is neither threatening nor fantasy. As the Bible describes, there is an unseen spiritual world of good and evil (see more on this in Chapter 10). This can seem odd, yet we might normally talk about 'demon drink' to describe the way alcoholism has oppressed someone's life. Because of the power of cinema and media, we can feel uncomfortable with this language (me too). But we need some language to talk about the evil that oppresses people.

I always find this quotation from St Antony of Egypt, one of the original Desert Fathers (AD 251–356) very normalizing about demons:

> Even if they attack us and appear to threaten death, they ought to be laughed at rather than feared for they are weak and cannot carry out all their threats.[5]

We can find ourselves oppressed by evil, oppressed by evil spirits, especially at points of trauma. Note the important distinction from the cinematic sensations – we can be oppressed by evil, not inhabited. They might trouble us, but they don't live in us. Ignatius Loyola, founder of the Jesuits in the sixteenth century, was masterful at describing what this sort of oppression might feel like in practice. For example, sudden fear, sudden anger, sudden despair, which then lurks.[6] (See Chapter 10 below.)

In the church I come from, deliverance is conducted with care and wisdom, abiding by safeguarding guidelines, by authorized ministers, as only one aspect of healing among many, including the resources of medicine.[7] Jesus encouraged us to pray in the Lord's Prayer, 'deliver us from evil'. The beautifully simple thing is that praying in the name of Jesus in situations of demonic oppression really does work wonders. One of the experienced members of our deliverance team in the diocese said – we get used to not always getting immediate answers to prayer, but this ministry is different. It always works! God's peace always comes.

Here's the thing. Jesus had a PhD – in Preaching, Healing and Deliverance. This slogan is borrowed from another straight-talking Yorkshire evangelist, Canon Robin Gamble, who pioneered the Start Course[8] (a super introduction to the Christian faith). In today's church culture, I find we're happy to talk about the first of these (preaching), a little about the second (healing), virtually nothing about the third (deliverance). And yet in Mark's Gospel – in the eyewitness account of Jesus' closest friend, Peter – I notice the order is reversed. Jesus consistently encounters the forces of evil.

I lost touch with my lovely best friend from primary school when her parents divorced and she moved away. Fifteen years later, when we found each other again via the Friends Reunited website, I found out she had come to faith in Jesus as a young mum. This all happened because she was keen for her children to go to the local church school. She went along to church, the Alpha course and confirmation preparation. (Confirmation is a public celebration of Christian faith in the Church of England, where the bishop invites the Holy Spirit to fill the person, to confirm their earlier baptism, often as a child. It is one of my favourite services – the presence of the Holy Spirit is wonderfully sweet and peaceful.)

When the bishop confirmed her, something unexpected happened. She'd trained as a medium but, after her confirmation, she said it felt like her eyes were opened. She realized that the people she was contacting as a medium were not her long-lost family from beyond the grave. She was actually bringing high levels of fear into her house. And she found it was only praying in the name of Jesus that could deal with this and bring God's peace. One of my friends at vicar college came to faith in Jesus as a teenager because she'd been freaked out by what happened when she used an ouija board. Only the local priest, praying in the name of Jesus, could bring peace and stop pictures flying off the wall.

Healing also can easily slip off the radar. While I was writing this chapter, I went to watch my son play rugby. Such a pleasure (not least as he scored a try!). I got chatting to one of the dads in the bar afterwards. He had just stepped up into a very senior job. Articulate, charismatic, good at making his case. He was clearly well read on the less-than-savoury facts of church history. Under my breath, I asked for the peace of Jesus in our conversation and found myself saying I would be praying for him in his new role. The conversation changed gear. He told me about a friend of the family who had been miraculously healed in the last few weeks, against all the odds. Her church had been praying for healing.

When my dad was given six weeks to live after his treatment for leukaemia failed, he and my mum happened to be passing a gazebo on the streets in Bolton advertising prayer for healing by local churches. In desperation, they called in. Something significant happened. He wasn't miraculously cured, but there was a notable measure of healing – he lived another 18 months. My mum said: 'Why don't you advertise this more? Why don't you tell people that Jesus can heal today? Your churches would be full!' (I will write more about my personal experience of healing ministry in Chapter 8; and an influential healer in the Church of England, Dorothy Kerin, in Chapter 11.)

The first historian to write a history of the English people was a monk from Northumbria called Bede in about AD 731. His book, *The Ecclesiastical History of the English People*, is one of the bestselling and most comprehensive historical accounts of this period.[9] It is a gripping read, full of giants of faith, eye-witness accounts of healing and deliverance. As a famous old boy of the North East of England, Bede's tomb is just within the entrance of Durham Cathedral. When I was last visiting the Cathedral, there were queues of people filing to get past his tomb, pressing on to see an art exhibition of a scale-version of the moon. Yes, this was an impressive piece of art, but I suddenly felt quite overwhelmed. It felt as if the queue were sleep-walking past a much more potent story. Not pie in the sky, but real adventures here and now. I noted in my journal: 'Bede's tomb: deep sobs and tears. Pleading that people – men, women, boys and girls – might hear the gospel in their own language, might encounter healing and deliverance by Jesus the Rescuer, peace from heaven itself. C'mon!'

Unblocking the category error

All this talk of peace and healing and heaven drawing near could be in danger of sounding like a category error. A parallel universe. A fantasy film. How can we possibly be on the same frequency? How can it connect with our reality in this scientific secular age?

We will come back to secularism in Chapter 9, but a quick word on science. I remember a conversation in the lab with my boss when I was researching for my PhD in bio-inorganic chemistry in Oxford. To put it simply, our research was trying to work out how nature did such marvellous chemistry. If we could work out how metal centres in proteins catalysed complex chemical reactions at everyday temperatures and pressures, this would be revolutionary in the chemical and automotive industries. Well, that was the plan. But there were smaller revolutions. One day my boss, an internationally recognised professor, said to me: 'I used to be an atheist, but now I'm not so sure. Nature does such incredible chemistry.'

For all his rational, scientific training, it was as if he started to wake up. To honour our conversation, and the amazing chemistry I studied for three years, I prefaced my PhD thesis with a verse from the Old Testament which summed this up for me: 'And these are but the outer fringe of his works; how faint the whisper we hear of him! Who then can understand the thunder of his power?' (Job 26.14).

Just outside our lab in Oxford, there is a plinth commemorating the famous debate in 1860 between Samuel Wilberforce, Bishop of

Oxford, and London academic Thomas Huxley. What a shame that scientific discoveries have provoked arguments when there is so much more I could write about the beautiful resonances between science (which is answering the question 'How?') and faith (which is answering the question 'Why?'). But for the time being, if there's something warming your heart about all this, let's take a peek through the door of faith. Let's read to the end of the story that we started in Chapter 3 (Acts 2).

At the end of Peter's speech on the Day of Pentecost, after this epoch-shifting deluge of the Holy Spirit, many of his listeners 'were cut to the heart and said to Peter and the other apostles, 'Brothers, what shall we do?' (Acts 2.37).

It was as if they woke up. Their hearts were stirred.

Quite simply, Peter replies: 'Repent and be baptised, every one of you, in the name of Jesus Christ for the forgiveness of your sins. And you will receive the gift of the Holy Spirit.'

Repent. This is not a word we normally use today, is it?

It doesn't make sense – it conjures up that image again of shouty man on the streets of New York.

But throughout Christian history, the rediscovery of this word, a re-translation, has been the gateway into a flourishing of faith. It unblocks the category error. It seems to break the dams holding back those rivers of faith.

In the sixteenth century, a German priest, Martin Luther, saw a problem. In the Latin translation of the Bible used across Europe, the Greek word *metanoia*, meaning repent, was effectively translated as 'do penance' – undergo the Church's ritual of penance. Whereas repentance is about a change in our hearts, not doing religion. Jesus' words were getting lost in translation, no longer speaking to hearts, but telling us to do what the Church said.

It opened the door to fresh growth in faith in Europe; the dusty Bible came alive in fresh ways.

Today, the word 'repentance' is lost in the dust again. But it's too important a key to lose. It's often been the gateway to things of God's kingdom, the key to the door, the crack that breaks the dam. Jesus' opening words in public ministry were: 'The time is now, the kingdom is near. Repent and have faith, it's good news' (Mark 1.15, my translation). We might go instead for, 'Now's your chance, heaven is near, turn around, make a U-turn, reset, reboot.'

I attempted to put this into words in a video message during lockdown. It really travelled. Ten times the usual views. I was very surprised. In the days when the national slogan was STAY HOME – PROTECT THE NHS – SAVE LIVES, an ex-student of mine, Jonty, sent me a brilliant visual based on the same graphics (see Figure 2).

Repentance has a miserable-sinner, hair-shirt, depressing feel to it. Hard work. Like dig, dig, digging in our souls for dirt.

But in Scripture, repentance is always joyful. Zacchaeus throws a party; the Samaritan woman at the well runs to tell the whole village; the thief on the cross has a revelation that Jesus has done nothing wrong, while he is getting his just deserts: 'Jesus, remember me when you come into your kingdom' (Luke 23.40–43). Authentic, joyful repentance comes because of a *revelation* from Jesus, when the Holy Spirit shines his light and shows a better way of life. We can't do it ourselves.

A ship is lost at sea. The crew can't rescue themselves. They need *revelation* from outside their situation. They suddenly spot the lighthouse. There is joy as the captain turns the ship around, makes a U-turn, to sail towards the light, safe back home.

The peace breathed by Jesus unlocks forgiveness, a fresh start. To return to the account which started this chapter: 'He breathed

Figure 2

on them and said, "Receive the Holy Spirit. If you forgive anyone's sins, their sins are forgiven'" (John 20.22–23).

Our culture is used to 'calling out' evil, pointing the finger at others, but it doesn't offer any way of dealing with it. Sometimes with tragic consequences for those who are trapped in a cycle of very public condemnation.

Caroline Flack was one of my favourite winners when she lifted the *Strictly Come Dancing* glitterball trophy in 2014. She brought much joy to our screens, particularly with her unforgettable Charleston. Five years on and she hit the headlines in a less savoury way when she was released on bail for an incident of domestic violence against her boyfriend. She was shamed on social media. How low had a woman stooped that she'd physically attacked her partner? She responded with this Instagram post:

> For a lot of people, being arrested for common assault is an extreme way to have some sort of spiritual awakening . . . I've been pressing the snooze button on many stresses in my life – for my whole life. I've accepted shame and toxic opinions on my life for over ten years and yet told myself it's all part of my job. No complaining.
>
> The problem with brushing things under the carpet is they are still there and one day someone is going to lift that carpet up and all you are going to feel is shame and embarrassment.
>
> On December 12th 2019, I was arrested for common assault on my boyfriend. Within 24 hours my whole world and future was swept from under my feet and all the walls that I had taken so long to build around me collapsed. I am suddenly on a different kind of stage and everyone is watching it happen. I have always taken responsibility for what happened that night. Even on the night.
>
> But the truth is . . . it was an accident. I've been having some sort of emotional breakdown for a very long time. But I am NOT a domestic abuser . . . I'm so sorry to my family for what I have brought upon them and for what my friends have had to go through. I'm not thinking about 'how to get my career back'. I'm thinking how to get my life and my family's life back.[10]

The shaming continued. There was no way out. She was found dead at her home just a few weeks later. Suicide. Aged 40.

Caroline Flack's death was tragic. Unnecessary. But who hasn't felt trapped in guilt and shame, especially in the secret places of our relationships? In the pressure cooker of lockdown or raising a young family?

Quite simply, repentance is the gateway to the kingdom; it means we can breathe again. No matter how tightly we're cornered, even pinned to the cross like the thief. Turning around into the light of Jesus unlocks his peace from heaven. Yes, it's impossible to find our own way out of the mess. But God has sent a rescuer. It's going to be OK. Believe the good news. Trust that heaven can and is breaking in. Trust that one day it will be OK – evil doesn't have the last word; Jesus is here. As a friend of mine from a council estate put it: 'Jesus is my rescue-truck. He has all the kit on board to get me back on the road.' I smile when I pass roadworks with signs: 'Free Recovery. Await Rescue.'

We might come to it faster or slower, but there is always a moment of crossover on the journey. A moment of turnaround. A moment when we realize the rescue truck can be just a phone call away.

Let me give you a couple of examples:

A year ago, I felt prompted to FaceTime a friend of mine. I was a bit surprised when she laughed and immediately passed me over to her brother who was with her at the time. 'Haydn's got some news for you.' Last time I'd seen him, a couple of years earlier, he was in a very dark place indeed. This time his face was beaming: 'Tonight I have sworn an oath to Jesus. I have been swayed by what I've seen happen to my sister, I have now joined her church.' I confirmed him at the same time as the outdoor baptism service on the council estate allotment (see Chapter 1). He turned up to the allotment in a tatty T-shirt. At first I felt disappointment – was that a sign of his deteriorating mental health again? And then I read the slogan on the T-Shirt: 'Triumph'. He smiled: 'That's what's happened to me.'

Back in Widnes, some of the local women and I were enjoying meeting weekly to go through the Start Course which I mentioned earlier It's a few short video clips. You can watch over a cuppa in a front room, or down the pub. The clips prime the pump to get a discussion going. All views welcome. Suddenly, Jacqui got very upset; I could see tears were welling up, so I asked if she wanted to take a breather. We popped out to the room next door. She sobbed through her tears: 'I want what they've got.' I gently asked a few follow-up questions to find out what exactly it was she wanted; like many of my friends in that town, she'd been through a lot in her life. Finally, I clicked as to what she was after, and asked: 'You mean, you want Jesus to come into your life?' She nodded her head vigorously. 'Well, he's waiting. All you need to do is to invite him in.' I read her the beautiful passage tucked away at the end of the Bible: 'Here I am! I stand at the door and knock. If anyone hears my voice and opens the door, I will come in and eat with that person, and they with me' (Revelation 3.20). Then she formed a beautiful, open-hearted prayer to invite him into her life. A precious moment. A quiet moment, tucked away in a Widnes vicarage. But I like to think the heavenly anthems were roaring in celebration at a precious daughter, come home.

Going further

For group discussion

1 Where or when are you most at peace?
2 A dentist's consulting room might be an unexpected place for peace. Have you ever noticed a change in the atmosphere simply because you prayed?
3 The girls in Widnes were amazed that the tramp gave them exactly £3.60.
   (a) Have you come across stories of 'ordinary miracles'?
   (b) Have you come across stories of 'glorious miracles' of healing or deliverance?
4 'We can think the Golden Age for faith and the gospel is in the past. That's a lie. Faith has always risen and fallen over time.' If we met again in ten years' time,

(a) What would a Golden Age look like?

(b) What would the Dark Ages look like?

5 'And these are but the outer fringe of his works; how faint the whisper we hear of him! Who then can understand the thunder of his power?' (Job 26.14). Do you find science feeds your faith or challenges your faith?

6 Caroline Flack's story is tragic and heart-breaking.

(a) Do you have friends, family or colleagues who are trapped?

(b) How would you translate the word 'repent' for them?

7 'He's waiting. All you need to do is invite him in.' Have you found yourself in this sort of moment, like Jacqui? Would you like to?

For personal devotion

Read: John 14.18–27

Prayer to conclude: Jesus, Prince of Peace, I open my heart to you. Come in. Lead me home. I await your free recovery. Please bring your peace from heaven. Amen.

5

Who is key in lighting the beacons?

A best kept secret

Shhhh . . . Here's the best kept secret of this book . . . And in my view, it's dynamite.

The key beacon lighters are not who you expect!

This is writ large all over the Bible. And yet it's so counter-cultural, so topsy-turvy, so downright unbelievable that I confess I have had to see it for myself. Again. And again. But God's ways are not our ways: that's why we need Scripture – and need to be happy to eat a decent portion of humble pie. Again. And again.

The first 30 years of my life passed off happily in an achievement sort of way. As I get older, I've realized how life is so very different for different people. I had a happy childhood, with friends like me, and a school I enjoyed. Independent girls' school in Bolton. Cambridge University. Oxford University. Multinational company in Oxfordshire, then Surrey. International travel to most continents. Back to Oxford University to train to be a vicar. First Class. CV of gloriousness.

I'd never met a girl who wanted a baby at 16 so she could escape the nightmare of a dysfunctional family to achieve something laudable for the first time ever. I'd never met someone who had survived years of domestic and sexual abuse and yet cheerfully got out of bed refusing to be defined by her past. I'd never been to parties where within minutes people would come straight out with, 'I'm not good enough for God.'

But over the next couple of years, I met all these dear people. I was ordained in Liverpool Cathedral, to serve as curate – an apprentice vicar. We moved to live on a council estate in North Liverpool. A cross-cultural shock.

I'd never had someone come to faith in my front room, as I explained why Jesus died on the cross. I met Cathy on the streets of our council estate and got chatting. She was surprised to see a woman in a vicar's dog collar; I was surprised she already had five kids – we were nearly the same age. We became really good friends; we still text regularly. Her own tumultuous life story had washed her up so close to the gate of heaven. So hungry for home, it didn't take many steps for her to realize what an incredible offer it was that Jesus died to wipe the slate clean, to clear the bad debt from all her past darkness. She could finally face opening the door to come home to him.

Later, my husband was also ordained and we moved for him to be a vicar in Widnes, when our two boys were small. Rats. Break-ins. Loud music.

And yet the kingdom of heaven has never been closer in these two, seemingly 'forgotten', places dear to my heart.[1]

In short, I'd never met people who had survived with such deep cavities of pain and disappointment in their lives. And yet these cavities became the very channels for the grace of God and for Jesus to draw near. It was as if, with surgical precision, Jesus patiently navigated deep-root dentistry to remove rotten roots and heal abscesses. Then these gaping holes allowed so much more room for his love, faith and hope from heaven. They were fluent in repentance, that gateway to his kingdom (see Chapter 4); it came naturally – they were so conscious of their brokenness. I found myself like the self-righteous Pharisee affronted by Jesus' behaviour. Telling him under my breath that he was totally out of order ('Do you know what sort of woman she is?'). Then confronted by Jesus again and again: 'Look at that woman . . . Those who are forgiven much, love much' (Luke 7.36–50). He introduced me to brothers and sisters whose very egos had been crushed and crucified. Over again. When mine had been lauded and applauded. Over again. I noticed how much more trusting, loving and open to God they were than me. I didn't need to trust and love; I could manage with my glorious CV, thank you very much. I began to realize why Jesus spent his time with the 'outcasts' – the sex-workers and tax-collectors – who were entering the kingdom ahead of me.[2] I heard the gospel according to Jeff, ex-drug addict from Widnes, king of the one-liners: 'Jesus delivered what drugs never could.'

When the boys were school age, my part-time day job took me further afield to some of the higher echelons of the Church of England with our brightest and best academics. CVs of gloriousness to rival mine. And yet, again and again, wonderful colleagues as they were, they rivalled me with our feeble levels of faith, love and openness to God. Like me, they could usually manage everyday life without needing Jesus to turn up. But then going home of an evening to Widnes was like going to another world where I would meet giants of faith, with gaping holes in their fractured lives where the kingdom of God flooded in every day. After a while, I got used to the cross-cultural shock. But I never lost the frustration that we lauded pygmies of faith like me; I never got used to the tsunami of grace that flowed through those cavities of brokenness. I started to joke to my Widnes family: 'I come home to Widnes to be revved, all fired up for Jesus.' The wonder of God's upside-down, topsy-turvy kingdom.[3]

Peters and Pauls

I noticed these patterns in Scripture. One of my heroes, Paul, the academic with glorious CV, was three years in the wilderness before he was trusted by Jesus as an apostle (messenger of the gospel) (Galatians 1.17—2.1). Peter, the unschooled fisherman, was trusted with preaching on the Day of Pentecost – his apprenticeship with Jesus had been served in the school of hard knocks, where his ego had been beaten and bashed. It was Peter's job to explain all those fiery wonders (see Chapter 3). As the great philosopher Blaise Pascale put it: 'Not the God of philosophers and academics, but fire, fire, fire.'[4]

If you're a Peter reading this – brilliant. Can you hear Jesus' commissioning over you: 'You are Peter, and on this rock I will build my church, and the gates of Hades will not overcome it' (Matthew

16.18)? I bet you've felt the draught from the gates of hell: winds of elitism, intellectualism or racism, misogyny, clericalism or imposter syndrome? Winds blowing gale force at times have threatened to knock you off your feet. But listen to those words of Jesus. You are my rock. He needs you to be foundational in his building of his Church and renewing of his nation. Caedmon's heavenly song was a hinge moment in the gospel translating into the local Anglo-Saxon language (see Chapter 3).

Mechtild, a nun from the convent of Helfta, struggled with her calling in the thirteenth century. She was the first mystic to write in her own native language (German), rather than Latin. This is what she heard Jesus say to comfort her when men threatened to burn her book:

> Whenever I have bestowed my special grace
> I have always searched for the poorest, smallest and most hidden.
> The proud mountains cannot receive
> The revelations of my grace,
> For the flood of my Holy Spirit
> By nature flows down to the lowliest valleys.
> There are many so-called wise writers
> Who, in my eyes, are fools.
> And I tell you more,
> It greatly honours me
> and greatly strengthens holy Church
> That your unlearned lips should teach
> The learned tongues the things of my Holy Spirit.[5]

If you're a Paul, don't despair. This is not to say that Jesus has no need for CVs of gloriousness. I am confident he showers us with gifts for his glory. It is just that these natural gifts and talents, like Gollum in *The Hobbit*, can easily become 'my precious'. We can blindly elbow our way busily through life, projecting that it's our gifts that Jesus needs, looking down on others when, in actual fact, they are already feasting at the top table in the heavenly banquet. They are entering the kingdom of heaven ahead of us.

It can be hard for Pauls to realize they are not 'better' than Peters. But in time, in the wilderness years, Paul learnt to honour this upside-down economy of grace, and later wrote one of the most eloquent expressions of this in the Bible:

> For the foolishness of God is wiser than human wisdom, and the weakness of God is stronger than human strength.
>
> Brothers and sisters, think of what you were when you were called. Not many of you were wise by human standards; not many were influential; not many were of noble birth. But God chose the foolish things of the world to shame the wise; God chose the weak things of the world to shame the strong. God chose the lowly things of this world and the despised things – and the things that are not – to nullify the things that are, so that no one may boast before him.
> (1 Corinthians 1.25–29)

If you're a Paul, your gifts may naturally propel you into positions of power and authority, where Satan's lies are that much more believable. To paraphrase Luke 4.5–7, when Satan tests Jesus in the wilderness outside Jerusalem before the start of his public ministry: 'The devil led him up to a high place and showed him in an Instagram all the kingdoms of the world. And he said to him, "I will give you all their authority and splendour; it has been given to me, and I can give it to anyone I want to. If you worship me, it will all be yours."'

Satan loves to mess with our minds about the future. One of the biggest deceptions is that the Instagram future is bright. It's a red carpet. It's a spotlight. It's not a backwater. It's not fragile. It's certainly not a stable.

In the fourteenth century, hermit and mystic Julian of Norwich had a series of visions from Jesus. Her most famous one was a hazelnut.

> And I saw it that he is everything that is good. And he showed me more, a little thing, the size of a hazelnut, on the palm of my hand, round like a ball. I looked at it thoughtfully and wondered, 'What is

> this?' And the answer came, 'It is all that is made.' I marvelled that it
> continued to exist and did not suddenly disintegrate; it was so small.
> And again my mind supplied the answer, 'It exists, both now and
> forever, because God loves it.'[6]

In the fragile early days, when I was trying to start a church
from scratch (the technical term used nowadays is often 'church
planting'), a senior colleague whom I really respect, advised me: 'If
God's in it, it should be easy.' But he was wrong. I have learnt it's
the opposite. If God's in it, Jesus will lead you to the cross. (More of
this in Chapter 11.) The work of God is always fragile. He picks the
Peters to be his rock. But Peter's apprenticeship was served in the
school of hard knocks. He's enthusiastic, daring, devil-may-care;
he disrupts, denies, and even after the resurrection, at the tender
moment of recommissioning, he can't help comparing himself
unfavourably to another disciple.

'God chose the lowly things of this world and the despised
things – and the things that are not – to nullify the things that are'
(1 Corinthians 1.28). This is his heavenly wisdom which few wise
men and women seem to get.

The Lord of the Rings – beacon lighters

Back to the film clip which started this book, from *The Lord of the
Rings*. The amazing cinematography of a chain of beacons being lit
across the hills. Gandalf says that hope has been kindled.[7]

Who lights the beacons? It is the hobbits. The little people from
the Shire. Who can be trusted. Without the ambition and thirst for
power which hamstrings the race of men.

It makes me smile that the original Bishop of Lancaster's house
was in Shireshead, just south of Lancaster. Leafy lanes. Tucked
away. Exactly the sort of place where you might find a hobbit
contentedly smoking his pipe by the fire. Longing to be left alone
to write his books. Tolkien certainly spent a formative part of his
life just to the south in the beautiful Ribble Valley at Stonyhurst,

which to this day remains a stunning Roman Catholic college of international reputation.[8] Wonderfully, Lancashire has deep roots of Catholic faith, in what was, before the Industrial Revolution, an inaccessible but stunning part of the country. Happily out of the way. 'Make it your ambition to live a quiet life: You should mind your own business,' writes Paul (1 Thessalonians 4.11).

So, yes, the hobbits, the Peters if you like, have the starring role in the beacon-lighting, ring-of-power-destroying epic, but some in the race of men, the Pauls, do manage to find their part. Yes it may be that King Denethor's firstborn son, Boromir, is the first to break the Fellowship of the Ring – killed because of his ambition to bear the ring. But Aragorn plays a much more significant role, rallying the troops from all races in Middle Earth to support the fragile mission of the hobbits. So, what qualifies him where other men have failed?

Let me tell you the story of Norma, our lay reader in Liverpool. When she preached as she thought a Church of England lay reader should preach, it felt like the stilted regurgitation of a Bible commentary. But when she relaxed into her own way of speaking, she spoke with such witty imagination it was breathtaking! I can still remember her sermons 20 years on.

In her Christmas sermon, Norma asked: how should we choose parents for the Son of God? Well, they'd form a committee, wouldn't they? You always need a committee. They'd take a good hard look at their finances, education, maturity, stability of the marriage. Never in a month of Sundays would you have chosen Mary!

Norma's spot on. It's fair to say, Mary was an unusual choice. And yet when she rushes off to tell her cousin Elizabeth about her amazing news, the song Elizabeth's joy calls out of her says it all. Mary's song resonates with the perspective of heaven. She rejoices in God's upside-down kingdom. His great reversal:

His mercy extends to those who fear him,
  from generation to generation.
He has performed mighty deeds with his arm;
  he has scattered those who are proud in their inmost thoughts.

> He has brought down rulers from their thrones
> > but has lifted up the humble.
> He has filled the hungry with good things
> > but has sent the rich away empty.
> (Luke 1.50–53)

Three unlikely qualifications: being in *fear* (in the old-fashioned sense of being in *awe)*, being *humble*, being *hungry*.

The unlikely qualifications of Mary

Awe/fear. 'His mercy extends to those who *fear* him.' This is a radical challenge to our comfort culture with its narrative of self-justification. But the fear of God is the gateway to his kingdom. When the angel Gabriel appeared to Mary, she was frightened. He assured her: 'Do not be afraid, Mary; you have found favour with God' (Luke 1.30). Peter's first words after his first meeting with Jesus and the first miracle: 'Go away from me, Lord; I am a sinful man!' (Luke 5.8). Quite frankly, I only hear the fear of God on our council estates and urban areas. Nowhere else.

Let me share my favourite Christmas Eve story. It was when I was a curate in Liverpool. I'd been let off the Midnight service because I was eight months pregnant. At 10.30 p.m., one of our teenagers texted: 'Jill, I'm at a party near yours, please come.' She'd never invited me to a party before. With my baby nearly due, I pushed through all my middle-class mental barriers of squeamishness: lots of cigarette smoke, quite a bit of pot, loud music, lots of drink . . . But I went. I'm so glad I did. That evening's conversations were at the gate of heaven . . . Straight in . . . 'But why would God bother with someone like me?' 'I'm not good enough for him.' I was experiencing first hand that God is close to those who fear him.

Humble. Luke 1.52: 'He has brought down rulers from their thrones, but has lifted up *the humble.*' Aragorn is humble. He is

75

descended from the great Isildur and yet he carries his heritage lightly; and in the end is elevated from his anonymity. I have never studied the Hebrew of the Old Testament but by attending to the text in the original language, it's like moving from watching in 2D to 3D. It's the same plot, but the funny specs you get given in the cinema make you feel part of the plot in a fresh way. So when a dear colleague, James Halstead, showed me a paper he had written about how the word 'poor' in Hebrew can also be translated 'humble' – it was like putting on the 3D specs and becoming part of the plot in a fresh way. I wasn't excluded from a front-row seat by my glorious CV. There's no way I could be described as poor but, if I could learn to be *humble*, this was another way in. And this began a fresh tutorial in the school of the Spirit.

Bishops are hardly in pole position on 'the learning to be humble' stakes. But God has his ways and means. In the office Secret Santa, my Christmas present was a superb mug emblazoned with 'I can't keep calm, I'm the bishop'. It's just a mug, but it seems to say that being a bishop means being stressed and busy. Senior roles in any organization can become synonymous with stress and overburden – too many things on the job list. That original sin of pride – Satan's whispers that we're unlimited, we can be like God.[9] I have listened to these whispers at times. When the job list seems too long, or too difficult, I have tried to learn to lean into Jesus' invitation: 'Come to me, all you who are weary and burdened, and I will give you rest. Take my yoke upon you and learn from me, for I am *gentle and humble* in heart, and you will find rest for your souls. For my yoke is easy and my burden is light' (Matthew 11.28–29). When the job list is long, me working harder isn't the answer. What's needed is for me to be humbler and gentler. There is much in my role that invites me away from this. I keep asking him to coach me deeper into both.

The Carmelites know about this – they are monks and nuns who base their discipline on the pattern of Elijah at Mount Carmel. A wise prayer of theirs includes the phrase: 'Grant to us all the *humility* and trust that will allow you to do great things in us and through us.'

I have spent a significant portion of my working years hidden away as a mum to young children and as a vicar's wife. As I watched contemporaries take more and more prominent roles, while I was hidden away, my spiritual director spoke to me about the spiritual discipline of hiddenness. A time in the darkness, where the deep seeds of the Spirit germinate slowly. Henri Nouwen puts this in perfect pitch:

> One of the reasons that hiddenness is such an important aspect of the spiritual life is that it keeps us focussed on God. In hiddenness we do not receive human acclamation, admiration, support or encouragement. In hiddenness we have to go to God with our sorrows and joys and trust that God will give us what we most need. In our society we are inclined to avoid hiddenness. We want to be seen and acknowledged. We want to be useful to others and influence the course of events. But as we become visible and popular, we grow dependent on people and their responses and easily lose touch with God, the true source of our being. Hiddenness is the place of purification. In hiddenness we find our true selves.[10]

Perhaps you are finding yourself in a season of hiddenness at the moment? Caring for young children or elderly relatives? Unwelcome redundancy or retirement? Maybe out of choice, or maybe enforced?

Hungry. 'He has filled the *hungry* with good things, but has sent the rich away empty.'

As I spend Sundays in different churches each week across Lancashire, I wonder if you can guess where the hunger is? Last summer, one of our new churches on a housing estate had clubbed together with another similar church just across the border in Bolton. They had brought 80 people camping in the grounds of an old working men's club in Preston. A good number knew nothing about faith and were just along for the ride. I was invited to come to speak at the afternoon service, held in the club on site. Before I get to speak, the leader says, 'It's our good news slot . . . anyone share

77

anything . . .?' A 9-year-old jumps up to grab the microphone: 'I decided to give my life to Jesus and I'm telling my friends about it.' Then people start chanting, 'Pauline, Pauline . . .' Pauline staggers forward, supported by two friends. 'After our service yesterday . . . I knew there was a door I needed to go through. It was a red door. Jesus was waiting . . . and I said yes.' Then it was my turn to speak. Under a glitterball. On a dancefloor with lots of kids running around. Then afterwards, a queue of people – hungry for prayer for healing, confession, God's calling, imposter syndrome. I finish by praying with a young Albanian mum, with two small children, seeking asylum from sex-traffickers. She looks up, with tear-stained mascara: 'There is so much light here.'

My wake-up call

The vital role of the hobbits in the plot of *The Lord of the Rings* is often overlooked. Not just in lighting beacons but also in carrying the ring to Mount Doom. What a pathetic strategy to break the hold of darkness over Middle Earth. If you don't know the story, the ring is a weapon of great power, but the horrible truth is that wearing it turns people evil. Many thought that at the threat of invasion, in the last extreme, it could be used for good. But the truth is that it will always corrupt.[11]

I confess that, despite living in urban areas as a church minister for 15 years, I needed a particular wake-up call. To the vital role of the Peters. It happened at the New Wine summer festival.[12] It wasn't in the way you'd expect.

New Wine has been described as Glastonbury for Christians. With the strapline 'Local Churches Changing Nations', it's a Christian charity that supports local churches 365 days of the year. But its signature offering is a summer festival in big tents with bands, worship, art, fantastic work for teens and kids, seminars, prayer ministry. Often a significant moment in the calendar each year. I remember taking a group of unlikely folks from Widnes. Most had never camped before. I will never forget Jean's open-mouthed amazement when we made it to the Somerset showground, full of tents and caravans as far as the eye could see: 'Gosh, there must be a God!' That became a headline over the week, as people encountered the tender work of the Spirit in their lives, some meeting Jesus for the very first time.

I'd like to say the significant moment for me was a profound worship session, insightful prayer ministry, brilliant kids work . . . but the significant moment began when our tent leaked. I had been taking the boys for several years because the kids work was so inspiring, but going once a year, there was never the right moment to invest in a tent that 'worked'. Namely, a tent that was fully waterproof. And this year we came a cropper. When the heavens opened – literally – the sleeping compartments round the central core turned into pools, and my 9-year old son woke up in a pool of water. His pod had collapsed and his sleeping bag was soaked through. The rain continued that day, so the only way to sort this out was a trip to the local laundrette. It was frustrating, of course, I would miss some interesting afternoon seminars, but nothing for it.

When I got back to site, I kept getting accosted. You must hear Bishop Philip North's seminar – it was amazing. I was getting this in stereo. There was nothing I could do. But there's nothing like hearing a seminar, one you missed out on, repeated to you by ten different people with ten different takes. By the end of the week, I was piecing it together sufficiently that it felt like I had been there. And then it was reported in the church and national media. A month later, it was the topic of discussion at our St Mellitus College staff retreat. Then I found Philip being quoted in an essay I marked. A sure sign he'd made an impact.

What he said was this. The reason the Church is not growing is because we ignore the poor. Let the poor get hold of the gospel and this will transform our nation:

> We are all trying massively hard to renew the Church. We are working like crazy, we are praying like mad, we are trying every new idea under the sun. Yet the longed-for renewal does not seem to come. In fact decline just seems to speed up. Why? Why are we struggling so much?

I want to suggest that the answer is quite a straightforward one. It's because we have forgotten the poor.

. . . The lesson of Scripture, the lesson of the past is clear. If we want renewal, we must start with the poor. And yet in the Church of England we have a mission approach that is almost entirely focussed on the needs and aspirations of the wealthy. Rather than speaking good news to the poor, we are complicit in the abandonment of the poor.

This seemed to start a chain reaction. Two things happened to me shortly afterwards.

Another month later, Mark Ashcroft, Bishop of Bolton, came to speak to us at St Mellitus North West in Liverpool about his 'embarrassing data'. Given that Jesus came to bring good news to the poor and it's hard for a rich man to enter the kingdom of God, it's embarrassing that in Manchester Diocese the graph is precisely opposite to what you'd expect. Namely, the largest churches are in the richest areas, the smallest in the poorest. (This isn't just an issue for Manchester, by the way.) He said: 'We – need – to – repent.'

The previous week, I'd asked the students in class to listen out in prayer for, 'What is the Spirit saying to our nation?' Karen from Blackburn had come up to me that morning to say, 'I think we need to repent, repent, repent.' So, when Bishop Mark had finished speaking, I called her out to lead us in a prayer of repentance on behalf of our nation. It sounds grand. But it really seemed the only thing to do. There were people in tears. I think he deserves an accolade for that: we'd never had a bishop visit before who had made the students cry!

Then shortly after this, I was woken up in the middle of the night. Like everyone, I'm sometimes woken by the wind banging our gate, or by some niggle from the day. This was different. I was woken by something that had never happened before or since. I was woken by a dream I was seeing while I was awake. Maybe this is what people call a vision. I imagined a big wave sweeping the country, scouring out an underground army trapped under the sediment and depositing them on the beaches. From there they would start to light beacons. I sensed this was from God, but for me it is essential that any vision or prophecy is tested and supported by Scripture. So I remember asking God directly: I'm not sure what's happening, but what is the Scripture? More to the point, who is this underground army? Instantly, I was led to Isaiah 61. I pulled out my Bible and read with fresh eyes.

> The Spirit of the Sovereign LORD is on me,
>   because the LORD has anointed me
>   to proclaim good news to the poor.
> He has sent me to bind up the broken-hearted,
>   to proclaim freedom for the captives
>   and release from darkness for the prisoners,
> to proclaim the year of the LORD's favour
>   and the day of vengeance of our God,
> to comfort all who mourn,
>   and provide for those who grieve in Zion –
>   to bestow on them a crown of beauty
>   instead of ashes,
> the oil of joy
>   instead of mourning,
> and a garment of praise
>   instead of a spirit of despair.
> They will be called oaks of righteousness,
>   a planting of the LORD
>   for the display of his splendour.
> They will rebuild the ancient ruins
>   and restore the places long devastated;
> they will renew the ruined cities
>   that have been devastated for generations.
> (Isaiah 61.1–4)

It's also the passage that Jesus chose when he stood up in the syna-gogue in Nazareth to preach his manifesto sermon at the start of his public ministry.

In the dim light, my attention was drawn to verse 4: '*They* will rebuild the ancient ruins and restore the places long devastated; they will renew the ancient cities that have been devastated for generations.'

Who are the underground army? Who are 'they'? They are the poor, the broken-hearted, the captives, the prisoners. Restoring the nation is not done by the confident and powerful. Renewing cities is done by the poor, the broken-hearted and the captives. They are the ones trapped underground, and the good things we all long for are only going to come through them.

I had never seen this before.

It echoed with the Great Reversal in Mary's song we mentioned just earlier.

My heart sang too. And it still sings. Here's my heartfelt prayer to this day:

> May there be a wave through our country that brings up this swell of people from the underground and deposits them on the shore, like a mighty army – that brings down rulers from their thrones and lifts up the humble. May there be a Year of Jubilee[13] for those captives, trapped underground, desperate to dig their way out, because they have the gifts that will renew the Church and restore the devastated cities.

What is trapping them underground?

But how are we stopping the poor and humble getting hold of the gospel? How are we excluding them from the banquet table? What is trapping them underground?

I have given this a lot of thought since that night. And the answer in my heart is not so politically correct, because we like to blame others. Never take the blame yourself; and never take the blame as an organization.

But I think it's basically the sin of the Church that is trapping the poor and humble underground. And I can only speak from my vantage point on this in the Church of England. Here are three of the boulders on their heads: elitism, intellectualism, imposter syndrome.

Elitism – we favour the rich.

Quite simply, we invest half the national average in ministry in our poorest areas. 'Nationally we spend £8 per head of population on ministry. In some rural areas that figure rises to £24 per head. On the estates we spend just £5 per head, by far the lowest.'[14]

Jesus' brother James was scathing about this:

> Don't show favouritism... If you show special attention to the man wearing fine clothes and say, 'Here's a good seat for you,' but say to the poor man, 'You stand there' or 'Sit on the floor by my feet,' have you not discriminated among yourselves . . . Has not God chosen those who are poor in the eyes of the world *to be rich in faith* and to inherit the kingdom he promised to those who love him?
> (James 2.1, 3–5, NIV 1984)

Intellectualism – we cut off our most courageous leaders.

I am not so convinced that Peter – the rock on which Jesus built his Church – would easily navigate his way through selection and ordination training. I am grateful for efforts being made now to tackle this. But I want to hold out a shining example within living memory in the North West – St Aidan's College, Birkenhead, which was closed in 1969. When it opened in 1846, it was ahead of its time. These were the days when you trained for ordination at either Oxford or Cambridge. St Aidan's College had the vision of training the ordinary man for ordination in the C of E – dockers, labourers, postmen. You still see this in the St Aidan's old boys today. The vicar who founded it, Joseph Bayliss, saw the growing need for the gospel on the other bank of the River Mersey, across the water in the burgeoning city of Liverpool, so trainee vicars would spend their afternoons at the coalface of ministry with the poor in the slums.

A verse that was important to us at St Mellitus North West in trying to revive the St Aidan's story is Acts 4.13. It's set in the incident where Peter and John heal the lame man, get into trouble with the authorities who in the end decide that if it's from God, nothing can stop this. The story continues:

> When they saw the *courage* of Peter and John and realised that they were *unschooled, ordinary men,* they were astonished and they took note that *these men had been with Jesus.*
> (Acts 4.13)

I so much wanted our trainee vicars to leave St Mellitus to astonish people with their *courage* because they have *been with Jesus.*

My brother-in-law Chris was involved in church planting (that is, enabling local people to start churches from scratch) in Central Asia for 20 years, bringing the Christian message for the first time as the country emerged from the Soviet empire. I once asked him: 'What makes a church-planting movement?' In some cities, there'd been church plants but they limped on or petered out. In other cities, they had become church-planting movements (where churches readily go on to plant other churches as a normal part of their lifecycle). I was interested to know – what made the difference? His answer was this: *extreme courage* of local believers. This is not what we train for in a context where essay marks dominate the culture.

St Aidan has become one of my heroes. As mentioned earlier, he is often pictured with this torch of the gospel – lighting beacons across the North. Bede, who wrote the first history of the English people, tells us:

> Aidan's life was in marked contrast to the apathy of our own times . . . if the wealthy ever gave him gifts of money, he either distributed it for the needs of the poor or else used it to ransom any who had unjustly been sold into slavery. In fact, many of those whom he ransomed in this way afterwards became his disciples; *and when they had been instructed and trained, he ordained them to the priesthood.*[15]

So here we have it. The great saint, who did so much to reach England by sending out many priests and leaders, started with slaves. That is how the church in England got started. This is not where we start today, which leads me on to my third boulder.

Imposter syndrome. One of the simplest and most accessible definitions of Anglicanism I've come across is the strapline on the Church of England website: 'a Christian presence in *every* community'. On our best days, I hope we are the church for the people round here. Every vicar is not just the vicar for those who come on Sunday; but we want to 'care for the souls' of everyone in that parish. Root for them, grieve with them, celebrate with them, work for the coming of the kingdom of heaven in that place.

This is a wonderfully welcoming ambition. In the Church of England, sometimes we might give the impression we're like the Vicar of Dibley or the Revd Timms from *Postman Pat*. Revds Granger and Timms are merely a façade disguising the astonishing real-life reach of what is one of the nation's largest all-age volunteer-based charities. With our aspiration to be a living, breathing manifestation of 'peace on earth and goodwill to all' in every city, town, village, estate, suburb in the country. Fifty years ago, many villages had a pub, a post office and a church. Today only the church is left. And then there are our wonderful chaplains, serving on the frontline of our hospitals, prisons, universities and in the armed services.

But every gift has its shadow side. And the shadow side of this welcoming vision is imposter syndrome. I often come across people being told they're not 'Anglican enough'. I never quite pin down what that means: too catholic, too charismatic, too this or that . . . It can easily become code for, 'You don't belong here.' The exact opposite of our calling. A shadow sign of insecurity.

I remember my first College of Bishops. This is the gathering of all the bishops in the C of E. Dress code: casual. Without much thought, I turned up in a summer dress, something I'd worn at the weekend. I instantly felt like an imposter – I was the only one in a summer dress. But then I realized that a lot of the men, who were wearing the right clothes and looked like bishops, also felt like imposters. Next College of Bishops at Lambeth Palace (HQ of the C of E), one of our more senior bishops got up to preach and spoke about how intimidating it was to speak to a chapel of bishops – he spoke about imposter syndrome. Then another year or so passed and we were meeting on Zoom. In my break-out group, a new colleague mentioned his overwhelming sense of imposter syndrome. At this point, I started to preach: 'It's the shadow side of our calling to be a church for people round here!' When the Zoom room closed, I felt I'd been a little over the top. Immediately – a serendipity of the Spirit – a text came in from one of my old students – mixed race from a poorer background. 'Bishop Jill, I am really struggling with imposter syndrome, please would you pray for me?' Darkness had revealed itself. I take great pleasure in hoovering up imposter syndrome wherever I spot it now (see Chapter 8).

Who's at the front of the queue?

When Jesus was asked, 'Who are the greatest people in the kingdom of heaven?', he called over a toddler and put them centre stage. 'Unless you change and become like little children, you will never enter the kingdom of heaven' (Matthew 18.1–5). As a mum of toddlers, I found this wonderfully reassuring. Even today, having a toddler with you has amazing benefits. It can also make you want to melt away in embarrassment in any mixed-age social gathering that's not in a soft-play area!

One of the aspects we have loved about New Wine is the amazing commitment to children's work. In our Pebbles group (ages 3–4), there was one boy who was getting upset. His leader tried to find out why. He had just had a baby brother, so the leader was assuming it was something to do with jealousy that had unsettled him. Yes and no. When his leader listened carefully, the 3-year-old told him: 'I'm really upset with Harry. He won't tell me what Jesus is like. And I'm starting to forget.' When my son was about that age, we happened to be looking at a picture of the statue of Christ the Redeemer on the hill above Rio de Janeiro. He said simply: 'Jesus is putting his arms out for the children.'

Children are incredibly open to the things of heaven and the things of the word and the Spirit. I wonder if the teacher who simply pinned up pictures of Jesus on the wall in a 1970s classroom in Bolton knew the impact it had on me as a 4-year-old, introducing me to Jesus. I love Archbishop John Sentamu's sense that our job is simply to lead people to Jesus and leave them there.

Have you noticed that wonderful whisper about the greatness of children when John the Baptist's birth is announced – way before Jesus – the first trailer of the coming kingdom in the Bible? 'He will go on before the Lord, in the spirit and power of Elijah, to turn the hearts of the parents to their children' (Luke 1.17). The first sign of the coming of the kingdom is not that children listen to their parents, but parents start to listen to their children. Hearts are turned *down* a generation. The fiery torch of Elijah is passed down. Fire is catching. I love it that every time I commission a new vicar or leader that these are the words of our shared calling with Christians everywhere:

> The Church of England is part of the One, Holy Catholic and Apostolic Church worshipping the one true God, Father, Son and Holy Spirit. It professes the faith uniquely revealed in the Holy Scriptures and set forth in the Catholic creeds, which faith the Church is called upon to proclaim afresh in each generation.[16]

Here's the hope . . . the Great Reversal, the great escape, beacons of hope lit from the sea . . .

Imagine if . . . this underground army – waiting to renew our country with the gifts that the Spirit of God – has – already – given – them . . . were called out of hiding. Imagine if . . . they were so full of the Spirit of God precisely because they were so hungry for him that they had been 'filled with good things'. Imagine if they split the rocks apart in our country; imagine if they broke through the strata of heavy sediment that is pressing down the poor and keeping them fossilized in position.

In the words of 'The Vision' poem from the 24-7 Prayer movement:

> This is the sound of the underground . . . Foundations shaking . . .
> Don't you hear them coming? Herald the weirdos! Summon the losers
> and the freaks. Here come the frightened and forgotten with fire in
> their eyes . . . Their words make demons scream in shopping centres.[17]

Sometimes, as I drive round Lancashire, I imagine this underground army, trapped underground by the sin of the Church, but full of fire. I play the theme tune from *The Great Escape* film on Spotify and pray for them to break through the ground. And here's the funny thing. I told this story to one of our estate church planters and she laughed. 'Do you know what? One of our women came to church in the allotment last week. She said: "All the manhole covers are off in our street."' The underground army are on the loose! Maybe it was a coincidence. I have got used to quietly enjoying these 'ordinary miracles' or serendipities of the Spirit.

The time is now. I am praying for an earthquake. Tidal wave. That turns us upside down and washes on to the banqueting table people so hungry for Jesus and the gifts of God that they show us how to feast again. Why? Quite simply because they have been with Jesus.

Going further

For group discussion

1 In your networks, where can you spot Peters? Where can you spot Pauls? Which one do you identify with most?
2 Mary's song brings the heavenly perspective of the Great Reversal bringing the humble and hungry centre stage (Luke 1.46–55). Mechtild writes that 'The flood of my Holy Spirit by nature flows down to the lowliest valleys.' Why do you think this is? What examples would you give?

3 Jesus speaks tenderly to us: 'Come to me, all you who are weary and burdened, and I will give you rest. Take my yoke upon you and learn from me, for I am *gentle and humble* in heart, and you will find rest for your souls. For my yoke is easy and my burden is light' (Matthew 11.28–30). How do these words affect you?

4 Are you in a season of hiddenness at the moment? In the dark, seeds germinate. 'Hiddenness is the place of purification' (Henri Nouwen). How does this feel?

5 Isaiah 61.4: '*They* will rebuild the ancient ruins and restore the places long devastated; they will renew the ruined cities that have been devastated for generations.' Where do you see this happening? If not, why not?

6 Acts 4.13: 'When they saw the *courage* of Peter and John and realised that they were *unschooled, ordinary men*, they were astonished and they took note that *these men had been with Jesus.*' Where might God be calling you to step out with courage? What feeds courage?

For personal devotion

Read: Isaiah 61.1-11

Sit with this important passage. See what Jesus highlights to you.

Prayer to conclude: Jesus, may there be your wave of the Spirit through our nation that washes up this swell of people from the underground and deposits them on the shore, like a mighty army – that brings down rulers from their thrones and lifts up the humble. Please set free those captives, trapped underground, desperate to dig their way out, because they have the gifts that will renew the Church and restore the devastated cities. Amen.

6

Fanning beacons into flame

Hobbits are often at the forefront of carrying the fire to light the beacons. Less ego, more room for the fire of the Holy Spirit.

Lighting beacons is a work of God; beacons don't spontaneously combust. But there is a part for us to play.

We carry more fire the more we make room for God, the more we offer ourselves to him as Lord.

On first blush, this could sound off-putting and restrictive – submitting to someone's lordship sounds feudal, even oppressive. But here's the wonderful thing. The more we offer ourselves up to his fire, the more freedom we find. We actually become more and more ourselves. I quoted Catherine of Siena earlier, but she's well worth a repeat:

> Be who God called you to be and you will set the world on fire.

On a cold night, being closer to the fire is no hardship. Fire warms, fire frees up those frozen muscles. This freeing is part of God's character, as the Bible highlights: 'Now the Lord is the Spirit, and where the Spirit of the Lord is, there is freedom' (2 Corinthians 3.17)

And that's why hobbits are often so good at carrying the fire to light the beacons (see Chapter 5). Less ego, more fire. More fire, more fruit – love, joy, peace, patience, kindness, goodness, faithfulness, gentleness, self-control.[1] It is this fruit-filled character that speaks volumes about God.

How do we offer more of ourselves? How can we be more hobbit? (Don't worry, I'm not talking hairy toes.) How can we fan our beacons into flame?

Three ways: prayer, Word and sacraments. Let's look at these in turn.

Prayer

I am convinced that beacons are fanned into flame by prayer.

This was summed up brilliantly in one of our Half Nights of Prayer at St Mellitus North West. In Chapter 1, I mentioned my surprise when student Rachel, who knew nothing about my beacons story at that point, said: 'As I am praying, I imagine beacons being lit across the North, fanned into flame by prayer.'

As a scientist, I love spotting patterns in the data. Joining the dots. There's no such thing in science as absolute proof. Just theories that seem to fit the data, as we have it.

And it's the same with the beacons and prayer. There seems to be a pattern I spot again and again that links prayer to fires being fanned into flame – from fired-up lives to fired-up regional transformations.

You can try to describe prayer using so many analogies. But wonderfully, prayer always escapes any possible theory. At the end of the day, the best way is to ask Jesus to coach you (see Chapter 7). But here are some very rough analogies.

There was a short-lived trend in my brother's school for illicit use of magnifying glasses. Really? On a sunny day in Lancashire, all you need is a handy magnifying glass and a bored moment in class. Then it turns out it is scientifically possible to surreptitiously focus the rays of the sun on the back of the boy's blazer in front of you. Holes just like mini cigarette burns mysteriously appear. Parents went mad.

But you could say, that's a bit like praying: we slip out our magnifying glass to focus the power of the Almighty.

All that said, prayer isn't just a schoolboy prank; it isn't a scientific mechanism. The ways of God are always beyond us. Scientists like me become frustrated because we can't pin down cause and effect. At the end of the day, the effect of our prayers is totally down to God. The best way is just to do it and let Jesus coach you.

It seems our prayer muscles are best stretched when God leads us into the fragile place where everything is beyond us and all we have to do is open our hands in prayer. The work of God is always birthed in fragility. When our egos are at their lowest ebb. This isn't the way we like, or the way we'd have gone about it, but then, we're not God.

Let me give you some examples. Big scale from history, then small scale from my own story.

Big scale

We finished Chapter 1 with the famous lines of Foreign Secretary Edward Grey. In 1914, on the eve of the First World War, as he watched the lamps being lit in The Mall from his office in Whitehall, he said: 'The lamps are going out all over Europe. We shall not see them lit again in our lifetime.'

His lifetime lasted till 1933. The same year that Hitler was appointed Chancellor of Germany. But scroll forward nearly 50 years to 1982.

Pastor Christian Führer at the Nikolai Church in Leipzig, East Germany, started holding prayers for peace every Monday evening. At first there were only a dozen people, huddled into this great Gothic church where J. S. Bach had once premiered some of his finest choral pieces. But they had the courage to persevere. And word got out.

On 8 May 1989, the authorities barricaded the streets leading to the church, hoping to put people off, but it had the opposite effect. The congregation grew. On 4 September, the day of the annual Leipzig Autumn Fair, Western camera crews had been granted permission to film all over the city. Lots gathered outside the church and filmed the Stasi (East German secret police) tearing protest banners out of the hands of the peaceful pray-ers. Now the world was watching.

On 7 October, the fortieth anniversary of the founding of East Germany, hundreds were arrested from the crowds in front of the Nikolai Church. News then leaked out that more brute force was to come. Doctors told them that hospital rooms had been made

available for patients with bullet wounds. The Christians were terrified, but did not give up praying.

On 9 October, around 8,000 people crammed into the churches
in central Leipzig, with a total of 70,000 gathered in the city from
all over East Germany (GDR). Pastor Führer tells the story:

> Everyone was holding a candle, a symbol of non-violence – you need
> to hold a candle with both hands to keep it from going out, which
> makes it impossible to throw stones.
>
> Later, a member of the SED Central Committee said: 'We had every-
> thing planned. We were ready for anything – except candles and prayers.'
> The police had not been briefed for this possibility. Had we thrown stones,
> they would have known what to do: They would have attacked. But the
> tanks had no choice but to withdraw without a single shot being fired,
> and that's when we knew that the GDR would never be the same again.
>
> We had a sense that something extraordinary had happened, but
> we only really understood the enormity of it later.[2]

We have seen many other turnarounds in European history in
answer to prayer.

On 4 August 1918, the late Queen's grandfather George V called
a National Day of Prayer for Peace. Exactly 100 days later, the armi-
stice which ended the First World War was signed.

A generation later, his son, the late Queen's father George VI,
called a National Day of Prayer for the British Army trapped
at Dunkirk. On 26 May 1940, there were extraordinary scenes
outside Westminster Abbey as people queued round the block to
pray. Two events immediately followed. First, a violent storm arose
over the Dunkirk region, grounding the Luftwaffe, which had been
killing thousands on the beaches. And then, second, a great calm
descended on the Channel, the like of which hadn't been seen for a
generation, which allowed hundreds of tiny boats to sail across and
rescue 335,000 soldiers, rather than the estimated 20–30,000. This
was known as 'the miracle of Dunkirk'.

In times of national trauma, prayers have been answered in
extraordinary ways. In 1536, William Tyndale was strangled and

burnt at the stake for translating the Bible into English. At the time, the Bible was only available in Latin, inaccessible to ordinary people, and indeed not so understandable by most clergy. Tyndale's final words were famously: 'Lord, open the King of England's eyes!'[3] Three years later, the King of England ordered English Bibles to be placed in all the parish churches across England.

In the words of the twentieth-century academic theologian Thomas F. Torrance: 'The prayers of the saints and the fire of God move the whole course of the world. They are the most potent, the most disturbing, the most revolutionary, the most terrifying powers that the world knows.'[4]

Small scale

I notice quite a few of my 'ordinary miracle' answers to prayer revolve around money. Maybe because it is such a tangible way in which God provides. Whether that was as a church treasurer, ending each year with 'just enough' in the bank account, just in time, or as a bishop, finding the same story but on a much bigger scale after the decimation of Covid-19. Here are two other heart-warming miracles on a small scale. Both happen to be about money – though not in the way we might want it!

One of my dear friends in Widnes came to a living faith in Jesus when she cried out, 'God, if you're there – help me!' from a drug-dependent low in her life. It wasn't a Damascus Road conversion, but God gently wooed her over the next five years – first by watching God TV (a Christian broadcasting channel), then being invited to come on an Alpha course with us in Widnes by one of the staff in the offices where she cleaned. She has many money miracles, but a rather charming one is about her grandson, who was given an old penny. He polished it till it shone and treasured it as his proud possession. He took it into school to show the class. But when the end of the school day arrived, the penny was mysteriously missing from his school bag. His teachers searched everywhere at school. His classmates were cajoled to own up and return it, no questions asked. But the penny was nowhere to be seen. We got praying that Jack's penny would turn up. Nothing. A week passed by. Then my friend phoned. 'You'd never believe this. Jack was coming round for his tea. He spotted something glinting by my gate. It was the Old Penny.' 'Nan – that's a miracle. I lost it at school.'

A couple of years ago, I was passing through Euston station on my way to catch a train to a speaking engagement. There wasn't much slack in my schedule, so I was walking at a pace to the Underground when I was prompted to go back. 'I want to show you something behind that pillar.'

I have got used to tuning in to such prompts. Sometimes they turn out to be a figment of my imagination. But what's to lose? Joan of Arc winsomely said: 'Of course [God speaks in our imagination]. That is how the messages of God come to us.'[5]

So I retraced my steps to the pillar. Behind it there was a plaque dedicated to a member of staff from the station who had been awarded a Victoria Cross for bravery in the Second World War 'for taking ground behind enemy lines'. When I came to buy my Tube ticket, there in the change I received back was a 50p, with the Victoria Cross on it. I tucked it away safely in my pencil case, as a reminder of this 'coincidence', and continued on my way. The speaking engagement was a meeting of church leaders from across the country. Appropriately, the title I had been given was: 'Fearless Leadership: How to be leaders who are led by the Spirit'. One of the church leaders came up to speak to me afterwards. He was in a very tough situation, not of his own making; he was needing to summon up immense amounts of courage. After I had prayed for him, I felt I had to give him my special 50p piece. A few months ago, I was facing a situation where I needed to dig deep for courage. I spotted something glinting on the carpet under my desk. It caught my attention because I was positive it hadn't been there a day earlier. I retrieved it. A 50p. A special Victoria Cross 50p. Two weeks later, I was having a Quiet Day at home. I spotted something glinting outside our back door. I was sure it hadn't been there when I'd fed the birds first thing. I picked it up. Another 50p. I love these underlinings, coincidences or 'serendipities of the Spirit'.

When I was writing this chapter, one minor irritant was that my son's passport was stuck in an anonymous backlog at the Passport

Office. I had resorted to emailing my intercessors' list to pray. There was just over a week to go till our holidays. I was right up to the very last moment before I needed to wheel into action to go to get him a replacement passport. The phone rang. It was the MP's office who had been chasing it – it had been found. I was having lunch at the time with a dear mum friend who had been reading a draft of my book. Helen summed it up brilliantly: 'Woohoo! The power of prayer.' And she proceeded to tentatively share with me some of her own incredible answers to prayer; another PhD scientist quietly marvelling at the wonders of God – his ordinary and extraordinary miracles. Our hearts were warmed.

Big scale, small scale, there is an undeniable connection between prayer and beacons being fanned into flame.

No damp wood!

In my early days as a bishop, I found myself mentioning the beacon story a few times when people asked me about my hopes – it has so much resonance in Lancashire with our beacon sites. I remember with fondness a meeting in Head Office in London, when a more experienced colleague smiled and said: 'Well let's hope there's not too much damp wood on those beacon sites in Lancashire.'

Just a few years on, if we met again, I could absolutely assure him that Lancastrian wood is not damp!

During our Covid-19 pandemic, I noticed an acceleration in openness to the things of God. Maybe it is because we were facing death and trauma in ways we had been cossetted from before. Was this waking us up from under our 'blanket of unbelief'? Perhaps. Whatever the case, my experience is that, in conversations, many of us are happy to dig deeper into realms of faith and the so-called supernatural.

After one Zoom meeting, I stayed online with a colleague in one of our hospitals. She had been looking drawn and haggard, not her usual bubbly self. 'I hardly slept last night. I've had this pain in my leg and hip for nine months; it won't go away and it makes it very difficult to sleep.' She isn't a woman of faith, but I have found that isn't a reason not to offer help. 'I believe that Jesus can heal today.

Would you like me to pray for you?' 'Ooh, yes, I'd be delighted.' So I prayed a simple prayer for peace and for healing, in the name of Jesus. I assured her it was on his authority not on mine. Next day, an email pinged in, headed, 'Amazing!!!' She had had the best night's sleep in nine months. The pain had completely gone. 'You must have a direct line!'

I met a man in a pub. That sounds worse than it is. On a busy Sunday, I stopped at a pub restaurant chain for a breather and some lunch. I got chatting to the man who was serving me: he hadn't served a bishop on her lunch break before. 'Do you work here often?' It turned out that this was just his seasonal job. Alan's career was organizing large music festivals round the country. Goodness me, that wasn't something I knew anything about. Why don't you come and see? I'd love to. So I found myself an invited VIP behind the scenes at the largest punk festival in Europe, held at the stunning Winter Gardens in Blackpool each year. A whole world, a whole family community I knew nothing about: the dress, the music, the art, the piercings . . . and the hair! My mum would have quipped: 'It was enough to make your hair stand on end!' I loved it. I received such a warm welcome, with wonderful comedy moments, for example, when someone came up to me and asked if *I* was in fancy dress. Here was me thinking I was looking reasonably normal in a jacket and dog collar. The punks and I had more in common than first appearances: we were all reaching out for a world beyond this. It was extraordinarily generous of Alan to give me so much time. As I left, I offered to pray for him. I gently asked Jesus to bring his peace from heaven. I looked up and there were tears.

Scroll forward 18 months. I had just finished filming my Christmas message outside the artificial ice rink in Dalton Square, an attractive Georgian square in the centre of Lancaster. I grabbed a cheeky burger and chips from the food stalls and sat under the outdoor gas lamp to keep warm. The door of the townhouse next to me opened, and out came a man and a woman. He instantly recognized me. 'It's Alan from the punk festival,' he offered, as I tried to place him. 'I didn't know you lived in Lancaster?' 'Oh, we don't, we're just on holiday for a couple of days – it's been such a tough year. And if things don't pick up in the summer, that will be the end of the music festivals.' 'Can I pray for you again?' Amid the bustle of a Christmas square, in a coincidental meeting of serendipity, the peace of Jesus gently descended. Alan and his girlfriend wiped tears from their eyes. 'Gosh, that was a coincidence,' he smiled. 'What were the chances of meeting you here?'

We can easily dismiss these moments as 'just another coincidence'. But as Archbishop William Temple put it: 'When I pray, coincidences happen, when I don't, they don't.'[6] I enjoy treasuring these generous encouragements and 'serendipities' of the Spirit.

Word

These moments of coincidence (or 'godincidence') are lovely and make good stories. But sometimes they can seem like the fairy-tale trails of bread in the woods.

Wonderfully, there is a proper road map for the journey home. It is that bestselling book of all time, the Bible. The Word of God. It's been a living book to me since, aged 11, from a family without faith, I first invited the Holy Spirit to open my eyes as I read it. And Jesus walked off the page of the Bible and into my life as a real and living person.

If you want to see beacons lit, if you want your faith to be fanned into flame, the Bible is your fuel. Your daily bread. Literally. 'You can't live on bread alone, but on every word from the mouth of God,' said Jesus (Matthew 4.4, my translation).

I read the Bible every day. I try to get to know parts off by heart. It feeds me in ways that are hard to describe until you experience it for yourself.

It's a hammer that smashes rocks into pieces.[7] Its perspective can clear away those boulders that collect in the road, making the way ahead seem impossible and impassable.

It's so sharp, it's like a sword that performs open-heart surgery.[8] Reading it can bring revelation about hidden sin, about darkness nestling in our lives. Its words can unlock the door to joyful repentance, that turnaround to a better way of freedom (see also Chapter 4).

It's a light,[9] lighting up the path ahead, often just step by step; shadows come to nothing. God is not who we think he is (see Chapter 2). And God's ways are not what we think they should be either.

His ways of operating are worlds away from ours. The best example of this is the cross. Absolutely nonsensical. Even in its own day. I have a lot of sympathy for Jesus' friends and family at the time, when he kept saying he had to die in Jerusalem. 'You're out of your mind.' It was only after his resurrection – and only when Jesus coached them from the Scriptures that this was the big plan all along – that the cross finally started to make sense. It was at this point that eyes were opened and hearts began to burn: 'Were not our hearts burning within us while he talked with us on the road and opened the Scriptures to us?' (Luke 24.32). We find his followers making sense of his death by working back from the fact of his resurrection. Over the next years, the intellectual Paul reaches for a whole variety of images from his day trying to put into words why Jesus died. Nothing ever fully explains the universe-shattering implications of his resurrection from the dead. We reach for analogies today. My favourite in school assemblies, in football-loving Lancashire, is that Jesus paid the ultimate transfer fee for us to join his team. Astronomical. His life for ours. But incredibly he thinks we're worth it. And not for our soccer skills. But because we're his long-lost beloved sons and daughters, whom he loved before the dawn of time, and he longs for us to come home (see Chapter 2).

The Bible is like fire.[10] Hearts began to burn when the risen Jesus coached people from it. This famously happened to Martin Luther and John Wesley. Both their hearts were 'strangely warmed' when they listened to Paul's letter to the Romans being read. (My favourite of all Paul's letters. Some stay away, finding it too complex; for me, it's a beautiful tapestry weaving together why Jesus came and had to die on the cross, inviting us into ways of living by the Spirit now in the light of the horizon to come.)

We met Augustine in Chapter 1. As a young man, he held one of the most respected academic positions in the known world at the time, professor of rhetoric in Milan. But his life is restless and empty. One day, in his garden, he hears a child's song, floating over the wall, *tolle, lege*, 'take and read, take and read'. He takes this as a divine prompt to open the book next to him, and randomly reads Paul's letter to the Romans: 'Clothe yourselves with the Lord Jesus Christ, and do not think about how to gratify the desires of the flesh' (Romans 13.14). He takes this as a direct word from God and devotes himself to following Jesus. He eventually becomes Bishop of Hippo in North Africa and one of the most influential theologians in the Western Church.[11]

Wales has been a nation which has brought the light of the gospel to nations across the world, a place where many beacons have been lit and fanned into flame.

From the age of 9, Mary Jones saved up for six years, then walked 26 miles across the hills to Bala to buy her own copy of the Bible in Welsh in 1800. Inspired by Mary's story, and by the need for reduced-price Bibles for Welsh speakers, the Revd Joseph Hughes asked a daring question to other church leaders: 'If for Wales, why not for the kingdom? And if for the kingdom, why not for the world?' This in turn inspired the founding of the Bible Society. It inspired the vision of William Wilberforce and the Clapham Sect in their campaign to 'make goodness fashionable': their hope was to inspire people to fall in love with the Bible and a biblically inspired lifestyle. Their work continues across the world today, even in languages that are not yet written down.[12]

A pattern I notice is how Wales is a nation that has brought the light of the gospel to nations across the world, a land where many beacons have been lit and fanned into flame. One more recent example is a beautiful story that made the secular media back in 2016. A delegation of Koreans came to thank the people of Wales for sharing the gospel with them. The story started 150 years earlier with Robert Jermain Thomas, who was serving as a missionary in China when God put Korea on his heart. At that time, Korea was closed to foreigners, so in 1866 he hired a passage on an American naval boat and threw snippets of key Bible passages off the boat as it sailed up the estuary. One government official took these scraps of paper home and used them to wallpaper his house. His home saw many regular visitors. People read them and started to trust in Jesus. The touchpaper was lit.

As a teenager, I was gripped by reading stories by Shirley Lees about mission to tribes in Borneo – *Drunk before Dawn*.[13] The tribes were literally this – drunk before dawn on the local brew, with terrible implications for family, social and economic life. Shirley's books are her real-life account of her life as one of the missionaries in the 1950–60s. At great personal cost, her husband Bill brought medical expertise, while Shirley, as a linguist, reduced the language of these remote tribes to writing, then translated the New Testament so they could read about the gospel in their own language. Many encountered Jesus, and found he still has the power today to release them from dark chains binding them to destructive patterns of life inherited over generations. You might imagine my surprise when, 30 years on, I found that my new boss, Bishop Julian Henderson, was married to Shirley's daughter, Heather! There was a moving moment after one Christmas holiday when Heather and Julian travelled to meet family in Australia. There they were joined from Borneo by a childhood friend of Heather's, who had married a Bornean tribeswoman. Unexpectedly, this Bornean woman made a point of thanking Heather personally as a missionary kid, 'who sacrificed so much of your childhood so we could have the Bible in our own language, and see the life of our community transformed so wonderfully'.[14]

There could be libraries and libraries of stories about the difference that access to a Bible in your own language makes.[15] Heather's parents' story is astonishing. Worth a read.

Sacraments

Beacons are fanned into flame by prayer, by reading God's Word and, often-overlooked perhaps, by his sacraments.

Over the centuries, the Church has appreciated how certain physical actions seem to carry the fire of God's grace in special ways. We call these 'sacraments'. Some churches recognize quite a number of these actions (e.g. confession, marriage, ordination, anointing for healing, confirmation). In the Church of England, we give priority to just two: Holy Communion and baptism. But I think they are so important to fanning beacons into flame that church isn't church without them. Our definition of church is simply this: 'The visible Church of Christ is a congregation in which the pure Word of God is preached, and the Sacraments be duly ministered according to Christ's ordinance.'[16] It's a simple definition I love. I find it helps me travel light; it allows plenty of room for rich local improvisation, translating into many different frequencies, so people can find a welcome at the family table wherever they find themselves. I love the sheer physicality of the sacraments in helping communicate the wonders of God, when we might otherwise be too much caught up in our heads.

Holy Communion

Two thousand years of Christian history have led to a range of understandings about what exactly happens when we celebrate Jesus' Last Supper – also known as Holy Communion or the Eucharist. Much ink, and indeed blood, has been spilt. But, as ever, God's ways are beyond all our understanding. In practice, I have come to appreciate the spiritual potency of what might appear at face value to be a seemingly simple act of remembrance. Jesus is especially present, as he promised, and just as Paul wrote in Scripture.[17] His past victory, his presence with us now and his future guarantee of the heavenly banquet appear to come into focus. 'Jesus Christ is the same yesterday and today and for ever' (Hebrews 13.8) And in particular, just as he said at the time, there seems to be a potency for the forgiveness of sins. After all, this is why Jesus died on the cross. This is the ultimate distillation of the good news that the beacons signal: 'that Christ died for our sins' (1 Corinthians 15.3). All is dealt with; we can come home.

My heart is warmed by the number of people I come across who have come in from the cold, simply because they received Holy Communion. And something precious happened in their lives:

Jesus becoming more real, more alive, more present. Often beyond words. A friend of mine was struggling with a messy divorce and in desperation she found herself in church one Sunday. Hadn't been for years. When she received Holy Communion, it was as if her eyes were opened for the first time ever. She had opened the door to the world of faith. I think there are hundreds of such encounters quietly happening, without fuss or fanfare. I love it that God respects those of us who prefer the soft *lighting* rather than the dramatic *lightning* Road to Damascus turnaround that gets more showy likes on Instagram. One of our teenagers in Blackburn recently experienced Communion for the first time. He commented: 'I really liked the blood and the bread bit. It made me feel I was part of the family.'

My dear colleague, Archdeacon David Picken, until recently chaired On Fire Mission.[18] Their dedication to see renewal in local parishes flows out of being renewed by the fire of God's Spirit in worship. My experience of their gatherings is that they are simply super refreshing, blending catholic spirituality with contemporary charismatic renewal. Spiritual gifts move from niche to normal. And, wonderfully, at the heart of any On Fire Mission gathering is the Eucharist.

On the night before Jesus died. At his 'last supper' with his friends. Highly symbolic, the night when the lambs were slaughtered for the Passover feast. High octane. Highly significant. Jesus simply asked them to do one thing, as he broke the bread: 'This is my body given for you; do this in remembrance of me' (Luke 22.19). 'This is my blood of the covenant, which is poured out for many for the forgiveness of sins' (Matthew 26.28). What is about to happen to him in the next 24 hours is so traumatic and devastating for his friends and followers, Jesus is giving them a route through this. A way to start to make sense, even if they cannot comprehend it at the time. He's warning and reassuring them. It will be bloody, make no mistake. But not to lose heart. Somehow that blood will pay for the forgiveness of sins.

After the resurrection, Jesus' followers found that that when they obeyed this command, Jesus was somehow especially present in the breaking of bread. For example, on that first Sunday, two followers on the road out of Jerusalem invited a mysterious stranger into their home for a meal. The Bible puts it like this: 'When he was at the table with them, he took bread, gave thanks, broke it and began to give it to them. Then their eyes were opened and they recognised him, and he disappeared from their sight' (Luke 24.30–31). Some years later, Paul wrote to the young church in Corinth who were in danger of over-spiritualizing everything, doing away with the physical (a common mistake over the centuries to come to dismiss the earthy reality): 'Is not the cup of thanksgiving for which we give thanks a participation in the blood of Christ? And is not the bread that we break a participation in the body of Christ?' (1 Corinthians 10.16).

And here's the thing, Jesus asked us to do this often. It seems so simple, it can slip off the radar. And yet, the presence of Jesus brings wholeness not just to human hearts but also to churches and communities.

Baptism

Again, much ink has been spilt over baptism – where, when, who, and who by? (Most of the things that have potency in firing up beacons – the Bible and the sacraments – seem to cause a spilling of ink.)

In short, baptism marks a public welcome into God's family of faith. Last Sunday, at a small church in one of our towns, the vicar and curate baptized and then I confirmed people from six different nations. On the wall of the upstairs prayer room of the church were the words: 'Ask me, and I will make the nations your inheritance' (Psalm 2.8). There was so much joy, as this promise was becoming a tangible reality. In Chapter 1, I described the sense of an open heaven over Paisley's baptism. This sums up how I experience baptisms – an open heaven. Ordinary everyday things – the water, the words – wonderfully echo the baptism of Jesus. They become a taste of the heavenly reality of the Father's love and welcome to that child or adult, mediated in the gentle presence of the Holy Spirit.

> At that time Jesus came from Nazareth in Galilee and was baptised by John in the Jordan. Just as Jesus was coming up out of the water, he saw heaven being torn open and the Spirit descending on him like a dove. And a voice came from heaven: 'You are my Son, whom I love; with you I am well pleased.'
> (Mark 1.9–11)

Baptism through history, this washing in water in the name of the Father, Son and Holy Spirit, has been closely linked to deliverance from evil. (For more on deliverance, see back to Chapter 4.) It's not just a symbolic act. Like Holy Communion, in some mysterious way God's power is mediated through ordinary physical things – bread, wine and water. I like to imagine that one day, in heaven, I will be able to grasp this fully. For now, like Mary in John 2, I'm just trying to 'do whatever he tells [me]'.

Beacons are fanned into flame by prayer, the Word and sacraments. It may appear from all my examples that I have a 'hotline' to God. This is not true. I have simply developed the habit of journalling these 'godincidences', noting Scriptures that resonate, giving thanks for answers to prayer, pushing past that internal dismissing of, 'Oh, that's just another coincidence.' Try it. I bet you'll be more than pleasantly surprised.

I love looking back periodically on what I call 'stones taken out of the Jordan'. This was God's instruction when the Israelites had miraculously crossed the Jordan. God told them to take stones from the dry riverbed (Joshua 4.3). He knew they would quickly forget the miracle and start grumbling. We have selective memories and tend to dwell on the difficult bits. We tend to be rather forgetful and short-sighted. We'll be picking this up in Chapter 9. But before then, let's go deeper with the most excellent coach.

Going further

For group discussion

1 'When I pray, coincidences happen, when I don't, they don't' (Archbishop William Temple). Do you have stories of 'ordinary miracles' or even big-scale examples?

2 The Bible: can you give an example of when reading the Bible has been like a light? Like a fire? How do you read the Bible?

   Idea: you might want to try reading the Bible with one person. Start, say, with Philippians or Luke's Gospel. Always ask the Holy Spirit to open your eyes before you start. Then see what strikes you both. What confuses you? What warms your heart? Let Jesus coach you from there.

3 Holy Communion: can you put words round what this means to you?

4 Baptism: have you been baptized? Do you remember it? Have you seen a memorable baptism – what made it so special?

5 Remembering: do you keep a journal? What are you most thankful for today?

For personal devotion

Read: Ephesians 3.14-21

St Columba's Prayer: Kindle in our hearts, O God, the flame of love that never ceases, that it may burn in us, giving light to others. May we shine forever in your temple, set on fire with your eternal light, even your Son Jesus Christ, our Saviour and Redeemer. Amen.[19]

7

Let Jesus coach you

Jesus: the best teacher

One day Jesus was praying in a certain place. When he finished, one of his disciples said to him, 'Lord, teach us to pray, just as John taught his disciples.'
(Luke 11.1)

Quite simply, that's the bottom line. He will teach you.

You could watch the slickest video on prayer, read the most erudite book on prayer, but the secret of the Christian life is what happens in secret: 'When you pray, go into your room, close the door and pray to your Father, who is unseen' (Matthew 6.6 – the other record of Jesus' teaching on prayer in the Gospels).

There's a beautiful line on this theme from Augustine, fourth-century Bishop of Hippo in North Africa, whom we met earlier in Chapters 1 and 6. He is writing about his mother, Monica, grateful that when he was the arrogant young Professor of Rhetoric in Milan, with the world at his feet but his heart so empty he was searching in all the wrong places for satisfaction, still his mother prayed doggedly for him.

Augustine wrote of his mother after her death: 'Monica was the kind of person she was because she was taught by you, Lord, her inward teacher, in the school of her heart.'[1]

Let Jesus teach you in the school of your heart. Let him teach you to pray. Let him teach you to read the Bible. Let him teach you to be fed by the sacraments.

I wonder, when did you last learn a new skill? I asked this question recently with a group of preachers in Preston. One was learning to sing. One was trying out stand-up comedy. Imagine if you turned up for your first singing lesson, and your teacher was Andrea Bocelli? Imagine if you went to a class on stand-up comedy and found your coach was Peter Kay?

Your coach in prayer is Jesus himself. There is no expert in the universe who is better placed. It's beyond an honour to be taught by him, in the school of your heart.

For those who were closest to him, during his public life on earth, prayer was one of the few things they asked Jesus to teach them. His praying must have intrigued them. For a start, it was so counter-intuitive. When he was most in demand, when the crowds were literally at the door, Jesus often went AWOL, up a mountain, to a desert place to spend time in secret with his Father. When they urged him to eat something because he'd skipped his lunch by wasting time at a well with a woman, Jesus put things into a totally different perspective: 'I have food to eat that you know nothing about.' They take him at face value – gosh, someone else must have brought him food. So Jesus gently corrects them. 'My food . . . is to do the will of him who sent me and to finish his work' (John 4.31–34).

Prayer tunes us in to the will of God. The really important stuff. More important than satisfying our immediate needs, ticking the next thing off *our* job list. Prayer lifts our eyes to the further horizon (see Chapter 8). Even to horizons that might seem impossibly distant. I love that when Pope John Paul II became Bishop of Krakow in his forties, the people in his diocese said: 'We want a bishop who prays.' He spent till 11am praying each morning. In the last chapter we heard the story of how a Monday prayer meeting helped crumble the Berlin Wall. Even secular historians credit Pope John Paul II's fiery furnace of faith with the melting of the Iron Curtain, which was thought at the time to be fixed across Europe for generations.[2]

More often than I expect, people ask me how I pray personally. I am no hero, but the image which captures how I have been coached in prayer is based on St Aidan's story, from when he was Bishop of Lindisfarne. (We first met him in Chapter 3.)

Bede writes: 'Aidan was a man of deep prayer, who meditated on the words of Scripture, equipping himself in quiet for an active and highly effective apostolate.'[3] (Apostolate is another way of saying bishopping.)

Lindisfarne is also known as Holy Island. It's a beautiful place, cut off from the mainland by the tide twice a day. I have two phases of prayer: prayer with the tide in; prayer with the tide out. Prayer that is focused inwards and prayer that is focused outwards.

Let's take a look at these in turn.

Prayer with tide in

This is those times of solitary prayer when the tide comes in and it is just us and God. It's a lifetime's work to grow in this prayer. Here are three headlines that have helped me.

First, it's God's work. As I go on in prayer, I'm finding it's not so much about me doing the work, but simply inviting the Holy Spirit to pray in me. Less ego, more fire. 'Pray in the Spirit on all occasions' (Ephesians 6.18). Pete Greig, founder of the 24-7 Prayer movement, often winsomely asks what is on the agenda of the heavenly prayer meeting? By the way, his book *How to Pray*[4] is one of the best 'how to' books on prayer I've come across. Another top pick is Matthew Porter's book, *A to Z of Prayer*.[5] Matthew is Vicar of St Michael-le-Belfry in York. Take a look.

Second, silence. I often spend time in silence, still – not trying to listen to Jesus – but to simply *be* in his presence. As he says to Martha, who was feeling overwhelmed by all she had to do: 'Martha, Martha . . . you are worried and upset about many things, but few things are needed – or indeed only one. Mary has chosen what is better' (Luke 10.41–42). Over the centuries this type of prayer has had many different names: centering prayer, contemplative prayer, silent prayer. One of the best contemporary books on this is Martin Laird's *Into the Silent Land*.[6] There are many heroes and friends who have explored the territory and left their own maps.

One top tip: don't be discouraged when, the moment you sit down, your head is filled with the latest job list, or you're distracted by noises around (Teresa of Ávila wittily calls them the reptiles and cockroaches who rush in when you open the door!). Going deeper in silence is like going underwater – there's often lots of noisy waves at the surface, but persist, stay with it, and you will find you can go deeper and deeper. Or like starting to exercise. There's often a pain barrier at the beginning that makes you want to give up, but stick with it, build up your spiritual muscles and it's incredibly rewarding. Just because we're only Park Run standard doesn't mean we can't learn tips from the Olympic athletes of our faith. They are our friends, not competitors to make us feel fat and flabby.

Third, quiet days. I try to take a quiet day once a month – I go to a local convent, no agenda but to sit with Jesus. When John Stott became Rector of All Souls' Langham Place aged 29, he found himself caught in a cycle of stress dreams – he'd wake up imagining he was in the pulpit with no sermon to preach. He happened to go on a London Diocese clergy training day and comments that all he remembers was the advice to put the letter Q in his diary once a month . . . and take it to be with the Lord. He said this: 'I followed this advice, and the weight of administration lifted and never returned.'[7]

If you feel overwhelmed by the weight of all the things you have to do – be counter-cultural. Don't work harder; take time out to be with Jesus.

Stott went on to grow in prayer to dedicate an hour a day, a day a month and a week a year.

Luther said he had so much to do it was impossible without first spending two hours a day in prayer.

Benedict spent three years in silence in a cave, then spent the rest of his life setting up a monastic movement which transformed the culture of Europe.

I don't think this is a coincidence.

Cuthbert, a successor of Aidan at Lindisfarne, resisted being made a bishop for most of his life, because the call on his life was so strong to spend time alone in prayer, first on the Inner Farne, an island near Lindisfarne, then on the Outer Farne, an island further out to sea. Shortly after he died, Bede recorded the eye-witness accounts of his healings, preaching and wrestling with demons. My favourite Cuthbert story is of how a fellow monk noticed he seemed to appear damp in the morning. So one night he followed him and watched him stand in the sea up to his neck with his arms outstretched. All night. Warmed by the fire within. The monk was overcome with guilt for having spied on so secret a time of prayer. He confessed this to Cuthbert who asked him not to tell anyone about this story until after his death.[8] Miraculously, Cuthbert's body remained undecomposed for years after his death in AD 687, and eventually found a resting place in 995 on the site of what is now Durham Cathedral. Thousands of pilgrims have visited his tomb over the centuries and found it a place of healing and hope. Is this the legacy of so much sustained prayer in the secret place? I would say so.

It turns out that living in silence can have remarkable effects. TV presenter, journalist and social commentator and *Strictly* winner Stacey Dooley MBE was filmed by BBC3 in 2021 as she spent time in a convent. With the same Anglican nuns in Whitby who made me so welcome on retreat before becoming a bishop. At the end of the week, she spoke generously to the nuns that she loved the idea of what it means to truly believe because of the impact it makes on their lives – why wouldn't people want that?[9] Previously the BBC filmed five men searching for meaning in their lives, who joined Worth Abbey and lived according to their Benedictine Rule for 40 days.[10] It was so popular they made a follow-on, *The Convent*, filming four women living with the Poor Clare sisters in Arundel.[11] In the silence, with the gentle rhythm of chapel prayer and daily spiritual direction from an experienced monk or nun, deep wounds surfaced and were tenderly healed by Jesus. Seared on my memory is one young woman, who, late at night, creeps into the candlelit chapel, alone. After some time in silence, she bursts into this beautiful a cappella singing of 'Amazing Grace'. After all she'd been through in life, she had finally unfurled her wings and found her voice. Maybe Jesus is inviting you deeper into silence in the secret place to unfurl your wings and find your song.

Prayer with tide out

This is my second phase of praying: prayer with the tide out. Prayer that is focused outwards.

Let's return again to Jesus' teaching on prayer in Luke 11, better known as the Lord's Prayer. Have you ever noticed the ambition in it? 'Your kingdom come, your will be done, on earth as it is in heaven.'

The way it is put in the Greek is very directive: 'Your will – let it be done; Your kingdom – let it come.' It's not a genteel English: 'Do you think this might possible, if you're not too busy . . .?'

He is the King! And he is on your side. So much more willing to act than we are to ask. He's no pussy cat – all a bit nervy – the slightest sound can scare him off. No, he's a lion:

> As a lion growls,
>   a great lion over his prey –
> and though a whole band of shepherds
>   is called together against it,
> it is not frightened by their shouts
>   or disturbed by their clamour –
> so the Lord Almighty will come down
>   to do battle on Mount Zion and on its heights.
> (Isaiah 31.4)

Jesus wants us to be direct.

One way of praying with others, especially as a team with a common endeavour, which I've found very effective is Half Nights of Prayer: 6 p.m. to midnight. In slots of say half an hour – swap between times of worship, times of silence with simple prayer stations, times of praying together for particular intentions. As we get closer and closer to midnight, I always noticed that our prayers are more and more direct and ambitious. Sustained time in his presence gives our prayers a clarity and confidence. We are sons and daughters of the King! Augustine was always deeply impressed by the Desert Fathers and Mothers that they had no education but they could stand up and storm the gates of heaven. Jesus said: 'From the days of John the Baptist until now the kingdom of heaven has been subjected to violence, and the violent are taking it by force' (Matthew 11.12, NCB). I am sure that includes women too. I'm not a connoisseur of icons, but I have on my desk an icon of Mary (from a Greek Orthodox church we stumbled across on holiday in Rhodes). Mary is holding a hammer in one hand and the devil by his ears in the other. I love this striking image of aggression in prayer!

Here's the pragmatic point: where many beacons are being lit, individual lives or regions transformed, or churches planted across nations today, they are always accompanied by high levels of prayer. Fact. There is no short cut. We like to think it's down to us and our plans and our strategy. In Britain it seems as if we are inoculated to the power of prayer because we have the NHS, we have our pensions, we have our education. We don't need his help; we don't need to depend on him – thank you very much. But what if we looked out to the majority world with humility and looked to the saints of the past to learn about intercession, about how they prayed with the tide out?

John Hyde (1865–1912) was one such saint. Known as 'praying Hyde', he went out from Illinois to India in the nineteenth century, not as a teacher or evangelist but as an intercessor – to pray on location. One story originates from his time at the Sialkot conference.

Approximately two thousand leading missionaries – both European and native – were present. A powerful revival swept through the conference. Men and women who had toiled for years in the Lord's service wept over their sins. Why? The Spirit of God had utterly broken their stony, self-righteous hearts. Now they recognised the luke-warmness and self-confidence in which they had lived for years as their greatest sin. They acknowledged that their sin of indifference was hindering the spiritual progress of their congregations and blocking revival. They humbled themselves, and admitted their specific failures and mistakes before the whole assembly . . . People who had gone about the Lord's work with indifference experienced a release from their lukewarmness. They were renewed and gripped with ardour. This surge of new life did not stop there but flowed out into the entire mission field. What sparked off this revival? . . . Before the conference started, John Hyde and two other missionaries knelt down and prayed almost all day and night . . . the hearts of John Hyde and his two praying friends were set on fire.[12]

It brought tears to my eyes when I discovered, by chance, that my Pakistani friend traces the point at which her forefathers and -mothers came to faith (in what was then India) to the Sialkot conference. The ricochets of faith travel far across the globe and through time.

Closer to home, I recall attending a Leadership Conference at Holy Trinity Brompton (HTB) church in London back in 2012. I was intrigued that they had a 7 a.m. prayer meeting on the conference agenda. As I walked along the Cromwell Road from my hotel to the church, in my mind's eye I imagined a volcano with deep magma chambers. As the prayer meeting started, the leader said, we often think of this as the magma chamber under all our ministry. I am saddened when I stumble across negativity towards the HTB members of our family. In our UK culture of 'tall poppy syndrome', we cut down to size people who seem to do well (perhaps the opposite of US culture). They would be the first to admit they are far from perfect. But they have had an astonishing reach for bringing people to faith and church planting with the Church of England, and now internationally across a generous spread of denominations. I would think there is no coincidence with this 7 a.m. magma chamber and the 24-7 prayer shed that has been on the site for many years.

Let the fires go out in the boiler room of the church and the place will still look smart and clean, but it will be cold. The prayer room is the boiler room for its spiritual life.
(Leonard Ravenhill)[13]

More famously, the Moravian Christians under Count Zinzendorf started a 24-7 prayer meeting in 1727 and sustained this for 100 years. We can trace significant leaders and church growth movements that came out of this furnace of prayer, like John Wesley (see Chapter 3). Jesus was clear about this – leaders are called out by sustained prayer: 'Ask the Lord of the harvest to drive out workers into his harvest field' (Matthew 9.38, NIV UK 2011 adapted).

When I was a new bishop, I happened to be at a meeting in Preston. An older woman in her seventies asked me which church I came to faith at in Bolton. 'St Andrew's Over Hulton – I came to faith in 1983.' With tears in her eyes, she said: 'I left in 1976. We prayed and prayed that God would call out the next generation of leaders.' I soon had tears in my eyes too. In fact, the story is more lovely than that. A few months later, St Andrew's kindly invited me back to preach. It would be my first time back there since my mum's funeral. I hadn't noticed the date in my diary until it was upon me. So, on my first Mothers' Day as Bishop of Lancaster, the sixth anniversary of my mum's death, I was surrounded by spiritual mothers, who had brought me to birth. As the service finished, the organist struck up with an unusual tune, which I'd never heard on the organ before. Puccini! She had no idea this was my mum's favourite aria. Played at her funeral. Another serendipity of the Spirit.

Praying with the tide out can be hard work. I find it feels rather like praying through birth contractions (see further in Chapter 11). In 1949–52, there was a surprising awakening of faith in the Hebrides. The Revd Duncan Campbell was invited to preach. And the response was astonishing; people not just in church but in pubs, schools, fishing boats, woke up to the presence of God. This was associated with gentle unbinding of darkness in people's lives and a resulting transformation of these communities – crime and disorder dropped dramatically, families were reconciled. *Shalom.*

Was this simply because Duncan Campbell was a good preacher? No. He was the catalyst. There is no neat cause-and-effect formula for such visitations of the Holy Spirit. But there have been such awakenings which have transformed communities across the world, and they are always accompanied by a high level of prayer. Hidden away in the Hebrides, there were two octogenarian sisters, Peggy and Christine Smith, housebound spinsters. They had prayed and prayed and prayed. Interviewed about their prayer, they called it 'travail in prayer', like praying through the contractions of birth, while new lives are born.[14]

And another coincidence. In 2016, the Archbishops of Canterbury and York introduced an annual ten-day period of prayer between Ascension Day and Pentecost, following the pattern of Jesus who told his first followers to pray in Jerusalem until the Holy Spirit came. They have encouraged us to pray for five friends to come to faith in Jesus Christ. This invitation to prayer #ThyKingdomCome quickly spread in successive years, involving 172 countries and more than 80 denominations and traditions (see Figure 3).[15] Rather satisfyingly, the ten days end with 'Beacon events'. The online map shows pinpoints of light wherever people are holding a #ThyKingdomCome celebration. Each year there are more pinpoints. The light spreads.

Finally, I had to smile. Yet again. As I finished writing this book, I opened my email to read this picture from Mei in Preston. As #ThyKingdomCome encourages, I could tell she was a woman who spent time in the secret place of prayer. She wrote: 'The picture is

Figure 3

one of flickering lights in the distance. I sense that individuals, as well as groups around Lancaster, have been seeking God in prayer. When people seek God in prayer, in whatever form, open to listen, I believe the Holy Spirit will set the flickering lights ablaze, and a proper fire will be the end result. Imagine watching a fire dancing away in a hearth, this fire which I am describing has been set ablaze by the wind of the Holy Spirit. My breath and my mind is blown away . . . imagine this becoming a reality in every imaginable setting.'

May Jesus coach you in the secret place to fan many beacons into flame.

Going further

For group discussion

1 Prayer: what struck you in the patterns of prayer described in this chapter? How do you tend to pray?
2 How do you find silence in prayer?
3 'Monica was the kind of person she was because she was taught by you, Lord, her inward teacher, in the school of her heart.'[16] What might Jesus be wanting to teach you in the school of your heart?
4 'Ask the Lord of the harvest, therefore, to drive out workers into his harvest field' (Matthew 9.38, NIV UK 2011 adapted). Jesus spells it out: leaders are called out by prayer. What would this mean in your community/school/workplace/nation? Where do you see a lack of leaders? What vocation is he calling out in you?

For personal devotion
Read: Matthew 6.5–15

Prayer to conclude: Jesus, would you teach me in the school of my heart. Always for your glory. Amen.

8
Lifting our eyes

Blazing beacons on hilltops lift our eyes up to the horizon.

When Gandalf saw the chain of beacons being lit, he whispered that hope was kindled.[1] These are words of faith. The tiny spark on the horizon kindles hope precisely because it represents the potential for something much more – a chain of lights across the hills, rallying the troops, Middle Earth reclaimed under the rule of a good and worthy king. A chain reaction of light.

Visibly the beacon is still just a small spark. But it lifts our eyes up to the hills and beyond, it represents so much more, as yet unseen. The lighting of the Platinum Jubilee beacons across the Commonwealth represented so much more than good photo shots around the globe. The chain of beacons along the cliffs from Anglesey to Liverpool signalled to ships in the Irish Sea that port was within reach, home is near.

Let's take a page to lift our eyes from the text, now we're well past halfway. To sum up my hope for this book, it's this: it will kindle faith in your heart.

It may be that you are more of a spectator when it comes to faith, watching from the terraces, never on the pitch. Or, to be honest, like me with football, living in blissful ignorance, politely taking an interest when my son comes back from a match. My hope is that reading this will encourage you to take a step of faith. That might feel like stepping on to the pitch, discovering those faith muscles you never thought you had; or if you're more homely and less sporty, it might feel like stepping through the door, to come inside and warm your heart by his hearth. Home is nearer than you thought.

It may be that the spark of faith was lit in you some time ago, but you're out of the match through injury. Your faith has been doused by pain, disappointment, or simply lack of attention to the fire. My hope is that reading this will fan your faith into flame. What if you dared to have faith that the realities of our home in heaven can break into today?

It may be that your fires of faith are burning well. You are like an athlete on the pitch in the thick of the match. My hope is that reading this will build your faith muscles so you grow tall as a giant of faith who can see the transformation of society with the eyes of faith. What if you stepped up, out of hiding, with courage and faith so this heavenly transformation can begin to become a reality where you find yourself?

It may be that life is especially difficult or fearful for you right now. It may be that you feel trapped underground and need a spark of light to guide you to freedom. It may be that you feel lost at sea and your eyes are straining for a lighthouse or beacon through the raging storm to guide you safely back home. What if you looked up from the dark tunnel or the choppy waves and caught sight of that light you have been secretly wishing was there all along?

Here's the exciting reality: when we lift up our eyes with faith, the horizon stretches far into the distance and beyond in every dimension. We will look at each of these in turn: eyes up to heaven; eyes to the future horizon; eyes to the past horizon. Each dimension is beyond our actual sight. This is the reality of faith. But what we don't see is more real than what we do see. This was Paul's advice during a time of extreme pressure: 'So we fix our eyes not on what is seen, but on what is unseen, since what is seen is temporary, but what is unseen is eternal' (2 Corinthians 4.18).

Eyes up to heaven

What does it look like to dare to believe the realities of heaven can break in to today?

This is how Jesus coaches us to pray. With ambition (see Chapter 7). To storm the gates of heaven to call heaven down to earth. The heavenly Lancaster. The heavenly Britain. The heavenly version of ourselves. Even with limited sight, we can imagine glimpses of the realities beyond us. Even though God's ways and purposes are always beyond us, we can grasp in part. Our vision is partial, but it's not mistaken, like seeing through frosted glass. Paul put it this way: 'For now we see only a reflection as in a mirror; then we shall see face to face. Now I know in part; then I shall know fully, even as I am fully known' (1 Corinthians 13.12).

I love that Jesus invites us to be seated with him in the heavenly realms and look *down on* rather than be overawed by our earthly challenges. 'Since, then, you have been raised with Christ, set your hearts on things above, where Christ is, seated at the right hand of God' (Colossians 3.1). One of my intercessors compared this with watching Parliament on live TV. (Bear with me.) For much of the time, the chamber of the House of Commons is full of empty green seats. She said that's like us: we don't take up our heavenly authority. We are busy working away in our constituencies (so to speak). But the real leverage for change comes from taking hold of the authority that Jesus gives us. 'All authority in heaven and on earth has been given to me. Therefore go . . .' (Matthew 28.18f.). Korean Pastor Paul Y Cho advises: 'If I were just to get up and begin my days without spending the hours that I spend in prayer, I would only have my natural resources to depend on. Yet, having spent time in prayer, I can *trust* the unlimited resources at God's disposal.'[2] As we saw in Chapter 7, Pope John Paul II used to spend two hours in silent prayer every morning. He lifted his eyes up to heaven, and he went on to have a ministry that was instrumental in reshaping the landscape of Europe.

This heavenly dimension is one which our ancestors seem to have been more used to taking hold of. For example, hermit and mystic from the fourteenth century, Julian of Norwich, writes:

Remember this faithfully for truly it is God's will, that we should hope as securely for the bliss of heaven while we are here as we shall enjoy it securely while we are there. And the more pleasure and joy we take in this security, with reverence and humility, the more it pleases him.[3]

We can live now with full assurance of the heavenly reality that, with Jesus, one day, it will all be OK. The brokenness of creation is temporary. The first Bishop of Liverpool, J. C. Ryle, wrote eloquently:

> Now assurance goes far to set a child of God free . . . It enables him to feel that the great business of life is a settled business, the great debt a paid debt, the great disease a healed disease, and the great work a finished work; and all other business, diseases, debts, and works, are then by comparison small. In this way assurance makes him patient in tribulation, calm under bereavements, unmoved in sorrow, not afraid of evil tidings; in every condition content, for it gives him a FIXEDNESS of heart. It sweetens his bitter cups, it lessens the burden of his crosses, it smooths the rough places over which he travels, and it lightens the valley of the shadow of death. It makes him always feel that he has something solid beneath his feet, and something firm under his hands – a sure friend by the way, and a sure home at the end.[4]

As a friend of mine puts it, more snappily: 'There are no expiry dates on God's promises.'

Evelyn Underhill had the word 'Eternity' embroidered on a plaque on the wall in her study. She was a woman whose gaze was drawn to the things of heaven, about which she writes with such beautiful texture:

> It's true that we cannot conceive all it means and all it costs to stand in that world of purity and wonder from which the saints speak to us; those high solitudes where they taste the mountain rapture, the deeply hidden valleys with a vista of white splendour, torrents of living water, quiet upper pastures and tiny holy flowers.[5]

Eyes to the future horizon

We are invited to lift our eyes upwards to heaven, metaphorically. That said, the most ancient Jewish way of praying was to stand, arms open, eyes to heaven. Not hunched over, mumbling to our feet.

Jesus also invites us to lift our eyes to the future horizon – the future when heaven comes down to earth.

Here's a tale of two women who have become very important to me. They are beautiful examples of women who had eyes of faith to the future horizon. They welcomed the future from afar. They both lived in the fifteenth century.

The first is Lady Margaret Beaufort from the House of Lancaster, a major figure in the Wars of the Roses.

A descendant of King Edward III, she was an important aristocratic pawn, so was married off by age 12. A year later, she became a mother to her first and only son Henry. She was petite and too young to give birth and so her body was broken and never recovered from the ordeal. But I would say her heart was broken by this birth too. Her son was taken from her to be made a ward of another aristocratic family, because at age 13 she was widowed when her husband died from the plague after being taken captive during the Wars of the Roses. She therefore spent many lonely hours in prayer.

And by coincidence, this very same year, 1456, she heard stories of the Pope's pardon of Joan of Arc. Joan had been burnt to death at the stake for heresy 25 years earlier, in 1431.

Joan was a young woman who had visions that would change the course of a nation. Joan had been filled with a sense of righteous indignation that it was not right that there should be English soldiers on French soil. It seemed that the rulers of the day had quietly given up and resolved that there was 'nothing that could be done'. Joan rallied the troops, influenced the French king, and was burnt at the stake by the English as a witch. But 22 years after her death there was not a single English soldier left on French soil; the Hundred Years War was over.

And the Pope's pardon 25 years later meant her story became famed across Europe. Was it a coincidence that Lady Margaret found herself in a similar situation at a similar age to Joan of Arc, deeply conscious of the political turbulence of the Wars of the Roses, where many of the men who controlled her destiny had quietly given up and believed the lie that 'nothing could be done; you've just got to put up with it': Lancastrians would always be at odds with the House of York? Living with fear of impending destruction or civil war was just part and parcel of life, as it had been, one way or another, for so many previous generations.

But I sense that in the deep prayer life of Lady Margaret, she also saw a vision of a land at peace. Was this when she started praying against the odds that her son might be the king who would unite England?

Nearly 30 years later, her son Henry did become king in 1485, Henry VII, the first king of the House of Tudor. A year later, he married Elizabeth of York, uniting the houses of Lancaster and York, ending decades of rivalry.

I wonder if Joan of Arc's far-seeing and calling-into-being of a change of wind direction over the nation of France inspired the teenage Lady Margaret to also pray for a change in direction in the wind in the political turmoil of the Wars of the Roses. To pray, work and hope that one day her son would be king.

Lady Margaret holds a special place in my heart because she founded the college I studied at in Cambridge. Nearing the end of her life, in 1499, she took a vow of chastity before Archbishop Fisher and did what she always wanted to do – she devoted her time to prayer and study. It was during this period in 1505 that she founded Christ's College. As a woman, she wasn't permitted to attend college chapel. But as a woman of prayer, she took a keen interest in the spiritual heartbeat of the college and had a window fitted in her lodgings so she could see into chapel. So it seemed to me a beautiful serendipity of the Spirit that I was invited from Lancaster to preach at the anniversary service in chapel to celebrate 40 years of women at Christ's in 2018. As part of my preparation, I asked the college archivist to retrieve the founding documents. Exactly as I suspected. Very early on, the documents refer to the college as a place of prayer. I quote: 'The weight falling on the shoulders of the late king was so alleviated by prayers and devotions when dealing with the great dangers confronting him and his country.'

I am truly inspired by these two women, to be praying and interceding on a 25-year timescale. Why not? In our click-of-a-button instant society we can expect change quickly. I love the story of William Wilberforce and the Clapham Sect. They were keen young Christians, and they thought the anti-slavery bill would get through Parliament in 18 months. It took 40 years. On 26 July 1833, Wilberforce heard of government concessions that guaranteed the passing of the Bill for the Abolition of Slavery. He died three days later.

We're used to doing this on a much smaller scale, aren't we? When we invest in people, we don't expect to see instant success overnight. Who doesn't remember that inspiring teacher from school days? In 1999, the Department of Education even ran a recruitment campaign based on the strapline, 'Everyone remembers a good teacher'. I remember the strapline more than 20 years on.

The words we speak over people, particularly over children and young people, can have tremendous influence over a long arc of time.

I remember as a 5-year-old in the school playground, the teachers telling us it doesn't matter what other kids say about us. (Unofficial anti-bullying strategy of the 1970s!) We just had to shout back: 'Sticks and stones will break my bones, but words will never hurt me.' That is a complete lie. Broken bones mend without trace. Words spoken over us can stay with us for a very long time.

Kenny Blue was five when he was first put on a horse in his grandfather's paddock. His grandfather whispered in his ear: 'Kenny, you're a natural.' Ever after that, every time he got on a horse, he heard his grandfather's voice in his ear. 'Kenny, you're a natural'. Kenny Blue went on to win the Olympic Gold medal for horse-riding for the United States.

Abbé de Tourville, nineteenth-century French Catholic spiritual writer, describes this future horizon beautifully:

The duty of the pioneer is not easy but it is noble; it is to live in heart and mind with those who are to come. It is for them, rather than for himself, that each in this world works. One could separate mankind pretty clearly into these clearly defined categories: those who live for the past (what good is that?), those who live for the present (very brief and restricted), and those who live for the future (spacious and open, and the satisfaction in doing so increases as time goes on). Think of what little returns Our Lord, the Blessed Virgin and the Apostles gained from their labours . . . but seen from the future, what enormous results stemmed from their first efforts.[6]

A woman who had a tremendous influence from the hidden place was Winston Churchill's nanny, Mrs Elizabeth Everest. A devout Christian, she was his 'dearest and most intimate friend' until her death when Winston was 20 years old. She had a profound influence on him. He seemed to have some foresight from the Holy Spirit. This is a conversation Churchill had at school at Harrow in 1891, aged 16, recalled by his friend Sir Murland Evans:

We frankly discussed our futures . . .
'Will you go into the army?' I asked.
'I don't know, it is probable . . . But I have a wonderful idea of where I shall be eventually. I have dreams about it.'
'Where is that?' I enquired.
'Well, I can see vast changes coming over a now peaceful world; great upheavals, terrible struggles; wars such as one cannot imagine; and I tell you London will be in danger – London will be attacked and I shall be very prominent in the defence of London.'
'How can you talk like that?' I said. 'We are for ever safe from invasion since the days of Napoleon.'
'I see further than you do. I see into the future. This country will be subjected somehow, to a tremendous invasion, by what means I do not know, but I tell you I shall be in command of the defences of London and I shall save London and England from disaster.'
'Will you be a general then, in command of the troops?'
'I don't know; dreams of the future are blurred but the main objective is clear. I repeat – London will be in danger and in the high position I shall occupy, it will fall to me to save the Capital and save the Empire.'[7]

The Bible is full of heroes and heroines with faith for a long vision into the future.

The elderly Simeon has been promised that he will see the Messiah before he dies. He spots a young couple in the Temple and sees with the eyes of faith. He takes Mary's baby in his arms in wonder and worship, knowing he can die in peace because 'my eyes have seen your salvation . . . a light for revelation to the Gentiles, and the glory of your people Israel' (Luke 2.25–35).

One-time ambitious Joseph is crushed by years hidden away, forgotten in prison. There his gift of interpreting Pharaoh's dreams means he sees ahead to seven years of plenty followed by seven years of famine in Egypt. With God's favour he becomes prime minister to save nations from starvation.[8]

Then, most famously, Abraham, a childless old man without hope of an heir, hears from God, and has faith in a most profound way that has echoed over three millennia. '[The LORD] took [Abraham] outside and said, "Look up at the sky and count the stars – if indeed you can count them." Then he said to him, "So shall your offspring be." Abram believed the LORD' (Genesis 15.5–6a). As a teenager, my mind was blown by news about a supernova explosion in a distant galaxy. The light had left the explosion when we were in the Stone Age. Wow! It stoked my passion to study science. Abraham has stoked my passion to have faith – to take God at his word. His mind-blowing word.

And here's the more mind-blowing news. Visions and dreams, these beacons on the distant horizon. They're not just for celebrities of faith. Perhaps even more astonishing is the promise that became a reality on the day of Pentecost in Jerusalem. As we read in Chapter 3, these visions and dreams are for ordinary men and women. Now anyone can receive the Holy Spirit, who is the 'deposit guaranteeing what is to come', present and yet beyond time.

> Peter stood up . . . 'This is what was spoken by the prophet Joel:
>
> "In the last days, God says,
>   I will pour out my Spirit on all people.

Your sons and daughters will prophesy,
>   your young men will see visions,
>   your old men will dream dreams.
Even on my servants, both men and women,
>   I will pour out my Spirit in those days,
>   and they will prophesy.'"
(Acts 2.14–17)

Eyes to the past horizon

A confession to make. I have a short memory and I am self-centred. I tend to presume I am living through the most significant times now. I don't think I am alone in this. In our society, we look down on the past, and talk of our ancestors as if they were misguided 'men of their time' at best, idiots at worst.

It has been a humbling but delightful treat to make the acquaintance of past beacon lighters, men and women of faith who have carried the torch of the gospel before me. Not just intellectually, as stories in the history books, but, as Scripture hints to us, as a cheering crowd, seated in the stadium all around us, cheering us on in the race.[9] They inspire me to step up, stand taller with greater ambition.

In the oldest Christian creeds (statements of faith), the Apostles' Creed, dating from sometime in the second century, there is a line tucked away near the end. 'I believe in the communion of saints.' 'Communion' and 'saints' are both words that have fallen out of fashion. It's this past horizon which has become an increasingly living reality in my spiritual life.

This all began with a question from a good friend before I was officially made a bishop. He asked me enthusiastically: 'Which three saints are you going to dedicate your episcopacy to?' This question had never been anywhere near my radar before. He's from the Catholic strand of the Church of England, brothers and sisters who would draw on the rich river of faith that flows to us down through the ages from our past family.

For example, he winsomely talks of prophecy calling us back to the past, whereas I instinctively talk of prophecy calling the future into the present. (For example, I am writing this book with a future tilt towards the 'Land of light and glory' as the final chapter.) But when he asked me about which three saints, my heart leapt. The answer sprung to mind immediately: 'Mary, Aidan and Hilda'. They have already featured in this book repeatedly, because they all have deeply inspired me. Just as John the Baptist looked back in time to Elijah and carried some of his fire, 'in the spirit and power of Elijah' (Luke 1.17), I had already prayed that, in some small measure, I might carry the same mantles and giftings of these three heroes of faith.

My first Easter as a bishop, I held a night vigil in the chapel at Whalley Abbey, our ancient centre of prayer, tucked away in the Ribble Valley in Lancashire. I prayed in the chapel for as much of the night as I could physically manage. Just before the sunrise service in the grounds, I was packing away the Communion silver in the vestry. Out of the corner of my eye, my attention was drawn to something tucked down behind the radiator. I rummaged around and pulled them out. Two small-framed pictures: one of St Aidan, one of St Hilda.

What if, surrounding us, unseen, there is a company of friends. Wise brothers and sisters, mothers and fathers of faith, behind the veil of time, cheering us on in the race, pointing us always to Jesus.

As a wise priest in our diocese put it: 'There is no rivalry or tension between them and us, simply a mutual rejoicing. As you sing with these people you will increasingly trust the beauty of your own voice adding harmonies of its own.' I have loved reading their stories, reading their writings. There are too many to introduce. But some of my favourites among those who have left us their writings are our homegrown English mystics from the fourteenth century: Richard Rolle, Walter Hilton and Julian of Norwich.

I pray often that God would be calling out giants of faith across Lancashire. But what if my brothers and sisters from past horizons let me 'stand on the shoulders of giants'? Britain has a multi-million-pound spiritual inheritance in the bank. This is how my Egyptian friend in London, Iman, puts it. She would say that the

British Isles has had a pattern of giants of faith; those who have tackled the strongholds in the land; unique relationships with kings and authorities; holistic ministry (for example, monasteries incorporated school, hospital, library, evangelism); a missionary heart to the whole world; giving honour to the place of the word of God; formation of Christ in their lives and miracles.

And perhaps, like me, you have noticed that some places appear to be easier to pray in than others. Thin places. I have been instinctively unsure about giving emphasis to special places, surely 'the earth is the LORD's, and everything in it' (Psalm 24.1). Yes, of course. But I am intrigued by some words of Jesus that seem to relate to this. At that high point in Jesus' ministry, his popular entry into Jerusalem on a donkey on the Sunday before Easter, the religious leaders criticize the crowds for their childlike palm-branch-waving enthusiasm about Jesus. He is quick to answer back: 'I tell you . . . if they keep quiet, the stones will cry out' (Luke 19.40).

Finally, one great advantage of ensuring our eyes strain to past horizons is that it counteracts our natural spiritual amnesia. We are naturally pessimistic; we have short memories. Who would have expected the growth of the Sunday school movement from no children in contact with churches in 1780 to 300,000 eight years later?[10] Who would have imagined Africa's growth in Christianity from 5 million in 1900 to 380 million in just 100 years?

Strongholds on the past horizon

As I was writing this chapter, I had just decided not to include this section. Then a WhatsApp came in from one of my senior colleagues asking us to pray for a particular parish community. A man had thrown himself into the river very near to the house where just over a month earlier there had been a double murder. It was the same parish where two previous vicars had suffered from illnesses that brought them dangerously close to death. A month later, when I returned from study leave, I discovered that, in prayer walking round the parish, our team came across stories from the local mill where the past had been covered up. This was unlike other parts of the UK where the human death toll of the Industrial Revolution was well documented and acknowledged.

We have noticed coincidences and serendipities of the Spirit. It is always worth paying attention to these. I also find it is worth paying attention to dark patterns and coincidences. In lives, families, in communities and even in nations.

On a bigger scale

Argentinian church planter Ed Silvoso defined a *stronghold* as 'a mindset impregnated with hopelessness that causes Christians to accept as unchangeable situations that they know are contrary to the will of God'.

We have noted this attitude of hopelessness, 'just putting up with it' as we say in Lancashire. Satan's ashen grey face, hand-wringing, saying, 'There's nothing that can be done. It's mad to try – just accept the status quo.'

I admire those who are mad enough to try. And I note how there can be a 'force field' putting us off trying to tackle some of the significant boulders of our age: for example, family breakdown, loneliness, economic disparity, poor diversity in our leaders. Ten years ago, one might have included the environment in that list. The first prophets to raise alarm about the environment, going back many years now, were often denounced as mad to try.

Strongholds also have spiritual dimensions, which require a spiritual response. Scripture speaks clearly about this: 'The weapons we fight with are not the weapons of the world. On the contrary, they have divine power to demolish strongholds' (2 Corinthians 10.4).

Dr Kenneth McAll was a trained medical doctor, psychologist and Christian who served in China. After a close brush with death, he wrote about what he called his awakening in these terms:

My mocking tolerance of the implicit belief of the Chinese in ghosts and the spirit world was gone. I understood that the spirit world holds both good and evil influences . . . I knew that, however disturbed one's environment might be, a person who had committed his life to Jesus Christ would be safe.[11]

He tells a compelling story about the dark horizon of the Bermuda Triangle:

> For hundreds of years the Bermuda Triangle (an area of the Atlantic Ocean enclosed by an imaginary line from Bermuda to Miami to Puerto Rico to Bermuda) has swallowed ships and aircraft, often without trace. The sheer weight of books written on this subject would sink a small ship. Most sailors prefer to avoid this place but, like many other people . . . I scoffed at such irrational fears. In 1972, my wife and I were sailing through the 'triangle' on a banana boat when we were caught in a force 9 storm . . . one of the ship's boilers broke which left us silently drifting. In the quietness, my wife and I distinctly heard a strange sound, like a steady droning dirge . . . almost two million slaves were thrown overboard [into the sea at this point] . . . it occurred to us that we heard that mournful dirge for a purpose. Perhaps we had a responsibility to pray for those wretched slaves who died uncommitted to the Lord, and to repent of the cruelty of those who were the cause of it. So in July 1977, with some interested bishops and some members of the Anglican Community of the Resurrection, a Jubilee Eucharist was celebrated for the specific release of all those who had met with untimely deaths in the Bermuda Triangle . . . From the time of the Jubilee Eucharist until now . . . no known, inexplicable accidents have occurred in the Bermuda Triangle.[12]

On a smaller scale

Not unlike Kenneth McAll, a very formative influence on my Christian faith in early adulthood was a visit to India and then Kenya with my church in Cambridge, who had developed friendly links with colleges that trained pastors in Hyderabad and Nakuru. One might have presumed that a bunch of us Cambridge graduates were helping out our brothers and sisters in the Global South, who hadn't had the same privileged education as us. But the privilege was all theirs. I had never seen, never mind experienced for myself, someone healed in front of my eyes, or released from oppressive spirits. Simply because I had prayed for them in the name of Jesus. This was everyday church life. In Nakuru, a blind woman received her sight. I remember arriving back at Gatwick airport with such a disjunction in my faith. It seemed like Britain was covered in a 'blanket of unbelief', as Lesslie Newbigin put it on his return from India (see Chapter 2). Seven years later, training to be a vicar in Oxford, I remember one tutorial on the Gospels that ran on for twice its allocated time, when the lovely, gentle academic suddenly swore at me in a response to something I'd casually said. '***t! You believe in miracles – you're a scientist!' 'Yes, of course I do – I've seen them.' So much scholarship over the last 200 years has airbrushed the possibility of miracles from our colour palette of possibilities. It's not black and white. There are plenty of grey areas where simple faith-filled prayers seem to go unanswered; but there's certainly more colourful answers than we imagine.

My Egyptian friend from London once invited her Egyptian spiritual director to visit the UK. She picked him up at Heathrow and excitedly pointed out the lush green English countryside as they drove to her house. He was very quiet, you might say unimpressed. She felt rather disappointed. It was several years before he shared with her the reason for his quietness. He was sad about what we had done with our spiritual inheritance. As a land of giants of faith, who had sent people across the globe with the gospel, he was sad to see a nation asleep.

I would say I am finding about one in ten parish churches which have 'got stuck'. What marks them out are repeated negative patterns, often rooted in some darkness, sin or tragedy in the past. I don't really understand this, but it is what I observe. I am just saying what I see. A little bit like the British Transport Police catchphrase you hear on the railways: 'See it. Say it. We'll sort it.'

I remember a particularly special time on retreat at the convent in Whitby leading up to my start in Lancashire. A word kept returning to my prayer times, a word which hadn't been a ready part of my vocabulary. It was the word 'confession'. As if the Spirit were prompting me with a key. In fact, I was consecrated as a bishop on St Peter's Day. The Gospel reading set for the day was the account in Matthew 16.19 where Jesus gives Peter the keys to the kingdom of heaven: 'Whatever you bind[lock] up on earth will be bound in heaven, and whatever you loose[unlock] on earth will be loosed in heaven.' Again, this connection between heavenly heavy lifting and earthly reality seems so often overlooked.

In these parishes that have 'got stuck' or 'locked up', we are finding that confessing sin and asking for God's forgiveness is so key (and indeed for the forgiveness of living people, actual or representative). And a way of manifesting this heavenly heavy lifting is quite simply by repentance of key leaders as part of a Eucharist in that place. To break the cycle of darkness. I like to call it 'spiritual hoovering'. We have a team in Lancashire, from different traditions across the Church, each one deeply prayerful with the gift of discerning spirits, a gift listed by Paul in 1 Corinthians 14, and a gift deployed with such normality by Ignatius and the Jesuit movement (see Chapter 10). This is not a silver bullet. It must be part of a more prolonged season of prayer and fasting. But I am conscious that we can have a tendency to rely on techniques and processes that don't address a spiritual root of the problem.

My Egyptian friend Iman observes that we tend to treat these issues as a problem-solution, but, in ignoring the spiritual dimension, we only diagnose part of the problem. Then we proceed with an intervention that dismisses the incredible spiritual riches we have at our disposal, namely the authority of Jesus and his victory over death and hell on the cross. When Jesus sent his disciples out ahead of him, he spelt this out clearly and simply: 'I have given you authority to trample on snakes and scorpions and to overcome all the power of the enemy' (Luke 10.19). He wasn't talking about our local Reptiles R Us shop or handling my pet snake. (Who has now been found, safe and sound, curled up on top of the bookcase in my study.)

In their bestseller *Angels on the Walls*, Wallace and Mary Brown[13] tell the story of parish life on an outer council estate in Birmingham. It is a riveting read. They are hounded by a teenage gang, who have been driving them to distraction since they moved in a year ago. Then one night when Mary is calling out in desperate prayer, she has a sense out of the blue that she should ask for 'angels on the walls'. She obeys. Within two weeks the gang has dispersed.

Quite by chance, I happened to pass a seminar in which they were speaking, years later at New Wine. They had done some research into the history of the area. A gang of seven young men had been terrorizing the area since 1840. There had also been seven teenagers in a gang that terrorized them. The place where there had been a number of suicides on the estate turned out to be the site of the hangman's noose.

Some of us are glass half-empty people, some glass half-full. In planting a garden, you need to tackle the weeds but not get obsessed with them. What makes a lovely garden is planting new flowers and bushes, laying a lawn, rather than moaning about the dandelions. On the whole, I find in nine out of ten churches and communities, it's much more productive to focus on the positive. I have written about negative stories in detail here because this root cause of some problems often escapes our radar. But in your community, sphere of influence: where are the people of peace? What's in your hand? Where are doors opening? Where is hope? Where is light breaking in? Look back warmly into the spiritual history (eyes to the past horizon). Listen out for the rhythms of the heavenly anthem (to the heavenly horizon). What are his stories over the places and situations we find ourselves in (eyes to the future horizon)? 'The earth is the LORD's, and everything in it' (Psalm 24.1), and nothing is impossible for him.

And don't overlook worship. Worship has such potency for lifting the spiritual atmosphere, especially the worship of infants and toddlers: 'Through the praise of children and infants you have established a stronghold against your enemies, to silence the foe and the avenger' (Psalm 8.2).

Leadership perspective

A last word to those who find themselves in a leadership role – in whatever sphere of society. You are gifted with influence over others, so it is more critical that you are able to lift your eyes to the horizon (past and future). And yet, the more senior you are in leadership, the more territory you have oversight for, the more the view through the windscreen ahead can get clouded. The farmers have been ploughing fields near me. There's more mud on the road than usual. It splatters. It happens. It obscures the view. Don't spend time analysing why the mud is on your windscreen or why a simple walk across the fields has mired you in mud. Detach. Don't be distracted. Just keep going. Keep your eyes on the road ahead.

This is most eloquently put in the letter to the Hebrews, where the young church found itself under heavy persecution:

> Therefore, since we are surrounded by such a great cloud of witnesses, let us throw off everything that hinders and the sin that so easily entangles. And let us run with perseverance the race marked out for us, fixing our eyes on Jesus, the pioneer and perfecter of faith. For the joy that was set before him he endured the cross, scorning its shame, and sat down at the right hand of the throne of God. Consider him who endured such opposition from sinners, so that you will not grow weary and lose heart.
> (Hebrews 12.1–3)

Where are the muddy spots, so we can avoid driving straight into them? Our next chapter looks at five main fire quenchers that douse the flames of the beacons.

Going further

For group discussion

1 Given all this talk of lifting our eyes up to heaven, to the future horizon, to the past horizon, there is a valuable discipline of living in the present: 'godliness with contentment is great gain' (1 Timothy 6.6). What are you thankful for today?
2 My hope for this book is that it will kindle faith. At the start of this chapter, I used four illustrations of where you might find yourself in the arena of faith (you could reread this briefly): spectator, injury bench, athlete stretching out, trapped underground. Where do you find yourself at the moment?

3 'There are no expiry dates on God's promises.' But which do you find most difficult to have faith in?

4 Eyes to the future horizon. Which of the stories did you find most inspiring? What do you see on the future horizon?

5 Eyes to the past horizon. Which heroes of faith or saints particularly inspire you? And why?

6 Ponder your community or networks for a moment. Where are the people of peace? What's in your hand? Where are doors opening? Where is hope? Where is light breaking in?

For personal devotion

Read: Luke 2.22–40

Prayer to conclude: Lady Margaret Beaufort's translation of a prayer of Thomas à Kempis:

This day, good Lord
I offer unto Thee myself.
Perpetually, for evermore
to be Thy servant.
With my heart and soul fully
to continue. And I beseech
Thee to inflame me with
the burning fire of charity [love]. Amen.[14]

9
Fire quenchers

With a chapter heading like that, you might be thinking that, 'This looks like a depressing read.' One to skip. Feel free!

But how about a more hopeful angle? My boys, like most, went through a phase of being scared of the dark. There's a goblin on the wardrobe watching me. With the light on, it's such a relief – it's just the shadow of an old suitcase. When darkness is seen in the light, you see it for what it really is. It can be such a relief to find the shadows come to nothing.

Beacons can be doused. Fiery torches can be blown out. Little candles can be snuffed out. Damp wood can suffocate a flame. What is it that quenches our fires? What are the main 'fire quenchers' (as I like to call them)? It might turn out to be a relief when we see these for what they really are. In the light of Jesus, darkness has to reveal itself. Fire quenchers need not have the last word.

Bad news and good news

The bad news is that *we* are the main ones who quench the fire. It's about *us* not *externals*. We are the fire quenchers. (We will look at the things that quench our fire from outside in Chapter 10.) The good news is that we can also do something about it.

Sin is not a word that finds its way into everyday language. It used to be on-trend in the world of archery, when sin was a technical word for 'missing the target'. You might translate it today as missing the goal, missing the penalty. Again, a bit too sporty for most of us to fully connect with. Comedian Milton Jones, with his wonderful wordcraft, puts it this way: 'Persistent niggling sin is a bit like leaving the car glove compartment light on. Slowly it saps all the energy, so you can't get going at all.'[1]

There are numerous health warnings about this in Scripture. For example, Paul warns the church in Thessalonica: 'Do not quench the Spirit. Do not treat prophecies with contempt but test them all; hold on to what is good, reject every kind of evil' (1 Thessalonians 5.19–22).

In my experience, here are the top five quenchers.

1 Belittling the enthusiasm of others

In the early days of working in Christian leadership, I used to apologize for my enthusiasm. Often. When you're the new girl on the block, you don't want to appear naive. Surely, we'll all graduate to being hard-bitten and cynical when our enthusiasm hits 'the real world', right?

No. I still remember the moment I was brought up short by my spiritual director. I was in the middle of an apology for being so thankful for the favour of God which I was treasuring. 'Jill,' she said, 'don't apologize for your enthusiasm. Enthusiasm in the Greek means *en theos*, 'full of God'.

This is brilliantly portrayed in the 2016 Disney film *Zootropolis*. On the face of it, a laugh-out-loud children's cartoon film. But a deeper look, and it's a perceptive, masterful portrayal of racism, feminism, drug culture . . . and enthusiasm. Police officer Judy Hop is the tiny country bunny with big ideas for the city of Zootropolis. She has her enthusiasm ground out of her by buffalo Chief Bogo and then con-artist Nick, a fox. With her childhood dreams crushed, she finds herself back at home on her parents' carrot farm in Bunnyburrow. But she has one last enthusiastic idea. She even manages to rally cynical Nick. Together, the dreamer who dares to dream one last dream and the cynic who dares to hope join forces to save the day.[2]

Others will have their own coping mechanism, but when I have finished a big stage speak, I am spent. It is as if the fire has gone out of my insides. Literally. I joke with a friend that's it's like being a Lancaster bomber: you take off, fly over the dam, drop the bombs, then race back to hide in the hangar to be refuelled. I simply don't want to engage with anyone who's heard me speak. Especially people telling me how amazing my speaking was. If the words I spoke were meaningful, then the glory goes to Jesus. I am just 'his plastic straw', as my friend Iman describes herself.

So normally when I have spoken, I try to escape as quickly as possible. I notice that Jesus often did that too – disappearing off when the crowds were most pressing.

But I am thankful for a lovely, nameless couple who followed me out of a big speak I had just done at a conference in Leeds. The couple gently spoke to me: 'We might be wrong, but we think God wants you to hear: "Never apologize. Never be reticent."'

My story of reticence has a deep root, rooted in reticence over my birth. It is deeply personal, but I want to take the step of committing it to paper because it's a beautifully tender story of God's healing response when we allow darkness to be unearthed. It came to light when I least expected it to: Lambeth Palace, HQ of the C of E, during a meeting of all the bishops. As a way of offering us some much-appreciated space to pray, the dedicated praying community at Lambeth, the Community of St Anselm,[3] had converted parts of this ancient building into prayer rooms, based round Psalm 139, a psalm which speaks of God's care for us. It was a very restoring time.

One prayer room was called the 'womb room'. It had blacked-out windows, lit with soft red light, a heartbeat pulsing, based on the verse: 'For you created my inmost being; you knit me together in my mother's womb' (Psalm 139.13). I felt a sense of repulsion (talk of wombs felt out of place here in a predominantly male environment) and I judiciously avoided this room. Until the end. I felt I really had to go in there to pray. I sat down in the dark. And, quite unexpectedly, burst into floods of tears. I went to find one of the chaplains: 'I don't understand why I am so upset. I had a happy childhood. Except my mum didn't want children . . . Aha . . .' As the last words came out of my mouth, it was like something I hadn't ever vocalized came out into the light.

I was due to see my spiritual director, Jenny, a fortnight later. She has been like a spiritual mum to me over the last 20 years or so; her wisdom and spiritual discernment are spot on. So I brought up the story with her. Tears again. 'I don't understand why I am so upset.' 'Jill,' she said tenderly, 'listen to your tears.' In my head, I pushed back – what? I don't listen to tears; I think things through rationally. But I could make no sense . . . and so I listened . . . And deep out of my heart emerged a question: 'Am I wanted?'

'Am I wanted?' I had never realized I had been living with that question all my life. Since my conception. As Jenny gently prayed for me, I felt sick, very sick. It was as if I wretched out deep darkness, like vomiting the abscess in a tooth, rotten to its very core. Leaving a massive gap. 'I see an image of you as a baby with Jesus laughing and throwing you in the air in delight,' she whispered, and she prayed that where the darkness had left, I would be filled with his joy. Gosh! My heart felt fit to burst. An overwhelming sense of joy flooded in, almost bursting my lungs. In fact, the following day I was leading a quiet day for some ex-students of St Mellitus. 'Bishop Jill,' they commented, 'you are carrying so much joy.' Too right. I had just been to see the surgeon of our souls for deep-root-canal dentistry!

As we reflected on that deep, dark root, it was as if Jesus unravelled a dark thread of knitting that had connected me to my own mother and grandmother's story. As I will explain more in Chapter 12, my mum lived her whole life with the sense of not being wanted. Because she was a girl. It was as if I had picked up her reticence too – even before birth. But when darkness revealed itself in the light of Jesus, he wonderfully unravelled and uprooted it. And filled me with such joy and light that I couldn't help radiating.

> You are the light of the world. A town built on a hill cannot be hidden. Neither do people light a lamp and put it under a bowl. Instead they put it on its stand, and it gives light to everyone in the house.
> (Matthew 5.14–15)

Where there's been quenching in our lives, and we allow Jesus to fan us back into flame, there's no hiding our beacon!

Yes, like all gifts, there can be a shadow side to enthusiasm. St Teresa of Ávila, who received many fiery charismatic experiences, warned that we need to take care not to let the cooking pot boil over. To train ourselves in discretion. I am trying to pay careful attention here. Especially if I seem to hear something for another person. I pause to ask: is it really for sharing now? Often, I am led to wait, and pray it for them in the secret place. But even if I sense a green light for sharing in the moment, I try to share like the couple in Leeds, who framed what they'd heard so tentatively: 'We might be wrong . . .'

St John of the Cross was more circumspect of fiery experiences. He thought they could be a showy sign of immaturity. If the fire is burning maturely, it won't spit and crackle but glow gently. You might think the fire is quenched, but it's not. I found his wisdom very balancing. The gifts of Jesus don't exclude; they aren't for show. He is gentle and humble in heart.

But in all this, why should health and safety warnings mean we huddle away, settling for cold baked beans and no central heating? Besides, have you noticed who are the most belittled? The very ones who are so potent in carrying the gospel. The poor, the humble and children. Those with less ego, who make plenty of room to carry his fire (see Chapter 5).

Why belittle enthusiasm? Why do the powerful waste time putting others down? The answer, boring as it seems, is usually jealousy and threat. Subconsciously, we know that it's the enthusiastic ones through whom fresh life and change will come.

2 Cynicism about the word of God and the power of God

When I've had a bad day, I imagine Jesus smiling and saying, well at least they didn't call you the devil from hell. He was quite familiar with that. And just as Jesus is the best coach in prayer (see Chapter 7), he's also the best coach in dealing with cynicism.

Jesus was on the receiving end of torrents of cynicism. Mostly from the religious leaders of his day. (Herod, the local despot, and Pilate, the Roman governor, were simply intrigued by him.) This was his response to the religious teachers. It was bold and blunt: 'You are in error because you do not know the Scriptures or the power of God' (Matthew 22.29; Mark 12.24).

Do we know the Scriptures?

The Scriptures are wonderfully more accessible than ever – available on our phones and tablets. But do we *know* the Scriptures? I love how my heroes of the past had the word of God living in their hearts. Paul challenged his apprentice Timothy, in his final letter before his death: 'Do your best to present yourself to God as one approved, a worker who does not need to be ashamed and who correctly handles the word of truth . . . All Scripture is God-breathed and is useful for teaching, rebuking, correcting and training in righteousness' (2 Timothy 2.15; 3.16). I love the imagery this conjures up of being trained by the master swordsman to correctly handle the word of God which is 'alive and active . . . sharper than any double-edged sword' (Hebrews 4.12). To handle it like my hero of heroes, Jesus, who wielded it with such precision in the wilderness to strike down every one of Satan's whispered lies.

I love being part of a church family which aspires to take God's word seriously. In my role, I regularly find myself commissioning a new minister. We read a short statement of core beliefs that includes the line, 'The Church of England . . . professes the faith uniquely revealed in the Holy Scriptures and set forth in the Catholic creeds, which faith the Church is called upon to proclaim afresh in each generation . . .' Then the first question I ask each leader is this: 'Do you accept the Holy Scriptures as revealing all things necessary for eternal salvation through faith in Jesus Christ?'

Here's the thing I notice. Where there's cynicism about the word of God, there seems to be less experience of the power of God. The Spirit comes where he is welcomed as Lord. The Scriptures are 'God-breathed' (2 Timothy 3.16). Ignore his Lordship, and he moves on. More ego, less fire. Jesus found he couldn't do many miracles in his home town because the people were cynical (Mark 6.4–6). Paul commended the Thessalonian church for exactly the opposite (1 Thessalonians 2.13).

There is much in our 'God-breathed' Scriptures that is beyond our understanding. God, for example. But our posture towards them seems to unlock (or lock up) the power of God, so to speak. What is the posture of our heart when we don't understand the Scriptures, or they are perplexing or upsetting? Do we react with cynicism or respect?

Do we know the power of God? That's quite a question.

With all my heart, I believe that the power of God has not diminished over time. His strength is beyond our imagining: it is the power that made the universe, for example. In fact, the power that brought Jesus back from the dead, the Spirit of God, actually lives in us (Ephesians 1.19–21). The wonders and growth we see in the pages of the New Testament can absolutely happen today. Jesus specifically promised this before he left, that his followers would do even greater things than him, because his Father would send the Spirit:

> Very truly I tell you, whoever believes in me will do the works I have been doing, and they will do even greater things than these, because I am going to the Father. And I will do whatever you ask in my name, so that the Father may be glorified in the Son. You may ask me for anything in my name, and I will do it.
> (John 14.12–14)

Through history, those who have carried the fiery torch before us have taken God at his word. Nineteenth-century missionary to China, Hudson Taylor, said: 'God has spoken his word. He means what he says. And he will do everything he promised.' After 50 years in China, there was little to show for his work in terms of local Chinese people awakening to a living faith in Jesus, even though he mobilized many workers through his founding of the China Inland Mission. One hundred years later, China has the fastest-growing church on the planet. Hudson Taylor's faith was for fruit that was far beyond his lifetime. My wise Ghanaian friend, Maria, says: 'It's like a slap in the face when we don't trust God.' Maybe you've been in a relationship where you are not trusted: perhaps a boss at work, or, even more painful, a relationship within your family. When you're not trusted, it is demeaning and diminishing. Very quickly we wonder why we bother.

We are trained in cynicism. I am often embarrassed by my CV of earthly gloriousness. With my doctorate in chemistry from Oxford University, I am highly trained to question, to query, to distrust until I have the evidence, peer reviewed in international journals. This is all very well with metal centres in proteins. This is not the approach to take at home in my relationship with my husband. Imagine if my standard response to any of his suggestions was: 'Well, I'll start by presuming you won't keep your word, and then I can be pleasantly surprised when you do.' That would be saying, I don't trust you. And I imagine it wouldn't go down so well.

As a church in Western Europe, we train, we exercise – and we even compete – in cynicism on corporate scale. My dear colleague in the Diocese of Blackburn, Bishop Philip North, has coined a modern-day heresy about this. He calls it *Declinism*, and I have written a spoof lecture about it, which you can find on our website.[4]

Declinism presumes: 'The church is in terminal decline, because the power of God has declined. Even if you believed it really happened back then, there's no way the power of the Spirit which brought Jesus back from the dead can be as active now.'

Or, to put it another way, *Declinism* says: 'Come on – be realistic – grow up – that was then, this is now. They were more primitive. They weren't as scientific. They weren't used to rational thinking. They didn't live in a post-modern post-Christendom secular society.' We patronizingly frame faith within a world view of scientific advancement where it is self-evident that we arrogantly know more than the previous generation. This might work for a chemistry PhD, but it is not the way we operate in other spheres of life which are to do with people. For example, do we think that twenty-first-century mothers love their children more than mothers in the fourteenth century? Do we think first-century farmers cared less for their land than twentieth-century farmers?

We need to be humble. We have more technology but we're not better people. (Besides, we've got our facts wrong, as we cling to a supposed golden age in the past: where the Church is growing the fastest around the world, there's never been Christendom.)

The Holy Spirit comes where he is Lord. He stays where he is welcome, where his power is welcome, where his fire is received, where he is taken at his word. And Jesus didn't spend much time with the proud or cynical. He spent time with the humble poor who knew they needed to repent. The tax-collectors and sex-workers. They were under no illusions that they needed him. 'Those who are forgiven much, love much' (see Luke 7.47), and wonderfully they found themselves in some of the top seats at the heavenly banquet warmed by his fire. Because they took him at his word; they knew the power of God. This is still the case today.

Cynicism is one of the oldest quenching tricks in the book. I love this detail tucked away in Matthew's description of the resurrection:

> When the chief priests had met with the elders and devised a plan, they gave the soldiers a large sum of money, telling them, 'You are to say, "His disciples came during the night and stole him away while we were asleep"' . . . And this story has been widely circulated among the Jews to this very day.
> (Matthew 28.12–15)

Even on Day One of the Christian faith, the day of the resurrection, people were cynically spreading fake news, undermining the best news in the history of the universe.

The last 200 years of critical scholarship in the Christian West has buried essential life-giving strands of the Christian message which are deeply woven through Scripture (see Chapter 10). These are strands which were part of the everyday faith of our ancestors for centuries. These have been belittled from academic ivory towers as superstitious and naive. Whereas those on the frontiers of the new-budding life of Christianity see it very differently. Compared to the Church around the world, and indeed the Church through time, we are spiritual pygmies.

In my infant school in the 1970s, unbelievably, we had a 'slow table' in our class. I often sense I am on the slow table of faith. Elsewhere in the classroom, Christian brothers and sisters across the globe and back through time have a measure of trust in God that puts me to shame, with my lukewarm faith and stunted growth.

When theology or thinking about God is detached from open hearts in real life, it seems to develop a hard shell of cynicism, impermeable to the life-giving water of the Spirit. Theologians ossify when they are detached from exercising their faith in everyday life, especially if they don't come into contact with our key beacon lighters, the poor, the humble and children. It can easily happen in professional Christian circles, almost without noticing.

I recall one memorable lecture at Oxford University, which dissected the parable of the Prodigal Son. It was clear that the lecturer had never tried reading this Bible story with everyday people of faith, who instinctively knew what it might feel like to lose someone precious. Another example was at a meeting of bishops. I felt a stab of pain in my heart when a colleague said in one of our seminar discussions: 'When I was 18, I had a simple trusting faith. Then I went to college, and I was crushed as that faith was brutally dismantled.' Of course, our journey to maturity can be destabilizing as we let go of our false images of God, but it was like listening to an Olympic athlete describe a car crash that had mangled their legs. They didn't want to complain – they could at least hobble or jog on a good day, but they'd never again run with the strides of faith which they remembered in their prime.

In his last ever recorded interview in 1963, C. S. Lewis was wonderfully frank:

A great deal of what is being published by writers in the religious tradition is a scandal and is actually turning people away from the church. The liberal writers who are continually accommodating and whittling down the truth of the Gospel are responsible. I cannot understand how a man can appear in print claiming to disbelieve everything that he presupposes when he puts on the surplice [a white clerical vestment]. I feel it is a form of prostitution.[5]

Yes, of course apply your God-given mind to understand the Bible, to notice those coincidences, to tune in to the gentle whisper of God, and to weigh carefully what you hear; in other words, have 'faith seeking understanding', as Anselm, one of our great theologians from the eleventh century, put it. But it's simply not true that our minds can 'know best'; and that we live in the generation that 'knows it all'. That's just human egocentricity. Every generation suffers from it. We all want to think we're the centre of the known universe, living in the most significant time and culture shift in history. Of course, we're not. It can help to gain a more measured, humble perspective. Does your reading or do your thought processes ultimately bring joy and life? Do they make you more loving towards your neighbours? Or does this bring despair and death, and encourage withdrawal from those around you? That's a quick litmus test for the things of God. Or not.

3 Despair: the cloak of despondency

Perhaps you know the Aesop's Fable about the sun and the wind? It's an ancient Greek story about how the wind and sun see a man with a very heavy cloak on. They decide to have a competition to see who can get him to take his cloak off. The wind goes first. He blows harder and harder and harder. The man wraps the cloak round him tighter and tighter and tighter. Then it's the sun's turn. The sun shines gently and warms the man up. Eventually he gets so hot he sheds his heavy cloak. Warmed by the fire of the sun. I hope this might be one outcome from reading this book.

I often see people, especially leaders, struggling under this fire quencher of despair. I have named it 'the cloak of despondency'. Our instinct can be to be like the wind – come on, try harder – when what will make them shed their cloak is being warmed by the fire of the sun.

Julian of Norwich responds with much greater perception. Even in the darkest place, we are still with hope because of the cross. Although there was agonizingly no answer when Jesus cried out in absolute distress from the cross, 'My God, my God, why have you forsaken me?' (Mark 15.34), his death wasn't the end of the story.

In the words of Julian: 'All shall be well, and all manner of things shall be well.'[6]

I have spotted three common ways for this heavy cloak to descend upon us:

Disappointment. It starts with a disappointment. Then another and another. God has disappointed. Our hopes in his power, his care, his presence become dashed. We can soon get to a point where we don't dare ask God for anything in case we are disappointed again, and the cloak becomes even heavier. In our culture of instant answers, which avoids pain and death where possible, we can be unaware that following Jesus involves crucifixion. We can have unrealistic expectations, which in turn lead to disappointment (see Chapter 11).

Loneliness. Thinking we're the 'only one left' is a common way under the cloak of despondency.

We find this graphically portrayed in the Bible. My favourite pair of Old Testament heroes are Elijah and Elisha, prophets in Israel in the troubled times of the ninth century BC. After Elijah's fiery battle with the prophets of Baal on Mount Carmel, he slinks off in depression to a cave – 'I am the only one left' (1 Kings 19.10).

It happens again in the next generation. Elisha's servant woke up terrified to find himself and Elisha all alone, facing the King of Aram's army surrounding the city. Elisha rallied his servant's courage:

> 'Those who are with us are more than those who are with them.' And Elisha prayed, 'Open his eyes, Lord, so that he may see.' Then the Lord opened the servant's eyes, and he looked and saw the hills full of horses and chariots of fire all around Elisha.
> (2 Kings 6.16–17)

The King of Aram's army is puny compared to God's troops of fire.

Evil's way of making us feel that we're all alone is a recurring theme in *Star Wars Episode IX: The Rise of Skywalker*. There is a beautiful scene near the end of the film, when the distress call has gone out across the galaxy for help from all who stand for good. Millions of spaceships suddenly arrive on the scene – reminiscent of the tiny fishing boats who rescued ten times the expected number of Allied troops in the 'miracle of Dunkirk' in 1940, only days after King George VI, our King's grandfather, called for a national day of prayer.[7]

Predicting the future. We can have an extraordinary confidence that we are able to predict the future. It's often misplaced; it normally leads to despair. This is particularly so when it comes to predictions about church decline. I have heard countless times, 'Unless God turns up' (as if it's a joke), 'we need to plan on these decline projections.' The Church only exists because God turns up. It's like a scientist studying pond life who says, 'Unless the water turns up for the fish to breathe and feed in, we need to plan on death.' Fish can't live without water. Without God turning up, there's no Church and no faith.

As the story about the King of Aram's army continues, not only did Israel win but Elisha also brought about a victory with no bloodshed. The opposing soldiers were captured, fed and sent home – hatred averted, genuine peace. Amazing. Better than anyone could have imagined. Elisha's servant thought he could see the future. And it was terrifying. But he was wrong. God brought about a far better future.

The King of Aram's army takes lots of different manifestations. In Blackburn Diocese, the strategy in 2012 was called 'The Shape of Things to Come'. The thinking was that no one is interested in the things of faith in our so-called 'secular society' and there's no one wanting to be a vicar, so we need to manage the decline. Fortunately, this strategy was quietly shredded when the new diocesan bishop arrived in 2013, Julian Henderson. But I vividly remember a senior team meeting in 2019. Archdeacon Mark Ireland said: 'I was just doing some filing and found this old report.' He pulled it out of his bag. There was a ripple of nervousness in the room as we weren't sure where he was going with it. 'Do you know what was supposed to happen by 2019? We were supposed to have halved our number of vicars and be nearly bankrupt.' Then he broke out in a big smile. Neither had happened. At all. Of course, there are many threats in every generation, the work of God is always fragile, our natural temptation is to despair. We think we can predict the future. But the future hasn't happened yet.

4 Heresy and the fear of heresy

This fire quencher causes more fuss and fear than it really deserves – unlike our fifth quencher in the list, which I am saving till last.

Heresy – or false teaching – seems simply not to bear fruit. (The most popular heresies through time seem to have grown up around not taking Jesus at his word; or presuming on some secret revelation/knowledge beyond Scripture.)

Some people see it like discovering a cancer – fearfully leaping in, needing to cut it out with surgery. The excesses of Christian horrible history have some gruesome accounts of surgery – the Spanish Inquisition, for example. My experience is that heresy is more like a rotten branch. Without fresh green leaves, it dries up in the summer, there's no fruit in the autumn, then come the winter storms, and it tends to drop off. This doesn't happen overnight, not in a year or two as we might like. It can be disheartening to see branches slowly rotting, a worry that the whole tree will go that way, but in time the rotten drops away.

When I was a teenager, the then Bishop of Durham shot to fame with some provocative comments about whether or not the resurrection of Jesus was merely a 'conjuring trick with bones'. Nowadays, the kind of theology which appears to question the reality of the resurrection barely gets a hearing in the Church, nor in our culture for that matter. God brought Jesus back from the dead, living and breathing. This is a core belief of the Christian faith. Yes, the resurrection is a strange belief on first encounter, but there is no point in evading it to try to make it more credible. No one is interested in clever pretence that it might and might not have happened at the same time.

Fear of heresy is also a fire quencher. It doesn't bear fruit either. Instead, it tends to stir up arguments and fighting talk. In Paul's final letters before his death (2 Timothy and Titus) – his most distilled wisdom, perhaps – he warns repeatedly about the dangers of arguments. Sometimes I want to type this boldly on my social media accounts (but it might start an argument!) and write on a fluorescent sticky note to remind myself when I am tired. It is so easy to judge others. Heresy is a subtle invitation to do just this. I am more than fallible. I might be wrong. Criticizing others through fear of heresy seems to quench your own fire, with all the cold water you are pouring on brothers and sisters. The Holy Spirit convicts, God judges. It's not our job.

This more practical response to heresy is followed by one of my church-planting heroes of the nineteenth century, Bishop Selwyn, who helped catalyse new Christian communities across many of the Polynesian islands. He had a wonderfully pragmatic approach:

> But how, you will ask, shall the truth of doctrine be maintained if we tolerate in the mission-field every form of error, and provide no safeguard for the purity of the faith? I answer that, as running water purifies itself, so Christian work is seen to correct its own mistakes.[8]

I am conscious that those of us who teach will be judged by God more strictly.[9] I have made public promises to 'refute error, and hand on entire the faith that is entrusted to you'.[10] I intend to keep this promise, come what may. Let's be clear. I'm not saying false teaching doesn't matter. I'm saying don't fear heresy, because it will wither and die.

Let's keep our eyes on God's horizon. Don't get dragged down into despair, advised St Antony (AD 251–356), who faced one of the most destabilizing heresies of the early centuries of the Church – Arianism. (Arians believed that Jesus was created by God, so not fully man *and* fully God.) The Arians became very influential in the Church of his day, but St Antony puts it with poise, with his eyes to the future horizon:

> Do not give yourself up completely to grief. For just as the Lord was angered so he will again have pity. The Church will soon regain her

beauty and you will see that those who preserved the faith of the Lord during the times of persecution, shining once more in their former brightness. The serpents will return to their holes and our religion will spread further.[11]

Arianism was declared a heresy in AD 325 at the Council of Nicaea.

God needs us to be fire carriers, not fire quenchers. But let's not teach out of fear. The opposite. Teach courage. Hold our nerve. Like Gamaliel.

Gamaliel was a wise religious teacher in Jerusalem in the very earliest days after Pentecost when Jesus' disciples got into trouble with the religious authorities for healing people in the Temple (Acts 5.12–42). They were locked up in prison. But during the night, an angel unlocked the prison doors and led them to escape. He told them to keep speaking about this new life. They were promptly arrested again and brought before the ruling council to be questioned by the high priest. Ordered not to speak about Jesus, and when they refused, the plan was to execute them. Then Gamaliel intervened. This wasn't a new problem – he'd seen it all before:

Men of Israel, consider carefully what you intend to do to these men. Some time ago Theudas appeared, claiming to be somebody, and about four hundred men rallied to him. He was killed, all his followers were dispersed, and it all came to nothing. After him, Judas the Galilean appeared in the days of the census and led a band of people in revolt. He too was killed, and all his followers were scattered. Therefore, in the present case I advise you: leave these men alone! Let them go! For if their purpose or activity is of human origin, it will fail. But if it is from God, you will not be able to stop these men; you will only find yourselves fighting against God.
(Acts 5.35–39)

5 Disobedience

Finally, this is the quencher of fire we're most blind to, but the most blatant and insidious – disobedience.

In 2018, I heard a speech that woke me up. It was like an electric shock through my veins. It was in the most unlikely of contexts. A diocesan peer review. In the Church of England, from time to time, each diocese undergoes a 'peer review' (an evaluation of strategy and finance by peers in similar senior leadership positions elsewhere). It always starts with a 'state of the nation' address from the diocesan bishop. In a small, out-of-the-way meeting room, my boss, Bishop Julian Henderson, delivered his speech. He based it on 1 Kings 18 – looking at the stages needed before God sent fire to Elijah on Mount Carmel. He finished it with these words: 'We don't need an archdeacon's visitation, we don't need a bishop's visitation, we need a visitation of the Holy Spirit on the people of Lancashire.' Our lead peer reviewer was embarrassed; he didn't know what to say: 'Ahem . . . well, shall we start by looking at your finances?' Was it so shocking that explicit reliance on God was a key part of delivering strategy? But I was lit up – this is so important. Julian had hit the nail on the head. And that's what I started to pray in earnest.

Scroll forward in time a few months, and we were gathered as a senior team in Whalley Abbey. Above the altar in the chapel there was a painting of the Holy Spirit hanging down on chains. Bishop Julian whispered, 'It's like there are chains stopping the Holy Spirit from coming.' I started to ask God, what are those chains?

Scroll forward a few more months to May 2019, we were gathered as a team in the chapel again at Whalley for our three-day residential. At Evening Prayer, one of my colleagues read the set reading for the day. It was the Ten Commandments. I realized with horror how many of these commandments – just in the last week – I had dealt with in the diocese behind the scenes. At least I haven't had to handle a murder, I thought to myself. And then, fast on the heels, came the terrible reminder of the Lancaster Martyrs – these were 15 Catholic men killed for their faith by my predecessors at Lancaster. Their deaths are commemorated on 7 August.

I was left with the most awful thought. Is it the disobedience or, more bluntly, the sin of the Church which is stopping the visitation of the Holy Spirit? I could not escape this conclusion.

It has played on my mind ever since. I see boulders of structural sin which trap the poor and humble underground (see Chapter 5): for example, elitism, intellectualism, racism, misogyny, imposter syndrome. Of course, it's easier to spot the specks elsewhere than the logjams in my life. So I also try regularly to ask Jesus to reveal the sin and darkness in my own life. He teaches this practice in the Lord's Prayer: 'Forgive us our sins, as we forgive those who sin against us.' When there's been a renewal of faith in whole communities, this is always accompanied by repentance and fresh obedience (see Chapter 4).

This is beautifully expressed by Francis Xavier Nguyen van Thuan, who was Archbishop of Saigon in Cambodia. In 1975, he was arrested by the Vietnamese army, and he spent 13 years in a re-education camp, nine years of which were in solitary confinement. He managed to smuggle messages to his people out of prison on scraps of paper which were circulated then collected into his book, *The Road of Hope*, which I can't recommend highly enough, especially if you are facing challenging and fire-quenching times:

> You wish to see the whole world on fire, with the love that the gospel teaches; you wish to conquer the five continents. Then your every moment should be a flash of fire, the fire of duty, *obedience* and patience. Such a flame will burn bright and illumine the whole world.[12]

But make no mistake. Fire can be quenched. And we are usually the ones doing the quenching. The last 200 years of critical scholarship in the West has buried life-giving streams of the Christian faith under the rubble of rationalism, cynicism and secularism. Let's excavate important seams of buried gems in our next two chapters and become reacquainted with some of our family treasure.

Going further

For group discussion

1 With which of these top fire quenchers are you most familiar? Where would you disagree with what I have written?

2 Belittling enthusiasm of others: have you experienced this? Have you been tempted to do this?

3 'It is like a slap in the face when we don't trust God.' What does it mean to you to take the word of God or the power of God seriously?

4 Have you experienced the cloak of despondency? Are you under it at the moment? Could you trace when or why it descended?

5 What do you think of Bishop Selwyn's pragmatic approach to heresy?

6 'The Spirit comes where he is Lord.' Is it disobedience or, more bluntly, the sin of the Church which is stopping the visitation of the Holy Spirit? What can we do about this individually and corporately?

For personal devotion

Read: Revelation 3.1–22

Pay attention to what the Spirit is saying to you and to your church community through this passage.

Prayer to conclude: Jesus, may I have ears to hear what your Spirit is saying. May you bring to light what is quenching your fire in my life. Would you be the surgeon of my soul, even to those hidden abscesses, which I am blind to. Please unbind me through the power of your Name. Amen.

10
What is the battle?

Beacons are lit in response to danger.

As we saw in Chapter 1, in *The Lord of the Rings*, in the midst of the battle, Pippin the hobbit manages to scramble up to light the beacon at Minas Tirith. It signals the start of a chain of the Warning Beacons of Gondor throughout the White Mountains, beacons to rally the troops of the Rohirrim, to answer Gondor's call for help.[1]

On top of Rivington Pike, in the West Pennine Moors in Bolton, near where I grew up, there had been a beacon site on the hill since 1139, established as part of a chain of signals by the Earl of Chester. It was lit in 1588 to warn of the Spanish Armada in the English Channel. Historically, beacons were lit in response to danger.

In our chain of lighting the beacons, what is the danger? What is the battle?

The simple answer to this question is a strand of the Christian faith that has been muted and sidelined over the last 200 years by critical scholarship (see Chapter 9). There's a great example of this strand, which has slipped off the radar, in Ephesians 6.12: 'For our struggle is not against flesh and blood, but against the rulers, against the authorities, against the powers of this dark world and against the spiritual forces of evil in the heavenly realms.' Even today, in the world of theological training, few essay questions are set on this risqué subject. And that's odd when you think about it. If you are training soldiers for battle, or a rugby team for a match, an obvious topic to study is – your opponent. This is not to be morbid or ghoulish or defeatist. Simply pragmatic and realistic. Yes of course, don't take an unhealthy interest, so they obscure your vision to distraction. (In *The Lord of the Rings*, this is how the dark lord Sauron mastered wizard Saruman, simply by dominating his thoughts.)

All in moderation. But to ignore the enemy is simply naive. Scripture is clear: there's a war on. Sometimes I think I prefer to be tucked away, like First World War generals, safely sipping port in our oak-panelled senior common rooms, miles behind the lines, in blissful denial. Whereas C. S. Lewis, wrote in more balanced terms about the devil:

> There are two equal and opposite errors into which our race can fall about the devils. One is to disbelieve in their existence. The other is to believe, and to feel an excessive and unhealthy interest in them. They themselves are equally pleased by both errors and hail a materialist or a magician with the same delight.[2]

Textbook tactics

My teenage son bought himself an ancient textbook on war, *The Art of War* by Sun Tzu. My husband, who served in the British army, still has his *Serve to Lead* pocketbook.

'No plan survives contact with the enemy' is an army saying. Very popular in our household. Yes of course, life does not follow a textbook, but knowing what you can expect significantly reduces stress. Why else is Mumsnet so popular? When battling for sanity, it's reassuring to be reminded we haven't got the only baby who won't sleep through the night.

One helpful textbook I have found for enemy tactics is the book of Nehemiah. We're going to draw out the six textbook oppositions he experienced while rebuilding the walls of Jerusalem. Behind so much opposition are the evil spiritual forces. Their aim is to *dissipate our energy* – so once you know about their textbook tactics, it can save you giving them too much time. Evil is not creative – it follows the same pattern. Even patterns from the fourth century BC.

You may or may not have had much to do with the book of Nehemiah before. It's tucked away – about halfway into the Old Testament part of the Bible. The Old Testament is like a library of books – history, poetry, visions, laws. This is one of the history books. It was written about 450 years before Jesus was born. In 586 BC (we know this date precisely from history and archaeology) a terrible thing happened. The Babylonian army invaded the land of Israel. It was shock-and-awe tactics: they burnt the fields, demolished the walls of Jerusalem, burnt the Temple with fire and raided the treasury. They were brutal: they smashed people's heads to pieces and took many of the leaders away as slaves. Now, you might think the Babylonians were bad. They were then beaten in by the Persians.

Nehemiah was an architect and engineer, a leader and strategic planner, but when we meet him he's working as a cupbearer to the King of Persia, King Artaxerxes (465–425 BC). Presumably, for the king, this was a display of his power to have high-born foreigners serving at his table. In a rather precarious role. A cupbearer's job was to taste the king's wine before the king drank it. So when the king's enemies tried to poison him, Nehemiah was the one who would die first. If you're the King of Persia, you'd beaten up lots of people, you'd made lots of enemies. There were a lot of people who wanted to put poison in your cup. So you needed quite a few – disposable – cupbearers.

Summary of the plot

This book is Nehemiah's story. Here's a summary of the plot.

Plot starts in Susa in Persia (modern-day Iran). Nehemiah hears these terrible reports from back home in Jerusalem. He gets a lucky break and the king allows him to go back home. He gets there. He's heartbroken – it's worse than he thought. The walls of his beloved home city are demolished. The gates have been burnt with fire. But Nehemiah starts rebuilding the walls. He gets terrible opposition. He keeps on rebuilding the walls. He gets terrible opposition. He keeps on rebuilding the walls. He gets terrible opposition. He keeps on rebuilding the walls. He gets terrible opposition . . . Do you get the plot? But 52 days later, the walls of Jerusalem are rebuilt.

This reminds me of so much of the challenges we face in life – as individuals, as communities and as a nation.

Our walls are broken down. Not just physically but spiritually. When we take a closer look, things can often be worse than we thought. In our heart of hearts, we know it doesn't have to be like that. We want to see change for the better.

We start to rebuild.

We get terrible opposition.

We continue to rebuild.

We get terrible opposition.

I have been so heartened by reading the book of Nehemiah. It's like a textbook, a user manual for the types of opposition you will face when you try to rebuild. And it really helps to have these on your radar because otherwise opposition can be incredibly wearing. And that's the point. What's the biggest danger for the Church? It's not that the vicar runs off with the organist, or we all start following some heresy or false teaching, and like lemmings disappear off the cliff. It's much more boring than that. The biggest danger for the Church is that we just get weary and give up. What's the biggest opposition we face in community transformation or the transformation of society? It's the same – we get weary and give up. You find this again and again in the New Testament: 'Consider him who endured such opposition . . . so that you will not grow weary and lose heart' (Hebrews. 12.3).

In Western Europe, we can lull ourselves into a false sense of security with our comfort blankets and NHS. We can lull ourselves to sleep. We don't like to talk about the kingdom of darkness. We fall into the error C. S. Lewis noted, of disbelieving the existence of evil forces.

We also conveniently forget that Jesus invites us to 'take up our cross'. It's not even in the small print. More than one-quarter of Mark's Gospel is about Jesus' crucifixion. If you're following Jesus, you will be crucified. We'll look at this more in the next chapter.

If your vision is from God – at the very least – expect opposition. Jesus advised his disciples before he left: 'If the world hates you, keep in mind that it hated me first . . . A servant is not greater than his master (John 15.18, 20).

I love being a bishop in the Church of England. I love it that our vision is to be the church for the people round here: 'a Christian presence in every community'. But often our greatest strengths have a shadow side, don't they? One of our shadow sides is – we want to be liked. For people to always speak well of us, to be popular in the community. We're a little squeamish about opposition. And ultimately, you can't be free of opposition if you are following Jesus all the way.

This is wonderfully brought to life in *The Message* paraphrase of Jesus' teaching in Matthew 5.11–12:

> Not only that – count yourselves blessed every time people put you down or throw you out or speak lies about you to discredit me. What it means is that the truth is too close for comfort and they are uncomfortable. You can be glad when that happens – give a cheer, even! – for though they don't like it, *I* do! And all heaven applauds. And know that you are in good company. My prophets and witnesses have always gotten into this kind of trouble.

Reading Nehemiah's story has helped me recognize the patterns of opposition we can expect to face. It's helped me keep going and not be distracted. To waste as little energy on the opposition as possible. Because if you're trying to rebuild walls, if you're wanting to see a change for the better, I can guarantee you will face opposition. So learn to spot it!

That's been quite a long introduction, but it's important to set the scene. There are so many gems in the Bible, but we can miss out on them because they can sound like ancient history. But the Bible is living and active, and lights our way today.

The story begins . . .

The book starts with bad news. No opposition yet – it will come soon.

The words of Nehemiah son of Hakaliah:

In the month of Kislev in the twentieth year, while I was in the citadel of Susa, Hanani, one of my brothers, came from Judah with some other men, and I questioned them about the Jewish remnant that had survived the exile, and also about Jerusalem.

They said to me, 'Those who survived the exile and are back in the province are in great trouble and disgrace. The wall of Jerusalem is broken down, and its gates have been burned with fire.'
(Nehemiah 1.1–3)

This is 20 years on from what was called 'the exile' – the terrible time when the Babylonians had attacked and carried most of the Jewish leaders off to Babylon. One of Nehemiah's brothers comes from Judah – that's the territory around Jerusalem – with bad news about the 'Jewish remnant', bad news about the Jewish survivors.

How does Nehemiah respond? 'When I heard these things, I sat down and wept. For some days I mourned and fasted and prayed before the God of heaven' (Nehemiah 1.4).

What is breaking your heart today? What makes you want to sit down and weep?

That's not a thing we normally let ourselves do.

We tend to avoid emotion – keep calm and carry on. This is important. Coping mechanism. We numb the pain.

Let me remind you of an example I touched on earlier from Lancashire. My favourite comedienne, Victoria Wood, used to say something along these lines:

It's a very Lancashire thing – you 'put up' with everything. You don't show your emotions. You don't mind about anything.

If you look at the history of the North West of England –

They closed the mines and they just went – 'Oh well, there you go.'

They closed the shipyards – 'Oh well, fair enough.'

They closed the cotton mills – that's that then.

At least in the North East, in the 1930s they marched to London from Jarrow to complain.[3]

But Nehemiah didn't just 'put up with it'. To paraphrase Churchill, who famously said: 'There is something up with which I will not put.'

Nehemiah mourned, fasted and prayed. He brought his pain to God.

Maybe it's time to bring your pain to God. Bring your mourning to God. What is breaking your heart today? It is often mourning that gives birth to God's plans.

He fasted – he went without food. Fasting is not such a common practice at the moment for bolstering prayer life, but I do recommend this for short periods of time. I find fasting from my favourite things is a way of training my spirit – disciplining myself – saying to God, 'I'm really serious about this.' It's not just a quick prayer. I go for 21 days without alcohol, chocolate and caffeine. Three staples I really miss. As I feel the pangs of missing these, it is a prompt to pray.

Nehemiah's response to bad news is to start in prayer. His pattern is very much like the Lord's Prayer that Jesus taught us. Three top tips:

1 He lifts up his eyes: 'LORD, the God of heaven, the great and awesome God, who keeps his promises of love' (Nehemiah 1.5, NIV UK 2011 adapted). This is the reality. We can spend our lives looking at our feet, looking at our phones, mauling our problems in our heads. No. Start big. Lift up your eyes. Lift up your eyes today – he is a great and awesome God. He means what he says and he will do everything that he has promised.

2 He confesses sins: 'I confess the sins we Israelites, including myself and my father's family, have committed against you' (Nehemiah 1.6). The wrongs we have done, the patterns of evil that weave themselves into our lives, that have passed on through generations – bring these into the light of Jesus. Sin makes us ashamed. We want to hide. Maybe you've got a cupboard under the stairs where you just keep stuffing stuff in. It's like that in our lives. We can be afraid to open the door in case it all tumbles out and overwhelms us. Don't. When we bring the darkness into the light of Jesus – the darkness always loses, the

darkness always crumbles to pieces. Switch on the light and you find the monsters in the cupboard disappear to nothing.

3 He asks. And he asks big. "'Give your servant success today by granting him favour in the presence of this man.' I was cup-bearer to the king' (Nehemiah 1.11).

And, amazingly, the request is granted. Nehemiah's courage opens the door to incredible favour, and the king asks: 'What is it you want?' (Nehemiah 2.4). He's quick off the mark. He replies big. He asks to be sent back to Jerusalem to rebuild it; he asks for letters of safe passage, and a letter to be given access to timber from the royal park. 'And because the gracious hand of my God was on me, the king granted my requests' (Nehemiah 2.8). And more – the king sent army officers and calvary with him. My experience is that God's answers don't fall short of our prayers – they normally exceed them. I have a card on my desk from Sharon, one of my wonderful colleagues in our diocesan offices: 'God's work done in God's way will never lack God's supplies.'

Six textbook oppositions

Nehemiah records the six oppositions he faces as he rebuilds the walls of Jerusalem. For the rest of this chapter, I'll take these in turn. See if you can spot them in any opposition that you are facing.

Opposition 1: They are disturbed

Response: Say nothing – discreetly take stock of the reality with God

'People are disturbed.' 'People are saying.' You can sense disapproval – for something you expected to be good news.

> When Sanballat the Horonite and Tobiah the Ammonite official heard about this, they were very much disturbed that someone had come to promote the welfare of the Israelites.
> (Nehemiah 2.10)

Nehemiah had come to do a good thing – to promote the welfare of the Israelites and rebuild the walls of Jerusalem. A good thing for the Israelites. Not so good for the officials who preferred the status quo.

Does it matter? No. This isn't really opposition. A shadowy 'they' are disturbed.

Nehemiah responds by keeping out of their way, saying nothing until he's taken stock of the reality in quiet and rallied his team with the honest assessment of the situation they're facing.

Our culture, amplified by social media, can encourage us to waste time on self-justification. People are disturbed. So what?

Nehemiah took time to explore, to look and perceive (2.11–12). Visions of God are conceived in the secret place of prayer. 'I had not told anyone what my God had put in my heart to do for Jerusalem' (Nehemiah 2.12). When God gives you a vision, don't blurt it out. If it's from God, it will scare people – visions from God are always beyond us – be patient to sit with it. When a new idea comes, allow a gestation period, give it the test of time. This is the discipline of discretion.

- If it's not of God, it will wear off and die down.
- If it's from me, it will wear off and die down.
- If it's from God, it will be confirmed.

When we meet with opposition, sometimes even the hint of opposition, our instinct is to fight back.

Nehemiah had better things to do than expend his energy on the officials being disturbed. He took time to explore, to look and to perceive. He examined the walls of Jerusalem. He allowed his heart to prophesy over dead bones. Sometimes we get acclimatized to ruins. Sometimes we get used to the walls being reduced to rubble. We put up with it.

Opposition 2: Mocking words
Response: Act in the opposite direction
The most mocking words I have had to listen to have come to me *in my head*! 'Who do you think you are?' I found this most oppressive

when I was trying to lead the children's work as a vicar's wife in Widnes. Each Sunday, I'd wake up with a sense of dread. What I was preparing was rubbish. I was rubbish. There wasn't much point in bothering because it was rubbish. Oh, and did I say, I was rubbish?

It'd be wonderful to say, in reality I was having a downer on myself, and the children's work I was leading was amazing. That's not true. My wise husband reminded me, 'Jill, it's better than nothing. Leave your high standards behind. Offer what you can do, don't be overwhelmed by the A* vision of children's work you have in your head.'

G. K. Chesterton said: 'If a thing is worth doing, it is worth doing badly.'[4] Sometimes we have such astronomic visions, we dare not start.

I didn't give up as planned. I tried to copy the little boy in the Gospels with his five loaves and two fish. He wasn't overwhelmed by the crowd. He didn't belittle what he'd got. He simply offered the little he had to Jesus. Jesus blessed it and fed five thousand.

So, I did that. And looking back, incredibly, the children's work was an important way home for so many lost families, teens and kids. (In fact, 75 per cent of people come to faith before they are 18, but that would be another book!)

We see this pattern in Nehemiah's experience. Repeatedly.

> But when Sanballat the Horonite, Tobiah the Ammonite official and Geshem the Arab heard about it, they mocked and ridiculed us. 'What is this you are doing?' they asked. 'Are you rebelling against the king?' (Nehemiah 2.19)

But Nehemiah pressed on undeterred. He drew a line. It's not about us, but God: 'The God of heaven will give us success. We his servants will start rebuilding, but as for you, you have no share in [this]' (2.20).

He then starts rebuilding the Sheep Gate (chapter 3), but the 'nobles would not put their shoulders to the work' (3.5). This is typical. In the early days of enacting new vision, key people whom you think should be on board tend to be half-hearted – even suspicious.

Do not worry. This is exactly what you can expect. When Mary says yes to the incredible vision from the angel Gabriel – 'You will conceive and give birth to a son . . . He will be great and will be called the Son of the Most High' (Luke 1.31–32) – she goes home to tell Joseph, who is a man of God, and he wants to divorce her (Matthew 1.19).

Visions from God are usually so terrifying that even our Josephs – those closest to us – want to divorce us. Notice it takes time for Josephs to come on board. Joseph needs to hear *for himself – in his own right* – that this is from God. And in due time, an angel comes to him in a dream: 'Do not be afraid to take Mary home as your wife, because what is conceived in her is from the Holy Spirit' (Matthew 1.20).

Then we get mocking words again:

> When Sanballat heard that we were rebuilding the wall, he became angry and was greatly incensed. He ridiculed the Jews, and in the presence of his associates and the army of Samaria, he said, 'What are those feeble Jews doing? Will they restore their wall? Will they offer sacrifices? Will they finish in a day? Can they bring the stones back to life from those heaps of rubble – burned as they are?'
>
> Tobiah the Ammonite, who was at his side, said, 'What they are building – even a fox climbing up on it would break down their wall of stones!'
> (Nehemiah 4.1–3)

All you see is a heap of rubbish – even a fox could break this down.

Many of God's visions are aborted before they start, because of discouraging words and negative rumours.

I went to see a vicar in our diocese to suggest to her a potential vision that had emerged from us praying. I wasn't sure how she'd take it, for a variety of reasons. I plucked up the courage to share it in full. She said quietly – a holy moment, 'Well, Bishop Jill, back in 2014 I had that very same vision, but I was told it could never happen because other clergy in the area would never agree to it.' Then I knew we were on to something!

My experience is that if we ignore mocking words, avoid distraction and keep on building, opposition can actually *strengthen* us and our team. They see the threats come to nothing – again and again.

How do you recognize an enemy threat?

Some of the best tactics on this come from Ignatius of Loyola, sixteenth-century priest, missionary and founder of the Jesuit movement. He was a wounded soldier when he discovered the Bible and writings of the saints. (It was the only reading material to stave off the boredom in the house he was convalescing in for six months, after a cannonball shattered his right leg.) So, he wonderfully deploys lots of military analogies in his army textbook for spiritual growth, *The Spiritual Exercises.*

Ignatius trains his troops in 'discernment of spirits'. You can find this gift in the list of spiritual gifts in 1 Corinthians 12.1–11. (A book to recommend if you want to dig deeper here is *The Jesuit Guide to (Almost) Everything*, by James Martin SJ.[5])

In short, here's a top tip from Ignatius that's survived the test of time. If a conversation or encounter leaves you feeling alive – if you feel hope, joyful, more loving (or other fruit of the Spirit – love, joy, peace, patience, kindness, goodness, faithfulness, gentleness, self-control[6]) – then this is a spirit from God, a spirit of 'consolation'. If a conversation or encounter leaves you suddenly fearful or despairing or demeaned, then this is not a spirit from God – it's a 'spirit of desolation'. It's worth getting practised at noticing this. And noticing your moods after meetings or encounters. What are the conversations that inspire fear and make you anxious? Where are the conversations that inspire hope and bring peace?

Finally, my all-time favourite spiritual discipline is also from Ignatius. In the Latin it's called *Acte Contrare*, which means acting in the opposite direction to the prevailing spirit. In military terms, when a bomb goes off, most of us want to run for cover. But you need the soldier or police officer to step towards the conflict. To act in the opposite direction to the rest of the crowd.

What does this look like in practice? Let's take the three great Christian virtues: faith, hope and love (1 Corinthians 13.13). The spiritual discipline is this. If you suddenly feel fear, act in *faith*. If you suddenly become overwhelmed by that cloak of despondency, consciously act in the opposite direction with *hope*. If judgemental or critical thoughts start to plague your mind, consciously act towards that person in *love*. Try it. Like any discipline, it takes conscious practice.

An extreme, but inspiring, example of *Acte Contrare* is William Carey. He was called as a missionary to India and campaigned to end *sati* (the practice of widows throwing themselves on their husband's funeral pyre). His first wife died 1807, then his son died. Then in 1813 his printing press burnt to the ground. Any normal man would have given up and gone home. But he stood in the ashes of his printing press and 'acted against', proclaiming that, because of this, even more Bibles would be printed, and even more people would hear the good news about Jesus in India. This is exactly what happened.

Opposition 3: Ganging up
Response: Bind up fear

There's a comedy moment in the film *Chicken Run* (2000), when Mr Tweedy, henpecked by his domineering wife, declares that 'them chickens' are organized.[7] For good or ill, when people – or chickens – gang up against you, it inspires a certain level of fear.

This happens to Nehemiah:

> But when Sanballat, Tobiah, the Arabs, the Ammonites and the people of Ashdod heard that the repairs to Jerusalem's walls had gone ahead and that the gaps were being closed, they were very angry. They all plotted together to come and fight against Jerusalem and stir up trouble against it.
> (Nehemiah 4.7– 8)

Nehemiah's response? More prayer and more watchfulness. This is the tactic he's most famous for: 'But we prayed to our God and posted a guard day and night to meet this threat' (4.9).

'Watch and pray,' said Jesus to Peter, James and John in the Garden of Gethsemane, as he made the most crucial decision of his life (Mark 14:32–34, paraphrased).

Watch and pray. But also keep working. I love Jesus' response to threat. I have often been mindful of this in situations that verge on threatening, though never the blunt severity of this incident.

'Some Pharisees came to Jesus and said to him, "Leave this place and go somewhere else. Herod wants to kill you"' (Luke 13.31).

How does Jesus respond? He acts in the opposite direction, and keeps working: 'Go and tell that fox, "I will keep on driving out demons and healing people today and tomorrow, and on the third day I will reach my goal"' (Luke 13.32).

Nehemiah's workers come under more severe threat. The enemies plan a surprise attack (Nehemiah 4.11). Then they repeat false information. *Ten times* they tell them, 'Wherever you turn, there will be an attack.' Over and over again. Sound familiar?

Nehemiah responds with strategic cover – cast out fear. 'Don't be afraid of them. Remember the Lord, who is great and awesome, and fight for your families, your sons and your daughters, your wives and your homes' (Nehemiah 4.14).

May I put in a big plea – a big health warning – to watch out for fear.

Martin Luther said: you can't stop the birds flying over your head, but you can stop them nesting in your hair. Fear is natural – it stops us getting run over by a bus. Natural for fears to fly over your head. But notice when they start nesting.

And when fears start nesting – it's time to ask Jesus to 'hoover' them up. We looked at spiritual hoovering in Chapter 8. It is based on the keys Jesus gives to Peter (Matthew 16.18–19) and he says this to us:

> Whatever you bind on earth will be bound in heaven, and whatever you loose on earth will be loosed in heaven.
> (Matthew 18.19)

Jesus gives us keys. Keys to bind up the atmosphere of hell – fear, despair, anger, hatred. And keys to release the atmosphere of heaven – love, joy, peace, etc.

So, where you find excessive fear – nesting in your hair . . . it has no right to be there. Ask Jesus to bind it up. Ask Jesus to hoover it up. I gave a personal illustration about my visit to the dentist in Chapter 4.

Housework and hoovering is not my forte, but once you've asked Jesus to coach you on spiritual hoovering, you'll be astonished by the difference it makes. Yes, the atmosphere of hell starts to nest, but we can ask Jesus to release the atmosphere of heaven.

And remember – keys are usually tiny, aren't they? But you turn them, and they unlock big doors. Sometimes even bank vaults – with lots of treasure hidden inside.

Opposition 4: Distraction

Response: Obedience to God's commission

This is a very crafty opposition – it sounds very reasonable. The opposition of – *time wasting*. One of the most common factors in people not bearing fruit is *distraction* – time spent on things that are not as important.

> When word came to Sanballat, Tobiah, Geshem the Arab and the rest of our enemies that I had rebuilt the wall and not a gap was left in it – though up to that time I had not set the doors in the gates – Sanballat and Geshem sent me this message: 'Come, let us meet together in one of the villages on the plain of Ono.'
> But they were scheming to harm me; so I sent messengers to them with this reply: 'I am carrying on a great project and cannot go down. Why should the work stop while I leave it and go down to you?' Four times they sent me the same message, and each time I gave them the same answer.
> (Nehemiah 6.1–4)

This is such an easy opposition to fall into because it sounds so reasonable. This is one of the biggest traps for senior leaders. You're working hard building the walls. You know the type of thing – come over here . . ., meetings that don't go anywhere, all talk and no action, talking that seems to sap your spirit.

Steve Jobs, founder of Apple, made one decision early on in his working life that he said he never regretted. He always tried to be home for tea. At that time the tech industry was all about conferences – being seen to be in the right place, at the right time, talking to the right people. He had none of it. He wanted to be back home with his family for tea. Rather than being stuck in endless meetings. Placating lots of different people and committees. Notice where you're spending your time. Focus. Concentrate. Get on with building the walls.

The response to this opposition is *obedience*. Just do what God has commissioned you to do.

It's not so fashionable to talk about *obedience*. We prefer perhaps to talk about gifting or anointing, especially in leaders. But unless we work out our gifting/anointing with obedience, then all our plans and visions and gifts will come to nothing.

For example, Saul was anointed by God as king, but he wasn't obedient. He kept disobeying God. On the day of his announcement as king he was 'hiding in the baggage'. There was a repeated pattern of disobedience. And in the end God's purposes moved on and Samuel anointed David, the shepherd boy: 'a man after [God's] own heart' (1 Samuel 13.14), a man who would complete the battles God gave him to fight (1 Samuel 10—18). The best example is, of course, David's descendant, Jesus, who 'humbled himself by becoming obedient to death – even death on a cross!' (Philippians 2.8), and who completed the work his Father gave him to do, right down to his final breath: 'It is finished' (John 19.30).

The most striking talk of obedience comes from long-term prisoners who have had their characters shaped and refined in the fiery ordeal of prison. For example, Nelson Mandela spoke of 'the long walk to freedom'.[8] Francis Xavier Nguyen van Thuan (who we introduced in the previous chapter) wrote on a tiny scrap of paper from solitary confinement: 'Obedience is more important than sacrifice. Sacrifices can be of merely material things – fruits, incense, animals, money etc. When you obey, however, you sacrifice yourself, you kill your own will and pride, to become a living holocaust.'[9]

I love the detail in Jesus' first recorded miracle in John's Gospel. Turning water into wine. It's a well-known story. So much could be said which resonates with the themes of this book: extravagance, party; 'little people', the hobbits, trusted behind the scenes with this first-ever miracle. But most of all, I love the hinge-moment. And it's this: 'His mother said to the servants, "Do whatever he tells you"' (John 2.5). Mary had learnt obedience in 30 hidden years since that astonishing visitation from the angel Gabriel. She knew to do whatever God told her.

God is looking for men and women and children who are obedient. Who do whatever he tells them. Who become those fiery sacrifices for him, who 'keep in step with the Spirit' (Galatians 5.25) in the tiny minutiae of their everyday lives. He wants us to work out our anointing, our calling, our gifting in the little details of being obedient.

This is a great threat to the enemy, as C. S. Lewis puts it so fluently in his *Screwtape Letters*, which describe the advice from a senior devil to a junior devil:

> Do not be deceived, Wormwood. Our cause is never more in danger, than when a human, no longer desiring, but intending, to do our Enemy's will, looks round upon a universe from which every trace of Him seems to have vanished, and asks why he has been forsaken, and still obeys.[10]

Opposition 5: Open letter
Response: Laugh, but don't feed the crocodile

I confess that, thankfully, I haven't received many of these. But an open letter is particularly nasty. Seeing accusations in print gives them more credence than whispers, disturbance, even open mocking. And anonymous ones are even worse. It summons up in us an instinct to fight back, to justify ourselves, to explain our actions.

Don't. Don't feed the crocodile. The crocodile is never satisfied. I was with one of our vicars lately. He's been on the front of the local newspaper three times. Each time, the same false rumours. He'd been doing a great job. Building the walls.

Nehemiah is threatened with an open letter. Accusing him of rebellion. Falsely.

> Then, the fifth time, Sanballat sent his assistant to me with the same message, and in his hand was an unsealed letter in which was written:
>
> 'It is reported among the nations – and Geshem says it is true – that you and the Jews are plotting to revolt, and therefore you are building the wall. Moreover, according to these reports you are about to become their king and have even appointed prophets to make this proclamation about you in Jerusalem: "There is a king in Judah!" Now this report will get back to the king; so come, let us meet together.'
>
> (Nehemiah 6.5–7)

Open letter. False accusations. This is really nasty.

But here's Nehemiah's response. Note it. It's genius:

> I sent him this reply: 'Nothing like what you are saying is happening; you are just making it up out of your head.'
> (Nehemiah 6.8)

Try it! 'Nothing like what you are saying is happening – you are making it up!'

Martin Luther said this: 'The best way to drive out the devil, if he will not yield to texts of Scripture, is to jeer and flout him, for he cannot bear scorn.'[11] St Thomas More said: 'The devil . . . that proud spirit . . . cannot endure to be mocked.'[12]

I would thoroughly recommend laughter as a tactic when you face opposition. When I was a fairly new bishop, I got an email one Friday afternoon – copied into the rest of the senior team – saying how terrible a bishop I was. I'm far from perfect, but this email was so overdrawn I couldn't stop myself laughing at it. Twenty minutes later, my boss phoned . . . 'Jill – are you OK? I've just seen that email.' I replied: 'It was so ridiculous I couldn't stop myself from laughing.'

St Antony had a similar tactic, noted earlier: 'Even if they attack us and appear to threaten death, they ought to be laughed at rather than feared because they are weak and cannot carry out all their threats.'[13]

Notice the levels of laughter in your team? Are you taking yourself too seriously? When opposition comes against you – take it as a compliment! You must be on to something. See it for what it really is. And don't feed the crocodile.

Then finally . . .

Opposition 6: Betrayal by your own side
Response: Follow Jesus to the cross
This is the most painful of all the oppositions. When it happens, it can feel physically painful in your own body and incredibly difficult to speak about. The only response I have found to this is to silently follow Jesus to the cross. (I will explore this further in our next chapter.)

Jesus experienced this opposition from his closest disciples. First, Peter told him he must give up on his stupid plan to die on the cross. Jesus used his sternest rebuke ever: 'Get behind me, Satan!' (Matthew 16.23).

And then there was Judas in the Garden of Gethsemane, only hours after they had eaten the special Passover meal together.

A few years ago, we acted out the whole of Mark's Gospel in Blackburn Cathedral.[14] There were many comedy moments – not least as I was cast as Pilate, Bishop Julian as the chief Pharisee. But it was deeply spiritually moving. I wrote in my journal at the time: 'My heart feels enlarged for Jesus.'

Bishop Philip was cast as Judas Iscariot, the disciple who betrayed Jesus. If you know the plot, Judas arranged to bring a party of soldiers to arrest Jesus – he would signify who was Jesus with a kiss. There was a moment in the drama when he had to walk across the stage to kiss Jesus. He said it felt like walking down a dark tunnel to the only point of light and putting it out.

Nehemiah is told point blank that the only way forward is to go and do a wrong thing. This is the hardest opposition of all, because, like Judas, it came from his own side.

> One day I went to the house of Shemaiah son of Delaiah, the son of Mehetabel, who was shut in at his home. He said, 'Let us meet in the house of God, inside the temple, and let us close the temple doors, because men are coming to kill you – by night they are coming to kill you.'
>
> But I said, 'Should a man like me run away? Or should someone like me go into the temple to save his life? I will not go!' I realised that God had not sent him, but that he had prophesied against me because Tobiah and Sanballat had hired him. He had been hired to intimidate me so that I would commit a sin by doing this, and then they would give me a bad name to discredit me.
> (Nehemiah 6.10–13)

Nehemiah knew that, according to Jewish law, he shouldn't shut himself in the temple. Should he run away? Go opposite to the command of God to save himself?

Nehemiah was *obedient* to the word of God, and then realized this was false information. People had been hired to intimidate him. Nehemiah's character had been built already. He was obedient to God.

And the result of Nehemiah's obedience and perseverance: 'So the wall was completed on the twenty-fifth of Elul, in fifty-two days' (Nehemiah 6.15).

The wall was built – mission accomplished. This was done by God and not by Nehemiah. All the opposition – came – to – nothing.

But a final postscript on the book of Nehemiah. When the walls are built, Nehemiah gathers everyone and gets Ezra to read the book of the law – from daybreak to noon. (This is in Nehemiah 8). And the teachers explain the word to them.

Then he sends everyone off to party: 'Go and enjoy choice food and sweet drinks . . . Do not grieve. For the joy of the LORD is your strength' (Nehemiah 8.10). Laugh at the opposition. It all comes to nothing in the end. And it's always worth taking time to celebrate. Enjoy the breathers, enjoy the view.

Going further

For group discussion

1 What most strikes you about this chapter or confuses you?
2 C. S. Lewis talks about two equal and opposite errors: disbelief and excessive belief in the devil. In your setting, which is the more likely trap?
3 Jesus said about Satan: 'He is a liar and the father of lies' (John 8.44). Which lies are you noticing at the moment?
4 'The biggest danger in working for transformation is that we get weary and give up.' Would you agree?
5 'All the opposition came to nothing.' Can you give an example of this in your experience?
6 Which of these six textbook oppositions in the book of Nehemiah are you most familiar with? Which do you find most difficult or troubling?
7 'The joy of the LORD is your strength' (Nehemiah 8.10). Can you give examples of *Acte Contrare* – when you have found acting in the opposite direction has helped you overcome opposition?

For personal devotion

Read: Isaiah 35.1–10

Prayer to conclude: excerpt from St Patrick's Breastplate (I use the full version of this regularly, especially when aware of opposition)

> I bind unto myself the Name, The strong Name of the Trinity;
> By invocation of the same.
> The Three in One, and One in Three,
> Of Whom all nature hath creation,
> Eternal Father, Spirit, Word:
> Praise to the Lord of my salvation, Salvation is of Christ the Lord.[15]

11
Stepping into the fire

On the day of my consecration as bishop, as I mentioned, there were fires on the moors above my home town of Bolton and across the nearby moors above Blackburn. Fires can be dangerous if they get out of control, but intentional burning of moorland heather is actually a precursor to new life.

In some mysterious way, as we share in the sufferings of Jesus, we encounter resurrection and new life. Following the great beacon lighter, Jesus, will involve crucifixion as well as resurrection, joy and pain inextricably bound together in ways which can be overlooked in our culture. This overlooking is unwise: military experience demonstrates that post-traumatic stress disorder is much reduced when there is a realistic expectation of what lies ahead.

In many chapters, we have used the image of fire. In the previous chapter, we have asked, 'What is the battle?' These analogies are not used flippantly. Fire burns. In battle, people get injured or worse. And the battle is permitted to continue for now by the will of God. In this chapter, we will look at this head on. We will step into the fire, so to speak.

I realize that some dipping into this book might say: 'She's got lots of enthusiasm, but clearly everything worked out gloriously for her.' This is not true.

This came home to me during an enthusiastic speaking engagement. I'd been invited to encourage a team who had been starting a new church under quite difficult circumstances. I spoke of faith and courage, and ambition in prayer, weaving in some of the stories I've included in earlier chapters of this book. Then the church leader sighed: 'But what advice have you got when the going gets tough?' It was then I realized that I had completely missed out the painful depths that had been the furnace of my courage. I had forgotten to speak about the cross.

Mysteriously, the real glory of the Christian faith seems to come when Jesus invites us to 'share in his sufferings' (as we find, for example, in Philippians 3.10–11). When he invites us to follow him all the way. Not just resurrection, but death and resurrection. Not just glory, but suffering and glory.

There are lots of reasons why we avoid speaking about the cross and suffering. So much is beyond our comprehension. Take Colossians 1.24 for example: 'Now I rejoice in what I am suffering for you, and I fill up in my flesh what is still lacking in regard to Christ's afflictions, for the sake of his body, which is the church.' My husband Jeremy very nearly did his PhD on this verse, but decided it was too hard! It is one of the most perplexing verses in the New Testament, which scholars have tried to rewrite in so many ways. This is partly because we don't like the idea that Jesus' sufferings are incomplete (though, when Paul met Jesus on the Road to Damascus, Jesus was clear that because of Paul's persecution of the young church, Jesus was still suffering in his body). But it's mainly because we want to push away the idea that our suffering can bring good to us and to the Church. I understand that any talk of suffering being used in God's purposes might seem to support passivity in the face of abuse or oppression. But I think this verse is about us choosing to step into the fire, to follow Jesus to the cross. Paul was open-hearted, even rejoicing, in his willingness to suffer for the Church. If you read his story, it appears that what happened through his sufferings in turn brought so much life (see, for example, 2 Corinthians 1.3–11).

So, this chapter will feel a bit heavy. Come with me deeper into the heart of the Christian faith, which encompasses the hardest things in life. Even in the darkest place we can still be safe with hope, because of the cross. I am not the expert. I am just taking baby steps. Many in the school of the saints have been ahead of me in this stepping into the fire of sharing in his sufferings. I will introduce you to four friends who have walked this way before us, and whose stories or writings have consoled me and helped light the way in the darkest valleys: Polycarp, Gertrude, Teresa and Mary.

Polycarp

The title of this chapter was inspired by the second-century account of Polycarp, who literally stepped into the fire. He is honoured as one of the first Christian martyrs.

He had been Bishop of Smyrna on the west coast of Turkey for more than 40 years when the persecution of Christians began. He was arrested and brought before the Roman governor who gave him the option of renouncing his faith to save his life, saying: 'Take the oath, and I will let you go. Curse your Christ!' His response was this: 'I have served him for eighty-six years, and he has done me no wrong. How can I blaspheme my king who saved me?'

Then the eye-witness account describes his death in c. 155 with moving detail.[1]

Polycarp volunteered to stay at the stake just held by ropes which would soon burn away, not the usual nails. He looked to heaven and made this prayer of mature faith:

> I bless you for counting me worthy of this day and of this hour, so that I might be numbered among your martyrs and share the cup of your Christ, and so rise again to eternal life in body and soul and the immortality of the Holy Spirit.

When the flames were lit, an amazing thing happened:

> For the fire took on the shape of a great vault, like a ship's sail unfurling and billowing out in the wind, the flames forming a wall around the body of the martyr. Indeed, the body did not look like burning flesh, but like bread that is baking, or like gold and silver being refined in a furnace. There was also a pervasive sweet smell in the air as of incense of some precious spice.

It is from Polycarp that I have coined the phrase 'stepping into the fire'. Let's be clear, God didn't save Polycarp from death. But his death was so good and so wholesome, it was like freshly baked bread, as precious as gold, as sweet as incense.

It is a deep paradox that, as our faith matures, and the more we aspire to be giants of faith, God invites us to step into the fire. And with joy. Not to pass through the fire unscathed, but to step into it and be burnt. This is best put in Scripture by Peter, one of our closest witnesses to Jesus' sufferings:

> Dear friends, do not be surprised at the fiery ordeal that has come on you to test you, as though something strange were happening to you. But rejoice inasmuch as you participate in the sufferings of Christ, so that you may be overjoyed when his glory is revealed.
> (1 Peter 4.12–13)

We shy away from phrases like 'the fiery ordeal that has come on you to test you'. Not so much the fire (I am very conscious in saying this that any pain in ministry I've experienced is a world away from what our fellow brothers and sisters suffer and have suffered). We shy away from the inference that it is a test. When this is very much the experience of our ancestors. Paul wrote to the Corinthian church, who were so super-spiritual, that living everyday life caused a category error: 'No test has overtaken you except what is common to mankind. And God is faithful; he will not let you be tested beyond what you can bear' (1 Corinthians 10.13). Thomas à Kempis, a fifteenth-century writer, puts it like this: 'Jesus now has many lovers of His heavenly kingdom, but few bearers of His cross, many are desirous of consolation but few of tribulation.'[2]

This is an important strand in Christian experience, which we have a tendency to airbrush away today in our squeamishness about pain.

This fire for the beacons burns our insides. It is usually private. Often lonely. Like Jesus praying in agony alone in the Garden of Gethsemane: '*Abba*, Father . . . everything is possible for you. Take this cup from me. Yet not what I will, but what you will' (Mark 14.36).

Jesus' beloved disciple, John, especially close to his heart, puts this so eloquently: 'Unless a grain of wheat falls to the ground and dies, it remains only a single seed. But if it dies, it produces many seeds' (John 12.24). When a project very close to my heart died a sudden death (see Chapter 2), it was this verse that my wise boss quoted to me at the time. 'Sometimes, Jill, God's ways take the longer route.'

Isaac of Nineveh, a Syrian bishop writing in the seventh century, echoes this theme in John's Gospel that the lifting up of Jesus on the cross was the moment when the glory of God shone most powerfully.[3] We want to think God's power shines most brightly in the resurrection. But in Scripture, the first declaration of Jesus' divinity comes at his death: 'And when the centurion, who stood there in front of Jesus, saw how he died, he said, "Surely this man was the Son of God!"' (Mark 15.39). Jesus was recognized as the Son of God when he died – not through his miracles and wonders, or even his teaching, but through his death on the cross.

A wise priest in our diocese advised: 'I try not to be scared of pain.' I sense Jesus inviting me into sharing his sufferings, raising my eyes to the horizon, so that in the light of eternity our 'light and momentary troubles' will be seen to have achieved 'an eternal glory that far outweighs them all' (2 Corinthians 4.17).

Gertrude the Great

Gertrude the Great (or Gertrude of Helfta) was a thirteenth-century German nun, brought up by the Benedictine nuns of Helfta from the age of five. Aged 25, she had a vision of Jesus and spent the rest of her life in contemplation of this. She is known for her attention to the wounds of Jesus, which she wrote about in her book *The Herald of God's Loving Kindness*.

> Inwardly in my heart, as if in physical places, I realized that the Spirit had impressed the worshipful and adorable imprint of your most holy wounds. By those wounds you healed my soul and gave me the cup of the nectar of love to drink.[4]

This fascination with Jesus' wounds might sound quite alien today. Personally, I have a tendency to withdraw from words like wounds and suffering, the way you might wince and withdraw when you burn your fingers on the oven.

Ten years ago, when my mum was dying of cancer, at first I would resist my usual practice of being still in prayer – it was simply too painful. If I were still, my heart would hurt more. As I became conscious of my busy displacement activities, I found myself led to Philippians 3.10–11 (NIV 1984): 'I want to know Christ and the power of his resurrection and the fellowship of sharing in his sufferings, becoming like him in his death, and so, somehow, to attain to the resurrection from the dead.'

One day, slumped in a chair, exhausted with grief, stressed by the potential of more grief and the chaos of bereavement (I had lost my father to cancer 15 years earlier), I felt those words come alive in my heart: 'Jill, I am inviting you to share my sufferings.' There was such a tenderness in this invitation. Like the tenderness of being invited to touch someone's wounds.

After a recent quiet day, I was leaving Whalley Abbey, when a man with learning difficulties came up to me and simply asked out of the blue: 'Why did Peter deny Jesus?' My mind was on to the next place I needed to be, so I confess I tried to hurry the conversation: 'What do you think?' He simply replied: 'But you're the bishop, I want to know what you think.' Then, unbidden, from my heart came the reply: 'I think Peter was afraid of the pain.'

This is something that has been underlined to me in prayer as I have stepped into more senior roles. I have found my eyes opened to these verses about the place of pain. I had presumed that Jesus suffered so I didn't have to. Perhaps you can understand why I had completely overlooked this important seam in the New Testament about pain (for example: Philippians 3.10; 1 Peter 4.12–13, both quoted above).

I am intrigued that in these last years as a bishop, I have started to feel the pain of situations physically in my body. A heaviness of heart, an ache in my body. I can't say it's the same as Gertrude's experience of inward physical wounds. But my body certainly feels pain.

Normally we (rightly) presume that pain in our body is a sign of something going wrong – a headache, heartburn and so on.

But I am drawn to notice how pain in my body as a woman, in that unspoken but that highly significant moment of life – childbirth – is completely normal. In fact, it's a sign that something is going right. And when significant things are happening, I can find myself – even within one day – experiencing spiritual birth pangs, pain and relief in short succession. Good news, bad news in waves, which I feel in my body. It reminds me of the experience that Paul writes about: 'My dear children, for whom I am again in the pains of childbirth until Christ is formed in you' (Galatians 4.19).

This leaves me intrigued by what Paul means in the same letter by, 'I bear in my body the marks of Jesus' (Galatians 6.17). Is this also what Gertrude is referring too? A twentieth-century mystic, Dorothy Kerin, after a miraculous healing (which hit the front pages of the London broadsheets in 1912) later received the five wounds of 'stigmata', wounds in the same place as Jesus received them in his crucifixion (which were testified by a number of priests and C of E bishops at the time).[5] She went on to have an international healing ministry and received astonishingly potent visions.

In our post-NHS world where pain is an insult to our world view, a veil has been drawn over this mysterious world of spiritual-bodily pain, this path to the cross. I don't understand it, but I am intrigued. I love Gertrude's open-hearted simplicity across eight centuries.

Teresa of Avila

Teresa of Ávila (1515–82) wrote *The Way of Perfection* for women who were trying to live the religious life. She was one of the pioneers of spiritual renewal in the wake of the religious conflicts of her time.

I remember very clearly the first time I discovered Teresa of Ávila's advice on suffering in *The Way of Perfection*. I stumbled across it quite innocently. It was her feast day, 15 October, in 2020. At Morning Prayer on Zoom with my senior colleagues, we often volunteer to bring a reading about the saint of the day. For this purpose, I always have Bishop Robert Atwell's red book *Celebrating the Saints* at hand.[6] (If you haven't come across it yet, I thoroughly recommend it as a wonderfully selected compilation of the writings of the saints – well worth the investment.) So I said breezily, 'How about I do a reading from the red book about Teresa?' Fine. All sorted. Morning Prayer commenced.

I hadn't been prepared for what followed.

As I read aloud, unrehearsed, it was as if God were prising open the tightly shut clam of some of my lockdown pain.

I suspect many of us experienced our own quiet 'crucifixions' in lockdown. Every time I experienced a deeply painful wave, I would do all I could to surrender myself privately: 'Take this from me, but let your will be done.' Paradoxically by that point in 2020, I was experiencing my most potent 'resurrection': astonishing favour in my work and speaking; people I encountered were very open to faith and healing; beacons were catching fire in unexpected places. At the same time, I was dealing with some very private pain. The two seemed linked.

As I read these words with my voice cracking, the painful upheavals of the previous six months made perfect sense, as, even though questions remained crushingly unanswered, they were tenderly held within the will of God.

It seems very easy to say that we will surrender our will to someone, until we try it and realise that it is the hardest thing we can do if we carry it out as we should. The Lord knows what each of us can bear, and, when he sees that one of us is strong, he does not hesitate to fulfil his will in him.

Do not fear that he will give you riches or pleasures or honours or any such earthly things; his love for you is not so poor as that. And he sets a very high value on what you can give him and desires to recompense you for it since he gives you his kingdom while you are still alive.

Would you like to see how he treats those who make the prayer 'Your will be done' from their hearts? Ask his glorious Son who made it thus in the Garden. Think with what resolution and fulness of desire he prayed; and consider if the will of God was not perfectly fulfilled in him through the trials, sufferings, insults and persecutions which he gave him until at last his life ended with death on a cross. So you see what he gave to his best beloved, and from this you can understand what His will is.[7]

I realized that the very difficult pain I was experiencing was the cost because 'he gives [us] his kingdom while [we] are still alive'. In my heart and in real-life ministry, his kingdom had been breaking in astonishingly. My journals from that time were very full indeed. I felt honoured, relieved to make sense of the pain. (And very grateful for Zoom that I could switch my camera off, excuse myself to the bathroom via the chat, to cry in private.)

When I returned, it seemed there was a different atmosphere in the Zoom room. A tender vulnerability. It was as if Jesus were especially present, allowing us to touch his open wounds. I said nothing about myself or my story: I had no words. Besides, about some of the pain, I promised God to be silent, never to speak of it. But it was a very precious moment. Of great wordless relief.

Pain brings with it a chaos. Unexplained. Unboundaried. Out of control. Teresa has helped me to experience that underneath are his 100 per cent reliable everlasting arms; the darkness is not too dark for him. That pain is allowed in the will of God. There are no reasons given for this, this side of the grave. Even to the Son of God. Jesus cries out in heart-wrenching agony from the cross: 'My God, my God, why have you abandoned me?' (Mark 15.34, NLT: note how this cry was so seared into the memory of eye-witnesses that Mark records it in the original Aramaic). And there is absolutely no answer.

But if I give my consent to follow Jesus to the cross, I need not be scared of the pain that will inevitably follow. He will hold me tenderly. In some mysterious way, it is an honour that he trusted me to enter into pain that at the time seemed pointless, crushing and retrograde (and still does). And yet: *The Lord knows what each of us can bear, and, when he sees that one of us is strong, he does not hesitate to fulfil his will in him.*

This has given me more courage to step into pain. To step into the fire.

Mary, the Mother of Jesus

We've met Polycarp, Gertrude the Great and Teresa of Ávila. But one heroine of faith towers above them all for me. Our final giant of faith: Mary, the mother of Jesus.

How did she keep faith all those years? The overwhelming visit from Gabriel; the threat of divorce by Joseph; the chaos of birth; the flight to Egypt; 12-year-old Jesus seeming to reject her and Joseph, which was repeated publicly in front of crowds when she was trying to rescue him from this madness; watching her son die in agony on the cross.

I think Mary kept faith all those years because she knew from the start the cost.

She learnt it in a very special encounter, when she and Joseph went to the Temple in Jerusalem to present Jesus, like all Jewish baby boys, when he was 40 days old. A patient old man, Simeon, and a prophetic old woman, Anna, came out of the shadows to bless him. They had both waited a very long time, in faith, for the Spirit to prompt them at this moment. It is such a beautiful encounter, I will quote in full:

> Now there was a man in Jerusalem called Simeon, who was righteous and devout. He was waiting for the consolation of Israel, and the Holy Spirit was on him. It had been revealed to him by the Holy Spirit that he would not die before he had seen the Lord's Messiah. Moved by the Spirit, he went into the temple courts. When the parents brought in the child Jesus to do for him what the custom of the Law required, Simeon took him in his arms and praised God, saying:
>
> 'Sovereign Lord, as you have promised,
>   you may now dismiss your servant in peace.
> For my eyes have seen your salvation,
>   which you have prepared in the sight of all nations:
> a light for revelation to the Gentiles,
>   and the glory of your people Israel.'

The child's father and mother marvelled at what was said about him. Then Simeon blessed them and said to Mary, his mother: 'This child is destined to cause the falling and rising of many in Israel, and to be a sign that will be spoken against, so that the thoughts of many hearts will be revealed. And a sword will pierce your own soul too.'

There was also a prophet, Anna, the daughter of Penuel, of the tribe of Asher. She was very old; she had lived with her husband seven years after her marriage, and then was a widow until she was eighty-four. She never left the temple but worshiped night and day, fasting and praying. Coming up to them at that very moment, she gave thanks to God and spoke about the child to all who were looking forward to the redemption of Jerusalem.

(Luke 2.25–38)

The sight of Jesus calls this beautiful prophecy out of Simeon's heart. A chink of light becomes for him a full-blooded dawn on the horizon. He has trained his eyes with great faith on the far horizon: he will be a 'light for revelation to the Gentiles, and the glory of your people Israel' (Luke 2.32).

Then he is moved to turn to Mary for a word in private: 'This child is destined to cause the falling and rising of many in Israel.' This must have been a reassuring underlining – she had been given a similar song in her heart when she first said yes to becoming the mother of Jesus: 'He has brought down rulers from their thrones but has lifted up the humble' (Luke 1.52). God's great reversal.

Mary's heart must have been caught up in the wonder of this prophecy confirming everything she'd heard from the angel Gabriel a year previously.

But then came his final words. About the cost: 'And a sword will pierce your own soul too' (Luke 2.35).

If you've been on this adventure of lighting the beacons for a little while, my guess is many of our souls have been pierced by swords since we followed God's call. In our comfort culture, this is bewildering, disturbing, disheartening. Maybe, even today, you're in a place where it's been so painful, you're so weary, you're tempted to give up, lose faith, throw in the towel.

But this is the cost of following Jesus with Mary to the cross. Over and over again, she chose to surrender to the pain. But I don't think she ever regretted the cost of 'yes' to be the mother of Jesus. She tasted his kingdom while she was still alive.

'He gives us his kingdom while we are still alive' – pain and joy together

Mary gladly stepped into the fire, into pain, at a young age. She tasted the kingdom of God while she was still alive. If we're privileged enough to experience some of the astonishing resurrection of his kingdom, this seems to bring with it an undertow of costly pain. Joy and pain in close succession, often simultaneously, as I described above.

In Chapter 5, I introduced the story of St Aidan's College, Birkenhead. This college was set up in the 1840s, the first of its kind outside Oxbridge, to serve the industrial slums of Liverpool, training priests from all walks of life for the C of E. Its motto was *Via Crucis, Via Lucis – the way of the cross is the way of light.* It faithfully carried that blazing torch of St Aidan, with faith that even through the grimness of industrial squalor, the light of heaven can still shine.

When I was Director of St Mellitus North West, the staff team had grown quite rapidly. I remember a particular staff retreat away. I had invited the team to sketch a timeline of their lives, against a simple axis of joy (above the line) and pain (below the line), as a way to get to know one another's stories. An intriguing pattern emerged. At the point at which each of us had become involved in training vicars and church leaders, the traces on our graphs suddenly sparked up and down – joy and pain in close succession. Like a crazy trace on a heart monitor. Helen, one of our tutors, quietly observed: 'This is just like the St Aidan's College motto, isn't it?' *Via Crucis, Via Lucis – the way of the cross is the way of light.* The world of theological education is particularly prone to this pattern of pain and joy together: good training has the potential to bring so much resurrection to a region. As a wise intercessor observed, 'Jill, you are training shepherds for the North West – that is why it is so much more costly.' I have noticed that the more influence for resurrection Jesus gives me, the more painful the crucifixions.

I was transfixed to discover the story of Jesuit priest, Walter Ciszek. He sensed a call to Russia in the 1930s. He spent the Second World War in incredible hardship and deprivation in the infamous Lubyanka prison in Moscow and in Siberian labour camps. His story is a gripping read. Even more compelling is the wisdom distilled during this time:

> If you look on sacrifice and suffering only through the eyes of reason alone, your tendency will be to avoid as much of it as you can, for pain is never pleasant. But if you can learn to see the role of pain and suffering in relation to God's redemptive [saving] plan for the universe, your attitude must change. You don't shun it when it comes to you but bear it with the measure of grace given you. You see it as putting on of Christ in the true sense of the word.[8]

How fiery pain trains us

I was once on the phone to my friend Iman, with all her wonderful inherited Egyptian wisdom of the Desert Fathers. I was in the middle of quite a painful bout of crucifixion birth pangs. She replied pragmatically, 'Well, Jill, the Desert Fathers and Mothers saw crucifixion as much more effective than fasting and praying for purifying the soul.'

What are the benefits from these purifications of the soul? I'm no expert, but here are four that I have experienced:

1 Humility. Paul receives glorious revelations when he is invited up to the 'third heaven'. Immediately afterwards he also receives a 'thorn in the flesh' from Satan. Which he pleads with God to take away. He receives this humbling answer: 'My grace is sufficient for you, for my power is made perfect in weakness' (2 Corinthians 12.9). This was also the verse given to me at my confirmation by the

Bishop of Bolton in 1989. It's a promise I cherish. And a promise I rely on often. On a daily basis, I find I am operating out of a place of weakness.

2 *Detachment.* In pain, the heavenly realities seem to come more into focus than the earthly distraction. Through difficult times, we grow in resilience and stamina. This is a process that the mystics describe as detachment from our ego, or mortification. Less ego, more room to carry his fire. Teresa of Ávila's advice to learn more about detachment is to love Sister Angela (the most irritating person in your community). St Columbanus, seventh-century bishop and abbott, offers other practical tips which I have found helpful:

> Mortification . . . which is intolerable to the proud and hard-hearted, becomes the comfort of those who take pleasure only in what is humble and gentle . . . Thus there are three ways of mortification: not to argue back in mind; not to speak with unbridled tongue; not to go wherever we wish.'[9]

3 *Resilience.* Pain strengthens resilience. It seems as if Jesus has been coaching me to be more robust. Watching my son play rugby is a very useful lesson in this. Tackles happen. You find yourself face down in the mud. You need to pick yourself up again and get back in the game. Teresa of Ávila describes an experience she had in prayer of an angel with a spear of gold, tipped by fire, piercing her heart ('to pierce my very entrails; when he drew it out, he seemed to draw them out also, and to leave me all on fire with a great love of God. The pain was so great, that it made me moan; and yet so surpassing was the sweetness of this excessive pain, that I could not wish to be rid of it.'[10])

4 *Cauterizing.* I had just been reading how St John of the Cross spoke of the fire of the Spirit as cauterizing our wounds. This was new to me. Within the week, I had a quiet day booked in. The moment I sat down to be still, reading a psalm, tears bubbled up.

The sad and painful situation I had been experiencing bubbled to the surface. I was taking this quiet day at home owing to the lockdown restrictions, so an hour in I popped into our kitchen to make myself a cup of tea. My husband spotted me: 'Gosh, you look awful.' I explained why, and how I'd promised God not to speak of it. He wisely chimed in, 'Sharing your pain does not help the Church.' Later that day, I found myself simply praying: 'Jesus, may the fire of your love cauterize this wound.' It seemed there was a tender healing inside me at that moment. I found later over dinner I could talk with my husband about it without any sense of the internal pain.

I like to call this 'open heart surgery'. Sometimes the wounds are caused by our own brokenness or sin; sometimes by the brokenness of others. I like the idea that Jesus is the great surgeon of our soul. He can gently unravel the knitting of our lives, which has woven in dark shards of glass. Our repentance can draw the poison of sin. And his Spirit cauterizes the wounds, gently knitting and restoring. As mentioned earlier, I have found he can even do this with pain that happened very early in life (see Chapter 9).

Suffering is conspicuously absent from many of our contemporary worship songs, and indeed our more recent hymns. One recent exception, which caused controversy in itself, is Matt and Beth Redman's song 'Blessed be the name of the Lord' (2012), composed after a series of miscarriages. In the good times, and the times marked with suffering, they simply offer the refrain 'Blessed be the name of the Lord', which we find in the book of Job. This Old Testament book is seen by some as a compilation of different responses to why God allows suffering. Once you meet God, the questions don't matter.[11]

The cross is beyond our understanding. The silence from God in the face of Jesus' abandonment is beyond understanding. And yet mysteriously this is where we see and share his glory. Francis Xavier Nguyen van Thuan, Archbishop of Saigon, whose story of extreme suffering we read in Chapter 9, speaks with fluency, honed by his silent years of obediently stepping into the fire.

In times of suffering, avoid asking who was at fault, but rather simply give thanks to God for the instrument he uses to sanctify you. Also, avoid seeking merely human consolation; take your problems to Jesus. Then when the suffering is passed, resist any impulse to recrimination and vengeance. Forget about it, never speak about it again, except to say 'Alleluia'.[12]

Going further

For group discussion

1 'We don't like the idea that Jesus' sufferings are incomplete.' What do you think of the invitation in Scripture to step into the fire to share in Jesus' sufferings?

2 'Do not be surprised at the fiery ordeal' (1 Peter 4.12). Why do we find ourselves surprised by suffering? How does this affect our faith?

3 Reflecting on Polycarp: A wise priest said to me 'I try not to be scared of pain.' Why do we find pain scary?

4 Reflecting on Gertrude: 'My dear children, for whom I am again in the pains of childbirth until Christ is formed in you' (Galatians 4.19). Do you relate to this analogy with the bodily waves of pain in childbirth?

5 Reflecting on Teresa of Ávila: 'The Lord knows what each of us can bear, and when he sees that one of us is strong, he does not hesitate to fulfil his will in him . . . since he gives you his kingdom while you are still alive.' What did you make of this?

6 Reflecting on Mary: what most inspires you about Mary's example?

7 Fiery pain has helped train me in humility, detachment, resilience, cauterizing. My friend Iman observes: 'The Desert Fathers and Mothers saw crucifixion as much more effective than fasting and praying for purifying the soul.' What's been your experience?

[**Special note for our final chapter:** If you are reading this as a book group, do look ahead to Chapter 12, 'For group sharing', for our final week. It is fun homework, and you might want the opportunity to make time and space to enjoy.]

For personal devotion

Read: 2 Corinthians 1.3–11

Prayer to conclude: Jesus, thank you for the honour of inviting me to share your glory in your sufferings and to receive your kingdom while I am still alive. Amen.

12
Land of light and glory

In this final chapter, we step up on to the ridge to look over the plain into the distance ahead: a land of light and glory. All our senses alive in anticipation of light beyond the lightest of days. Glory meaning the atmosphere of heaven come to earth.

The vista ahead

On the broadest canvas, I have faith for a land of light and glory. My biggest and bravest prayers are for 'Thy kingdom come, thy will be done, on earth as it is in heaven.' I am sure that what I imagine is only the faintest shadow of the heavenly reality which we will one day experience in Jesus.

And from different places on this great canvas, we all imagine this future differently; we experience different invitations to different parts to play.

Maybe you find yourself relating to one of these five parts as you read this final chapter:

- It could be your part is as hopeful as lighting a beacon on a hilltop, to be seen by others. Some of you have a small sphere of influence, like my local beacon in Bolton. Some of you have a reach into wider spheres of influence across our culture; you are more like the beacons of Gondor on a high mountain range, rallying troops from across Middle Earth. Whatever the case, giving consent and obeying in faith opens your heart to fresh fire of the Spirit, which in turn kindles a chain of hope declaring the all-important message from the heart of God: 'We miss you, please come home.'

- It could be your part is as simple as striking a match to light your flickering candle of faith. It might appear there's not a lot to show for it, but even in its fragility it can bring a delicate circle of light, hope for others in the dark.
- It could be your part is as enduring as those warm stones, who have been in the heart of the fire for years. Unlike the wood on the beacon, they don't burn with leaping fiery flame, but they are so close to the hearth of home, they bring the enduring warmth of heaven. They draw home lost and bedraggled travellers to be warmed by his fire.
- It could be that your story has led you through forgotten tunnels, down the mines, into a very dark place. But if you are set on fire, this starts the 'Great Escape' of his crack troops who are trapped underground. Maybe the invitation to you is to dig that escape tunnel to break out many others with gifts to renew our nation, to restore and rebuild places which have been devastated for generations (see Chapter 5).
- It could be that the fire in your heart has died down to a smouldering wick or in some cases it has been brutally snuffed out. You are living with crushing levels of disappointment, despair, pain, rejection, shame, unanswered questions. The fire of the Spirit can cauterize your wounds (see Chapter 11). Don't give up now because of your pain.

The painful journey to resurrection

This last place of disappointment is a very common place to be.

The hope of this book is to stir faith in our hearts, but many of us start just below the ridge, just before dawn. Before we rush on over the ridge, I want us to pause for a moment to catch our breath.

Not simply to put sticking plasters on blisters before we step up on to the ridge, to see the vista ahead. The risk isn't sore feet, but serious injuries mean precious people give up on faith and hope altogether. My friend Chris sums up how he hears this failure of hope: 'If I have too much hope, I'll get disappointed and hurt again.'[1]

It's our instinct to avoid the minor key. But just for a moment, let's stay with the pain.

'*Abba*, Father . . . everything is possible for you' (Mark 14.36), prayed Jesus at his darkest moment. The darkest moment before the greatest dawn. How do we live with faith in our very darkest moments?

Everything is possible for our Father. This book is an invitation to ask for the gift of faith. Great faith. The faith of giants. To aspire to have the 'faith in God', faith that moves mountains (Mark 11.22–23). When Jesus is teaching about faith, the language is intriguingly ambiguous. I prefer my own more ambitious translation from the Greek: 'the faith of God'.

But how do we live with faith in our darkest moments?

Mary Magdalene

If you've not met her already, I want to introduce you to Mary Magdalene, one of Jesus' followers in the Bible. Some think she used to be a prostitute. Whatever the case, it seems she'd known a lot of pain and heartache in her life. A lot of disappointment. But the worst was yet to come.

As dawn was breaking on the first Easter Day, she went to the tomb where two days before they had buried the body of the man she loved the most – Jesus. It was the worst thing that had ever happened to her. The bottom fell out of her world when she'd stood at the foot of the cross, watching Jesus die the long and agonizing death of perfected Roman torture. The least she could do was anoint his body with some precious spices. But as dawn was breaking, she discovered something even worse. Jesus' body had been stolen from the tomb. Ransacked. The tomb had been prised open and all that was left was a pile of burial clothes.

In panic she rushes off to tell Peter and John, Jesus' best friends. They run to the tomb. Same thing. Body gone. The pain in their hearts is unbearable. They give up and go back to where they are staying. Soon we see them reaching for the only displacement activity that might numb the pain. By John chapter 21, they are back at work, keeping busy.

But for now, Mary stays with the pain by the empty tomb:

> Now Mary stood outside the tomb crying. As she wept, she bent over to look into the tomb and saw two angels in white, seated where Jesus' body had been, one at the head and the other at the foot.
>
> They asked her, 'Woman, why are you crying?'
>
> 'They have taken my Lord away,' she said, 'and I don't know where they have put him.' At this, she turned round and saw Jesus standing there, but she did not realise that it was Jesus.
>
> He asked her, 'Woman, why are you crying? Who is it you are looking for?'
>
> Thinking he was the gardener, she said, 'Sir, if you have carried him away, tell me where you have put him, and I will get him.'
>
> Jesus said to her, 'Mary.'
>
> She turned towards him and cried out in Aramaic, 'Rabboni!' (which means 'Teacher').
>
> Jesus said, 'Do not hold on to me, for I have not yet ascended to the Father. Go instead to my brothers and tell them, "I am ascending to my Father and your Father, to my God and your God."'
>
> Mary Magdalene went to the disciples with the news: 'I have seen the Lord!' And she told them that he had said these things to her. (John 20.11–18)

Mary stayed with the pain. And that's when she saw two angels. And that's when she met Jesus. He called her by name. And that's when she recognized him. All she wanted to do was to cling on to him, so she would never lose him again.

Maybe this dark place is a moment to listen out for Jesus calling your name. He knows your agony and he sees your tears, even if no one else would ever know. Let your God look at you. Let him light the fire in your heart again. His fire can cauterize your wounds. He heals deep pain today.

This is an important part of the journey to the land of light and glory. In fact, an essential part. In my experience. There is no short cut. To grow great faith, to grow to a place where you glimpse the resurrection, where 'he gives you his kingdom while you are still alive' (to quote Teresa of Ávila from the previous chapter), there is simply no short cut. The way is through the cross. Not a diversion around it for health and safety reasons.

Safety. It's understandable, it's natural to want to keep our hearts safe.

My mum was a past master at keeping herself safe from disappointment. I remember noticing as a child that she didn't ever get as excited about anything as I did. I asked her why not. 'I don't get excited in case it doesn't happen.' She had learnt to protect her heart from disappointment by not hoping for anything. I remember thinking, but isn't that half the fun of holidays? To get excited? To look forward to them? To enjoy the anticipation?

As I grew older, I realized there were deeper shards in her life to do with disappointment. When my mum was born, so she was told, my granddad looked away in disappointment. Because she was a girl. That sounds harsh and sexist. But there was a back story. Back in the day, my gran (who had already lived through bereavement of her own mum as a 6-year-old) gave birth to her first baby at home. It was a breach birth. Michael was stillborn. Then came my aunt. Then a last-ditch attempt, in her late thirties, to have a boy. If you had met my mum, I sometimes felt she had the word 'disappointment' written on her forehead. She assumed, from the day she was born, that she would disappoint.

No disappointment

We are not a disappointment to God. No one is. Here's the thing. The safest place for our hearts is in the hands of God, who knew us and loved us before the dawn of time. He is the master surgeon who does not break off the bruised reeds or snuff out the smouldering wicks.[2]

At the end of the day, God does not disappoint. There are no expiry dates on his promises. Yes, we see through a glass darkly for now. But all that he has promised will happen. One hundred per cent guaranteed.

We live in the tension that we haven't yet reached the end when Jesus comes again and 'the whole earth [is] filled with his glory' (Psalm 72.19). But we glimpse it. We glimpse his glory. Out of the corner of our eyes. A trailer of the 3D blockbuster film which is to come.

> Earth's crammed with heaven
> And every common bush afire with God,
> But only he who sees takes off his shoes;
> the rest sit round and pluck blackberries.
> (Elizabeth Barrett Browning[3])

Or, in words from 'The Vision' poem which appeared as graffiti on the wall in the very first 24-7 Prayer Room:

> And this vision will be.
> It will come to pass; it will come easily; it will come soon.
> How do I know?
> Because this is the longing of creation itself,
> the groaning of the Spirit,
> the very dream of God.
> My tomorrow is his today.
> My distant hope is his 3D.
> And my feeble, whispered, faithless prayer invokes
> a thunderous, resounding, bone-shaking great 'Amen!'
> from countless angels,
> from heroes of the faith,
> from Christ himself.
> And he is the original dreamer,
> the ultimate winner.
> Guaranteed.[4]

We mistakenly assume it is God who holds back from acting. He is so much more willing to act than we are to ask. 'His Majesty has the power to do whatever He wants and is eager to do many things for us,' assures Teresa of Ávila.[5]

But we pull back from asking with childlike open hearts, in case we are shamed, disappointed, in case he lets us down, just as the lies whisper that he will do. Have you been listening to those lies? Where are they from? The pit of hell. 'The thief comes only to steal and kill and destroy; I have come that they may have life, and have it to the full' (John 10.10).

But, mysteriously, the route ahead is through the thicket of shame and disappointment. The route to resurrection will normally involve shame and disappointment because it is the way of the cross. *Via Crucis, Via Lucis*. The way to the resurrection light is the way of the cross (see Chapter 11). The bigger the vista, the greater the cost. But with Mary, Teresa, Gertrude, Polycarp, and as all the giants of faith have found – it is absolutely worth it.

If we give our yes to enduring the cross with Jesus, this releases us to play our part on a much bigger canvas. We start to crest the ridge to the dawn of resurrection.

We will begin to see where the beacons lead.

Beacons lighting up every sphere of our society: our families, our church life, our education system, our government and legal system, arts and media, sports, economy, science. Beacons so that no one is too far from a witness to God's good news. No one is too far from coming home to a community of brothers and sisters who gather round the risen Jesus with his fiery hearth and heart of love.

For the joy set before him

My hope and prayer is that reading this book fires *faith* in your heart for the transformation of society. That you will be a beacon of his fiery faith. Faith to endure the cross now, because the joy of the kingdom of heaven breaking in now is so incredibly worth it. If we surrender ourselves to him whatever the cost, he gives us his kingdom while we are still alive.

> For the joy that was set before him [Jesus] endured the cross, scorning
> its shame, and sat down at the right hand of the throne of God.
> (Hebrews 12.2)

So what would this joy look like? What does it look like over the ridge? As we crest this final ridge on our journey, what do we see in this promised land of light and glory?

Blank pages?

I left these pages blank. Because now it's over to you.

I could describe my vision – it would be a rough and ready vision at that. I could try to put into words the vista I imagine, as I might try to describe a glass of fine wine, a fun holiday, my favourite piece of music or my good friend. The tasting notes are nothing like the experience of drinking that vintage claret; it's impossible to find words to do justice to my favourite piece of music (Ennio Morricone's *The Mission*). I could write a library about fun holidays. And you'd never begin to imagine my friend with all his quirks and qualities until you'd had a chance to meet him in person, and even then your experience of him would be unique. Each of us brings our own colour to all our relationships. We are unique. No one is a mistake or a disappointment. God created us to enjoy the richness of our family, our brothers and sisters, loved since the dawn of time.

So, I have resisted writing even a rough-and-ready vision.

If I take up space on the canvas, if I start painting first, I am pretty sure it will cramp your style. You'll take your cue from me. You will assume you have to paint like me, sing like me, speak like me.

But by the wonderful creativity of the Spirit of God, each of us can hear, see, taste in different ways. We each have different gifts and passions to be fanned into flame. His calling on our lives is unique. There is no one like us in the history of the universe. Maria, my Ghanian friend, puts it simply: 'God puts different visions into our hearts. We need to pray that vision into existence.'

Perhaps you were disappointed or even unnerved to find blank pages? Like a secondary school textbook, it helps to have the 'answers in the back'. It's interesting as we 'grow up', we like to have more certainty about what comes next. Infant children relish a blank piece of paper to colour or paint on; give the same to adults and it tends to make us rather nervous. Small children get ridiculously excited about going on holiday; their parents can tend to be anxious about all the things that might go wrong. But this is an invitation back, to mature to childlike faith. Just like Jesus said:

'Unless you change and become like little children, you will never enter the kingdom of heaven' (Matthew 18.3).

The Archbishop of York, Stephen Cottrell, tells an endearing story about one of his school visits. He was chatting to teachers in the staff room when one teacher arrived from her class, lit up with enthusiasm, she was bursting to tell a story. It went like this. She'd planned a game of 'blindman's bluff', so had chosen a girl to be blindfolded. The teacher covered up her eyes with a scarf and asked, 'Can you see anything?' 'Yes.' So she adjusted the scarf to make sure the girls' eyes were properly covered. 'Can you see anything now?' 'Yes.' The teacher tried a third time. 'Can you see anything now?' 'Yes' . . . big sigh . . . 'Ok, what can you see, then?' 'I can see trees and mountains, I can see rivers and flowers.' What beautiful imagination. The Archbishop reflected, 'I wonder when we'll tell her that she needs to grow up. She can't see anything.'

In the Bible, there are many visions of heaven come to earth: a heavenly banquet, a river of life with trees for healing on its banks, a time when creation will be at one – no animal will harm another, 'and a little child will lead them' (Isaiah 11.6), a city of light where God comes to make his home with us, where he wipes every tear from our eye, where there is no more death or mourning or crying or pain.

Or, in the words of an Old Irish Homily from the ninth century:

> . . . the kingdom which the saints and righteous strive for. It is a bright flower in its great purity, it is an open sea in its great beauty, it is a haven full of candles in its true brilliance, it is the eye's delight in its great loveliness and pleasantness, it is a flame in its fairness, it is a harp in its melodiousness, it is a feast in its abundance of wine.
>
> Blessed are all they who shall come into the kingdom, where God himself is, a King, great, fair, powerful, strong, holy, pure, just, knowing, wise, merciful, loving, beneficent, old, young, wise, noble, glorious, without beginning, without end, without age, without decay. May we enter the kingdom of that King . . . and dwell there unto the ages of ages. Amen.[6]

This book has been about inspiring faith. Childlike faith. The faith of giants. Whether you are a flickering candle, a warm stone or a blazing beacon. My hope is that each of us, warmed by fresh fire of the Spirit, finds new faith to see visions and courage to dare to dream dreams. Dreams of the heavenly version of the places where we live, the spheres of influence in which we find ourselves, the communities we belong to, the countries we love. What would it look like if #LoveLivedHere, if #ColourComes, if #PeaceFlowedLikeARiver, if #HopeSprangEternal? And then with gutsy courage and determined faith we offered our lives unreservedly to be his junior partners, fired by all 'his incomparably great power for us who believe' (Ephesians 1.19), to see that heavenly blueprint begin to break in as a reality while we are still alive.

You have your own unique contribution. He has chosen you. Let him call you out of hiding.

Can we catch a glimpse of what that might look like? God's visions are always beyond us. The canvas stretches on. The chain of beacons continues beyond the skyline. We have more colours in more beautiful hues than we can possibly imagine. In the heavenly city of light at the end of time, the light of God's presence is all we need to see by. It is a real place, where, finally, our restless hearts find perfect rest, where we come home to the place Jesus has been preparing for us, safe at last to our Father who has been loving us since the dawn of time itself.

The final words I will leave to the imagination of C. S. Lewis, at the end of his *Chronicles of Narnia* series.

'Come further in! Come further up!' shouts Aslan at the end of *The Last Battle*. And even the masterful storyteller C. S. Lewis himself runs out of language:

Their hearts leapt, and a wild hope rose within them . . .

[Aslan said softly] 'The term is over: the holidays have begun. The dream is ended: this is morning.'

And as He spoke, He no longer looked to them like a lion; but the things that began to happen after that were so great and beautiful that I cannot write them.

And for us this is the end of all the stories, and we can most truly say that they all lived happily ever after.

But for them it was only the beginning of the real story.[7]

Going further

For group sharing

Instead of a having a discussion, why not allow time and space in your week to be creative. Ask Jesus by his Spirit to inspire you in words, pictures, songs, music, of what it might look like for heaven to come to earth where you live or work, in your school, your village, your town, city or nation. How do you glimpse his land of light and glory?

Allow yourself to draw, write, compose, create on the winds of his Spirit. For his glory. You will have your own unique contribution to his heavenly symphony. May you find your voice.

Do be in touch to tell me what you see or hear, via the website: <www.lightingthebeacons.com>.

For personal devotion

Read: Revelation 21.1—22.5

Prayer to conclude: The Lord's Prayer

Our Father in heaven,
hallowed be your name,
your kingdom come,
your will be done
on earth as in heaven.
Give us today our daily bread.
Forgive us our sins
as we forgive those who sin against us.
Lead us not into temptation
but deliver us from evil.
For the kingdom, the power
and the glory are yours
now and for ever. Amen.

Notes

1 Lighting the beacons

1 *The Lord of the Rings* trilogy, directed by Peter Jackson, 2001–2003.
2 Augustine, *Confessions*, I, i, trans. Henry Chadwick (Oxford: Oxford University Press, 1991), p. 3.
3 Matthew 3.13–15.
4 Jean Darnell, *Heaven, Here I Come* (London: Marshall, Morgan and Scott, 1974), pp. 104–5.
5 'Shine, Jesus, Shine', Graham Kendrick © 1987 Make Way Music.
6 See YouTube channel for the Diocese of Blackburn.
7 <www.ywamvalues.com/the-seven-spheres-of-influence.html>.
8 <www.homeforgood.org.uk>.
9 Kate Wharton, *Single-Minded: Being Single, Whole and Living Life to the Full* (London: Monarch, 2013).
10 <https://safefamilies.uk/>.
11 See 'Transformations. Full Documentary – The Power of Unity, Prayer and Fasting; Transformations II': <www.youtube.com/watch?v=-MG-XBkCTDY&ab_channel=JojoFlorendo>.
12 *Hello Magazine* 1741, 13 June 2022, p. 55.
13 <https://www.archbishopofyork.org/news/latest-news/sermon-st-pauls-cathedral-celebrating-her-majesty-queens-platinum-jubilee>.

2 We miss you, please come home

1 See <https://www.youtube.com/watch?v=fQzWfMKXx9k&t=35s>: Victoria Wood, *Live at The Albert* (2001).
2 *Star Wars VII: The Force Awakens*, directed by J. J. Abrams, 2015.
3 *Bridget Jones's Baby*, directed by Sharon Maguire, 2016.
4 *Paddington 2*, directed by Paul King, 2017.
5 Bill Cahusac, *That Gentle Whisper*, 2021 (Edinburgh: Muddy Pearl, 2021), ch. 1.

6 Lesslie Newbigin, *The Household of God: Lectures on the Nature of Church* (Eugene, OR: Wipf and Stock, 2008).

7 Henri Nouwen, *Bread for the Journey* (London: Darton, Longman and Todd, 1996), p. 324.

8 Charles Gore, 'The Holy Spirit and Inspiration' in Charles Gore (ed.), *Lux Mundi* (London, 1889), pp. 331–2.

9 <www.bbc.co.uk/news/uk-45679730>.

10 Edwige Camp-Pietrain, 'Une église anglicane en mutation: portrait de Jill Duff, évêque Anglican de Lancaster' in *Outre-Terre: Geopolitique de Dieu* (Paris: David Reinharc, 2022), p. 61.

11 <https://alpha.org.uk/>.

12 C. S. Lewis, *The Complete Chronicles of Narnia* (London: Collins, 2000), p. 263.

13 <www.homeforgood.org.uk>.

14 Mary Porter, *Mary Sumner: Her Life and Work* (Winchester: Warren, 1921), pp. 29–31.

15 Jennifer Worth, *Call the Midwife* (London: Merton Books, 2002).

16 Milton Jones, *10 Second Sermons* (London : Darton, Longman and Todd, 2011), p. 58.

17 Francine Rivers, *Redeeming Love* (Oxford: Lion Fiction, 2013).

18 Revelation 21.1–4; 22.5.

3 Wonders of God in their own languages

1 Romans 10.13–15.

2 <www.smithwigglesworth.com.>

3 C. S. Lewis, *The Complete Chronicles of Narnia* (London: HarperCollins, 2000), p. 127.

4 Charlie Mackesy, *The Boy, the Mole, the Fox and the Horse* (London: Penguin, 2019).

5 The first biography of her life was only published in 2020: Arlin C. Migliazzo, *Mother of Modern Evanglicalism: The Life and Legacy of Henrietta Mears* (Grand Rapids, MI: Eerdmans, 2020).

6 Bill Cahusac, *That Gentle Whisper* (Edinburgh: Muddy Pearl, 2021).

7 Hebrews 12.1; Robert Atwell (ed.), *Celebrating the Saints* (Norwich: Canterbury Press, 1998), pp. i–xi.

8 *The Sayings of the Desert Fathers,* trans. Benedicta Ward (Kalamazoo, MI: Cistercian Publications, rev. edn, 1984), p. 103.

9 *Bede: The Life of Cuthbert,* chs. 4 and 16, in *The Age of Bede,* ed. D. H. Farmer, trans. J. F. Webb (London: Penguin, 1965), pp. 49–50, 66.

10 Richard Rolle, *The Fire of Love,* trans. Clifton Wolters (London: Penguin, 1971), p. 45. This is the best modern translation.

11 *The Book of Margery Kempe,* Book 1, ch. 35, trans. B. Windeatt (London: Penguin, 1985, 1994), pp. 124–5.

12 *The Life of Saint Teresa by Herself,* ch. 29, trans. J. M. Cohen (London: Penguin, 1957), p. 208.

13 *The Collected Works of St John of the Cross,* trans. Kieran Kavanaugh and Otilio Rodriguez (Washington, DC: ICS Publications, 3rd edn, 2017), pp. 640, 657.

14 The Moravians were an early Protestant movement that emerged in fifteenth-century Bohemia. They trace themselves back to Jan Hus protesting against some doctrines of the Catholic Church (liturgy only in Latin, only celibate priests, indulgences and purgatory). For an excellent introduction, try: Phil Anderson, *The Lord of the Ring* (Edinburgh: Muddy Pearl, 2020).

15 *The Aim of the Christian Life: The Conversation of St Seraphim of Sarov with N A Motovilov,* trans. John Phillips (Cambridge: Saints Alive Press, 2010), p. 36.

16 Samuel Chadwick, *The Way to Pentecost* (London: Hodder and Stoughton, 1932).

4 Breathing the oxygen of peace

1 See <www.24-7prayer.com/about/about-us/the-vision/>. 'The Vision', written by Pete Greig: <www.petegreig.info> (adapted).

2 Matthew 3.16; Mark 1.10; Luke 3.22; John 1.32.

3 Irina Gorainov, *The Message of Saint Seraphim,* Fairacres Publications 26 (Oxford: SLG Press, 2007), pp. 17–19.

4 *The Exorcist,* directed by William Friedkin, 1974.

5 *Life of Antony by Athanasius,* 27, in Caroline White (trans.), *Early Christian Lives* (London: Penguin, 1998), p. 26.

6 A great introduction to Ignatian Spirituality: James Martin SJ, *The*

Jesuit Guide to (Almost) Everything: A Spirituality for Real Life (New York: HarperCollins, 2010).

7 See <www.churchofengland.org/safeguarding/safeguarding
-e-manual/safeguarding-children-young-people-and-vulnerable
-adults/4-1>.

8 See <www.leadingyourchurchintogrowth.org.uk/the-start-course>.

9 Bede, *The Ecclesiastical History of the English People*, Oxford World's Classics, trans. Bertram Colgrave, Judith McClure, Roger Collins (Oxford: Oxford University Press, 2008).

10 <https://www.instagram.com/carolineflack/>

5 Who is key in lighting the beacons?

1 For an honest and insightful description of 'forgotten places', see Chris Lane, *Not Forgotten* (Watford: Instant Apostle, 2022).

2 Matthew 21.31.

3 Wonderfully, and coincidentally, this is the theme I have been invited to speak on at Spring Harvest 2023.

4 The original, of which this is a paraphrase, says: 'Feu. Dieu d'Abraham, Dieu d'Isaac, Dieu de Jacob, non des philosophes et des savants', *Le Mémorial*, in Blaise Pascal, *Pensées*, ed. Louis Lafuma (Paris : Éditions du Seuil, 1962), p. 361. A literal translation would be: 'Fire! God of Abraham, God of Isaac, God of Jacob – not that of the philosophers and scholars.'

5 Mechtild of Magdeburg, *Revelations: The Flowing Light of the Godhead*, II, 26; English translation in Robert Atwell (ed.), *Celebrating the Saints* (Norwich: Canterbury Press, 1998), pp. 712–13.

6 *Julian of Norwich: Revelations of Divine Love*, trans. Clifton Walters (London: Penguin, 1966), p. 68.

7 *The Lord of the Rings* trilogy, directed by Peter Jackson, 2001–2003.

8 See <www.stonyhurst.ac.uk>.

9 Genesis 3.1–5: the serpent's temptation is precisely, 'Eat this fruit and you will be unlimited, like God.'

10 Henri J. M. Nouwen, *Bread for the Journey* (London: Darton, Longman and Todd, 1996), p. 254.

11 *The Lord of the Rings* trilogy.

12 See <www.new-wine.org>.

13 The Year of Jubilee is described in Leviticus 25.8–54: a year of liberty, cancelling of debts, releasing of slaves, a Sabbath for the land.

14 Bishop Philip North, *New Wine Soundcloud*, August 2017. See <https://www.blackburn.anglican.org/storage/general-files/shares /Resources/Talks%20articles%20and%20sermons/Hope_for_the _Poor_-__P_article__Word_document_.pdf>.

15 Bede, *The Ecclesiastical History of the English People*, Oxford World's Classics, trans. Bertram Colgrave, Judith McClure, Roger Collins (Oxford: Oxford University Press, 2008), p. 117. Italics added.

16 The Declaration of Assent <https://www.churchofengland.org/prayer -and-worship/worship-texts-and-resources/common-worship /ministry/declaration-assent>.

17 See <www.24-7prayer.com/about/about-us/the-vision/>. 'The Vision', written by Pete Greig: <www.petegreig.info>.

6 Fanning beacons into flame

1 Galatians 5.22–23, NLT.

2 'Peace prayers helped bring down the Wall, says Leipzig pastor', <www.dw.com/en/peace-prayers-helped-bring-down-the-wall-says-leipzig-pastor/a-3805080>.

3 Robert Atwell (ed), Celebrating the Saints (Norwich: Canterbury Press, 1998), p. 572.

4 T. F. Torrance, *The Apocalypse Today* (London: James Clarke, 1960), p. 73.

5 These are the words given to the character of Joan in George Bernard Shaw's 1923 play, *Saint Joan* (London: Renard Press, 2022), p. 99:

> *Robert*: How do you mean? voices?
> *Joan*: I hear voices telling me what to do. They come from God.
> *Robert*: They come from your imagination.
> *Joan*: Of course. That is how the messages of God come to us.

6 Attributed to Archbishop William Temple, source unknown.

7 Jeremiah 23.29.

8 Hebrews 4.12–13.

9 Psalm 119.105

10 Jeremiah 23.29.

11 Augustine, *Confessions*, Book VIII, xii, trans. Henry Chadwick (Oxford: Oxford University Press, 1991), p. 152–3.

12 See <www.biblesociety.org.uk/about-us/our-history>.

13 Bill and Shirley Lees, *Is It Sacrifice? Experiencing Mission and Revival in Borneo* (Leicester: InterVarsity Press, 1987). Shirley Lees, *Drunk Before Dawn* (Sevenoaks: OMF International, 1979).

14 Personal conversation with Heather Henderson.

15 See <www.wycliffe.org>.

16 Article XIX, *Thirty Nine Articles of the Church of England*. See <www.churchofengland.org/prayer-and-worship/worship-texts-and-resources/book-common-prayer/articles-religion>.

17 1 Corinthians 10.16–17.

18 See <www.onfiremission.org>.

19 Prayer attributed to St Columba.

7 Let Jesus coach you

1 Augustine, *Confessions*, IX, xxi, trans. Henry Chadwick (Oxford: Oxford University Press, 1991), p. 170.

2 For an excellent biography, try George Weigel, *Witness to Hope: The Biography of Pope John Paul II* (New York: HarperCollins, 1999, 2020).

3 Bede, *The Ecclesiastical History of the English People*, Oxford World's Classics, trans. Bertram Colgrave, Judith McClure, Roger Collins (Oxford: Oxford University Press, 2008).

4 Pete Greig, *How to Pray* (London: Hodder and Stoughton, 2019).

5 Matthew Porter, *A to Z of Prayer: Building Strong Foundations for Daily Conversations with God* (Milton Keynes: Authentic Media, 2019).

6 Martin Laird, *Into the Silent Land: The Practice of Contemplation* (London: Darton, Longman and Todd, 2006).

7 Alister McGrath, *Beyond the Quiet Time: Practical Evangelical Spirituality* (London: SPCK Triangle, 1995), p. 13.

8 For a contemporary translation of Bede's account, try Simon Webb, *Bede's Life of St Cuthbert* (Durham: Langley Press, 2016).

9 Stacey Dooley: *Inside the Convent*, BBC, 2022.

10 Christopher Jamison, *Finding Sanctuary: Monastic Steps for Everyday Life* (London: Phoenix, 2006); St Benedict lived AD 480–548 and established monastic communities across Italy, who lived by the Benedictine rule, which in turn influenced the shape of monastic life in Europe to the present day.

11 *The Convent*, BBC, 2006.

12 M. Basilea Schlink, *Stepping into the Breach* (Radlett: Evangelical Sisterhood of Mary, 1973), pp. 4–5.

13 Leonard Ravenhill, *Why Revival Tarries* (Minnesota: Bethany House Publishers, 1987).

14 Colin and Mary Peckham, *Sounds from Heaven: The Revival on the Isle of Lewis, 1949–1952* (Fearn, Ross-shire: Christian Focus, 2004).

15 See <www.thykingdomcome.global>.

16 Augustine, *Confessions*, I, i, trans. Henry Chadwick (Oxford: Oxford University Press, 1991), p. 3.

8 Lifting our eyes

1 *The Lord of the Rings* trilogy, directed by Peter Jackson, 2001–2003.

2 Paul Y. Cho, *Prayer: Key to Revival*, 1987 (Nashville, TN: Thomas Nelson, 1987), p. 16.

3 Julian of Norwich, *Revelations of Divine Love* (Short Text), ch. 20, trans. Elizabeth Spearing (London: Penguin, 1998), p. 31.

4 See <www.jcryle.info/2015/11/assurance-by-j.html>.

5 Evelyn Underhill, *The School of Charity* and *The Mystery of Sacrifice* (London: Longmans, Green and Co., 1950), p. 101.

6 Abbé de Tourville, *Streams of Grace: A Selection of the Letters of the Abbé de Tourville* (London: Continuum, 2005), p. 60.

7 Martin Gilbert, *In Search of Churchill: A Historian's Journey* (London: HarperCollins, 1994), pp. 214–15.

8 Genesis 37—42.

9 Hebrews 12.1.

10 See, for example, <www.madeupinbritain/Sunday_School>.

11 Kenneth McAll, *Healing the Family Tree* (London: SPCK, 1982, 2013), p. 2.

12 McAll, *Healing the Family Tree*, pp. 65–6.

13 Wallace and Mary Brown, *Angels on the Walls: The Risk-taking Faith that Reclaimed a Community* (London: Kingsway, 2000).

14 Translated by Peter Cane for *Commemoration of Benefactor's Service* at Christ's College Cambridge, 2018.

9 Fire quenchers

1 Milton Jones, *10 Second Sermons* (London: Darton, Longman and Todd, 2011).

2 *Zootropolis*, directed by Rich Moore and Byron Howard, 2016.

3 See <www.stanselm.org.uk>.

4 See <www.blackburn.anglican.org/bishop-jill>.

5 See <www.cbn.com/special/Narnia/articles/ans_LewisLastInterviewA .aspx>.

6 Julian of Norwich, *Revelations of Divine Love* (Short Text), ch. 13, trans. Elizabeth Spearing (London: Penguin, 1998), p. 22.

7 *Star Wars Episode IX: The Rise of Skywalker*, directed by J. J. Abrams, 2019.

8 Quoted in Robert Atwell, *Celebrating the Saints* (Norwich: Canterbury Press, 1998), p. 189.

9 James 3.1.

10 *Common Worship Ordination Services: Study Edition* (London: Church House Publishing, 2007), p. 62.

11 *Life of Antony by Athanasius*, 27, in Caroline White (trans.), *Early Christian Lives* (London: Penguin, 1998), p. 61.

12 Francis Xavier Nguyen van Thuan, *The Road of Hope: A Gospel from Prison* (North Palm Beach FL: Wellspring, 2018), #85, p. 36. Italics added.

10 What is the battle?

1 *The Lord of the Rings* trilogy, directed by Peter Jackson, 2001–2003.

2 C. S. Lewis, *The Screwtape Letters* (1941), p. 2. Available online at: <www.lewis-screwtape-letters.pdf (preachershelp.net)>.

3 See <https://www.youtube.com/watch?v=fQzWfMKXx9k&t=35s>: Victoria Wood, *Live at the Albert* (2001).

4 G. K. Chesterton, *What's Wrong with the World?* (1910), part 4, chapter 14. See <www.chesterton.org/a-thing-worth-doing>.

5 James Martin SJ, *The Jesuit Guide to (Almost) Everything: A Spirituality for Real Life* (New York: HarperCollins, 2010).

6 Galatians 5.22–23.

7 *Chicken Run,* directed by Nick Park and Peter Lord, 2000.

8 Nelson Mandela, *The Long Walk to Freedom: The Autobiography of Nelson Mandela* (London: Abacus, 1995).

9 Francis Xavier Nguyen van Thuan, *The Road of Hope: A Gospel from Prison* (North Palm Beach, FL: Wellspring, 2018), #406, p. 108.

10 Lewis, *The Screwtape Letters.*

11 <https://theimaginativeconservative.org/2015/02/laughing-lucifer-lewis.html#:~:text=Luther%20says%2C%20%E2%80%9CThe%20best%20way,cannot%20endure%20to%20be%20mocked.%E2%80%9D>.

12 <https://theimaginativeconservative.org/2015/02/laughing-lucifer-lewis.html#:~:text=Luther%20says%2C%20%E2%80%9CThe%20best%20way,cannot%20endure%20to%20be%20mocked.%E2%80%9D>.

13 *Life of Antony by Athanasius,* 27, in Caroline White (trans.), *Early Christian Lives* (London: Penguin, 1998), p. 26.

14 See <www.themarkdrama.com>.

15 For the full version of this prayer, see <www.prayerfoundation.org/st_patricks_breastplate_prayer.htm>.

11 Stepping into the fire

1 *The Martyrdom of Polycarp,* 9–10, 13–16, 18–19; *Apostolic Fathers* II, Loeb Classical Library 25 (Cambridge, MA and London: Harvard University Press, 2004), pp. 307–46.

2 Quoted in the gorgeous Advent Book by Robyn Wrigley-Carr, *The Music of Eternity* (London: SPCK, 2021), p. 137.

3 John 12.20–36; 16.14; 17.1–2.

4 Gertrud the Great of Helfta, *The Herald of God's Loving Kindness,* Book 2, ch. 4, trans. Alexandra Barratt (Kalamazoo, MI: Cistercian Publications, 1991).

5 Dorothy Musgrave Arnold, *Dorothy Kerin: Called by Christ to Heal* (London: Hodder and Stoughton, 1965), pp. 32–8.

6 Robert Atwell (ed.), *Celebrating the Saints* (Norwich: Canterbury Press, 1998).

7 Teresa of Ávila, *The Way of Perfection,* ch. 32, trans. E Allison Peers

(London: Sheed and Ward, 1946), pp. 136–8 (abridged), quoted in Atwell (ed.), *Celebrating the Saints*.

8 Walter Ciszek SJ with Daniel L. Flaherty SJ, *He Leadeth Me* (New York: Image, 1973), p. 126.

9 Columbanus, *The Rule for Monks*, 9, trans. Oliver Davies in Oliver Davies (ed.), *Celtic Spirituality* (New York and Mahwah, NJ: Paulist Press, 1999), pp. 255–6.

10 *The Life of Saint Teresa by Herself*, trans. J. M. Cohen (London: Penguin, 1957).

11 Job 40.1–5.

12 Francis Xavier Nguyen van Thuan, *The Road of Hope: A Gospel from Prison* (North Palm Beach, FL: Wellspring, 2018), #700, p. 183.

12 Land of light and glory

1 Chris Lane, *Not Forgotten* (Watford: Instant Apostle, 2022).

2 Matthew 12.20.

3 Elizabeth Barrett Browning, 'Earth's crammed with heaven', from <www.goodreads.com/quotes/38640-earth-s-crammed-with-heaven -and-every-common-bush-afire-with>.

4 See <www.24-7prayer.com/about/about-us/the-vision/>. 'The Vision'.

5 *The Interior Castle*, part 6, ch. 11, in *The Collected Works of St Teresa of Avila, Volume 2*, trans. Kieran Kavanaugh and Otilio Rodriguez (Washington, DC: ICS Publications, 1980), p. 422.

6 'An Old Irish Homily', trans. Oliver Davies in Oliver Davies (ed.), *Celtic Spirituality* (New York and Mahwah, NJ: Paulist Press, 1999), p. 368.

7 C. S. Lewis, *The Complete Chronicles of Narnia* (London: HarperCollins, 2000), p . 524.

Copyright acknowledgements

Tyndale House Publishers, Inc., Carol Stream, Illinois 60189, USA. All rights reserved.

Lyrics from 'Shine, Jesus, Shine' by Graham Kendrick © 1987 Make Way Music. grahamkendrick.co.uk International copyright secured. All rights reserved. Used by permission.

Prince Caspian by C. S. Lewis copyright © 1951 C. S. Lewis Pte Ltd. *The Lion, the Witch and the Wardrobe* by C. S. Lewis copyright © 1950 C. S. Lewis Pte Ltd.
The Last Battle by C. S. Lewis copyright © 1956 C. S. Lewis Pte Ltd.
The Screwtape Letters by C. S. Lewis copyright © 1951 C. S. Lewis Pte Ltd.
Extracts reprinted by permission.

The Thy Kingdom Come graphic is reproduced by kind permission.

Extracts from the Vision Poem, written by Pete Greig, www.petegreig.info, are reproduced by kind permission.

Every effort has been made to seek permission to use copyright material reproduced in this book. The publisher apologizes for those cases where permission might not have been sought and, if notified, will formally seek permission at the earliest opportunity.